THE CRISIS OF CULTURAL INTELLIGENCE

The Anthropology of
Civil-Military Operations

THE CRISIS OF CULTURAL INTELLIGENCE

The Anthropology of Civil–Military Operations

David Hyndman
University of New South Wales Canberra, Australia

Scott Flower
University of Melbourne, Australia

World Scientific

NEW JERSEY · LONDON · SINGAPORE · BEIJING · SHANGHAI · HONG KONG · TAIPEI · CHENNAI · TOKYO

Published by

World Scientific Publishing Co. Pte. Ltd.

5 Toh Tuck Link, Singapore 596224

USA office: 27 Warren Street, Suite 401-402, Hackensack, NJ 07601

UK office: 57 Shelton Street, Covent Garden, London WC2H 9HE

Library of Congress Cataloging-in-Publication Data
Names: Hyndman, David, author. | Flower, Scott, author.
Title: The crisis of cultural intelligence : the anthropology of civil-military operations / David Hyndman, Scott Flower.
Description: New Jersey : World Scientific, [2018] |
    Includes bibliographical references and index.
Identifiers: LCCN 2018025076 | ISBN 9789813273634 (hardcover)
Subjects: LCSH: Civil-military relations. | Counterinsurgency. |
    Ethnology--Military aspects. | Political anthropology.
Classification: LCC JF195 .H96 2018 | DDC 322/.5--dc23
LC record available at https://lccn.loc.gov/2018025076

British Library Cataloguing-in-Publication Data
A catalogue record for this book is available from the British Library.

Copyright © 2019 by the Authors

All rights reserved.

For any available supplementary material, please visit
https://www.worldscientific.com/worldscibooks/10.1142/11082#t=suppl

Desk Editor: Karimah Samsudin

Typeset by Stallion Press
Email: enquiries@stallionpress.com

Printed in Singapore

Contents

Chapter 1: **Cultural Research in ABCA Armies Civil–Military Operations**   1

   Introduction   1
   Civil–Military Armed Conflict, Disaster Management, and Interventionism   2
   ABCA: The Alliance of Anglo-Saxon Armies   3
   Human Terrain System: ABCA Armies Operational and Tactical Tool of Counterinsurgency   6
   Settler Colonialism   10
   Militarised Anthropology   13
   Nations Against States Armed Conflict Among the People   14
   Research   17
   Conclusion   19

Chapter 2: **19th Century Evolutionary Anthropology as Colonial Intelligence**   23

   Introduction   23
   America: 19th Century Evolutionary Anthropology, Settler Colonialism, and Wardship of Indigenous Nations   25

Britain: 19th Century Evolutionary Anthropology
  as Colonial Military Practice 27
Canada: Anthropology and Settler Colonial Accession
  of Indigenous Land 30
Australia: Anthropology and Settler Colonial
  Frontier Wars 34
New Zealand: 19th Century Anthropology and
  Settler Colonial Maori Wars 38
Conclusion 41

Chapter 3: Early 20th Century Ethnography as Colonial Instrument for Government Planning 43

Introduction 43
America: Post-Frontier Settler Colonialism, Salvage
  Ethnography, and Anthropologists as Spies 45
Britain: Social Anthropology as Ethnography
  for Colonial Administration 49
Canada: Salvage Ethnography and Settler Colonialism 51
Australia: Applied Anthropology in Aiding
  Government Control of Aboriginal Peoples
  and the Colonial Enterprise 52
New Zealand: Maori Field-based Ethnography
  and the Colonial Division of Anthropology
  Research in the Pacific 54
Conclusion 56

Chapter 4: Militarized Anthropological Intelligence in the Second World War 59

Introduction 59
America: Wartime Militarised Anthropology 61
Britain: World War II Anthropology in
  Administering and Defending Colonial Outposts
  of Empire 67
Canada: Academic Anthropologists
  Post-World War II 72

	Australia: Militarised Anthropology and Managed Colonised Peoples in World War II	73
	New Zealand: Anthropology and Shared Wartime Colonial Intelligence in the Empire	82
	Conclusion	87

Chapter 5: The Cold War and the Demise of Colonial Empire — 89

Introduction — 89
America: Korean War, Counterinsurgency in Vietnam and the Ethical Rejection of Militarised Anthropology — 91
Britain: Structural Functional Juggernaut and the Colonial Encounter — 97
Canada: American Anti-war Political Exodus and Anthropology Engagement with Indigenous Activism — 104
Australia: Thailand Counterinsurgency Controversy and the Ethical Impact on Anthropology — 106
New Zealand: Post-War Professionalising of Anthropology and Maori Studies — 110
Conclusion — 111

Chapter 6: Socio-political Status of Anthropology and Indigenous Resistance — 115

Introduction — 115
America: Anthropology and the End of Parasitical Dependence on the Study of Indigenous Nations — 117
Britain: Anthropology after Empire — 124
Canada: The End of Self Appointed Anthropology Proprietorship of Indigenous Nations — 126
Australia: Demise of the Old Anthropology of Classicist Persistence — 131
New Zealand: Estrangement between Anthropology and the Maori Political Movement — 135
Conclusion — 139

Chapter 7:	Civil–Military Intervention in Armed Conflict Among the People	141
	Introduction	141
	CANZUS: Settler Colonial Opposition to the Declaration on the Rights of Indigenous People	142
	Militarized Nations Against States	151
	Nation Against State Armed Conflict Among the People	152
	Conclusion	156
Chapter 8:	Cultural Intelligence in the ABCA Armies	159
	Introduction	159
	Cultural Narratives	159
	Expanded Cultural Narrative	171
	Conclusion	176
Chapter 9:	Case Studies	179
	Operation Outreach: The Australian Army Domestic Civil–Military Intervention in the Northern Territory	179
	Introduction	179
	Operation Outreach Military Operational Space	180
	Humanitarian Operational Space	184
	Culturalisation of Political Conflict	186
	Conclusion	194
	Operation Bel Isi: The New Zealand Army Pacific Way Civil–Military Intervention in the Bougainville Nation vs PNG State Conflict	196
	Introduction	196
	Panguna Mining Invasion of Bougainville	196
	Bougainvillean Mobilization Against Mining	199
	The Emergence of the Bougainville Revolutionary Army	200
	Guitars not Guns: The Maori Cultural Initiative	204
	Conclusion	210

Chapter 10: Conclusion   **211**
     Settler Colonialism   211
     Militarised Anthropology   211
     Nation Against State Armed Conflict Among
        the People   214
     Targeting: Crisis of Cultural Intelligence   216
     Civil–Military Operations   217
     Operation Outreach: Unsuccessful Use of Cultural
        Intelligence   218
     Operation Bel ISI: Successful Use of Cultural
        Intelligence   219
     ABCA Commonality   221

References   **223**

Index   **243**

About the Authors   **257**

CHAPTER 1

Cultural Research in ABCA Armies Civil–Military Operations

Introduction

Civil and military organisations have typically attempted to understand the contemporary cultural environment of conflict zones through drawing on the expertise of anthropologists. There are only a small number of studies that examine current uses of anthropology (as a discipline) for civil–military purposes. The publication of the *Counterinsurgency Manual* (2006, 2014) galvanised debate over anthropology and the security state. More recently, anthropologists have addressed the increasing convergence and cooperation between civil/humanitarian and military organisations, and the role of anthropology and anthropologists across the gamut of military and humanitarian emergencies and interventions, such as: *Anthropology and Global Counterinsurgency* (Kelly *et al.*, 2010), *The New Imperialism: Militarism, Humanism and Occupation* (Forte, 2011), *Dangerous Liaisons* (McNamara and Rubenstein, 2011), *Anthropologists in the Securityscape* (Albro *et al.*, 2012), *Peacekeeping under Fire* (Rubenstein, 2008), *Humanitarians in Hostile Territory* (Van Arsdale and Smith, 2010), and *Contemporary States of Emergency: The Politics of Military and Humanitarian Interventions* (Fassin and Pandolfi, 2010).

Within the discipline of anthropology itself, proponents of the debate initially focussed on America's efforts to 'militarise' and 'weaponise' the discipline through the Human Terrain System (HTS), such as: *Weaponizing Anthropology* (Price, 2011), and *American Counterinsurgency: Human Science and Human Terrain* (Gonzalez, 2009). Within the ABCA Armies, Kirke (2005) has studied anthropology from inside the British Army culture and has taken an ethnographic approach to understanding authenticity (Kirke, 2009). Kirke (2010) has also argued that social psychology is more informative than culture for understanding cohesion in the British Army. Elsewhere in the ABCA Armies, Fosher (2013) has considered the practice of anthropology within the American Army.

Civil–Military Armed Conflict, Disaster Management, and Interventionism

The guiding principle of civil–military management is to strengthen a culture of multi-agency collaboration. Advancing multi-agency, whole of government coordination enhances civil–military capabilities for armed conflict and disaster management. Armed conflict between states has diminished since World War II, while intrastate armed conflict has increased. There are fewer challenges inherent in disasters than in responding to armed conflict. Host governments make early requests for assistance following a disaster, but less so for armed conflicts. Civil–military armed conflict prevention and peacemaking is ideally followed by peacekeeping and peacebuilding. Defence predominates in the armed conflict phase, with multi-agency, whole of government coordination occurring in the post-ceasefire and peace phases. Civil–military operations are rarely undertaken unilaterally and include host states, multinational coalitions, and UN missions. The culture of civil–military multiagency collaboration enhances the management of armed conflicts and disasters (Asia Pacific Civil–Military Centre of Excellence, 2010).

The vogue for thick descriptions and blurred genres in postmodern anthropology acted to depoliticise knowledge, and to shut and block out the clamour of voices from nations on the outside asking for their claims about empire, domination, and armed conflict to be considered (Said, 2001). As military campaigns shifted away from war between states to civil–military occupations of regions identified as "tribal" and "Indigenous", the ABCA Armies sought anthropological knowledge to understand the shifting characteristics of enemies and inform engagement with such adversaries (Price, 2011: 3).

Internationalised intrastate armed conflicts and disasters in the early 21st century have become embedded in the same global logic of interventionism, which is based on the temporality of emergency and the conflation of military and humanitarian operations used to justify a state of exception (Fassin and Pandolfi, 2010). The urgency of the situation and the danger to victims from war and disaster justify the exception of intervention. The principle of intrastate internationalised intervention constitutes an important political innovation of the early 21st century, namely a break with the doctrine of sovereignty. Following World War II, the UN Charter was based on the principle of "sovereign equality" of its members (Article 2-1) and proscribed intervention "in matters which are essentially within the domestic jurisdiction of any state" (Article 2-7). Decolonisation established the sovereignty of colonised peoples and their right to self-determination in conflict with the sovereignty of colonising states. Military and humanitarian actors structurally placed themselves under the same state of exception. Humanitarianising interventions naturalise conflicts, as if military operations did not originate in the defence of the interests of the state conducting them. Military resources of the interveners are much greater than those of the belligerents located in nation-against-state conflicts. Contemporary counterinsurgency operations and civil–military interventions in natural and human emergencies is still the law of the strongest. Given the need to ensure the imbalance between the actors involved, it has been the ABCA Armies, sometimes with NATO militaries of Western European countries, which have intervened in regions where economic and strategic issues have been at stake. However enveloped in humanitarian morality, interventions often involve a degree of coercion reflective of the existing power inequalities between interveners and intervenees (Fassin and Pandolfi, 2010).

ABCA: The Alliance of Anglo-Saxon Armies

"Men are not tied to one another by papers and seals. They are led to associate by resemblances, by conformities, by sympathies. Nothing is so strong a tie of amity between nations as correspondence in laws, customs, manners and habits of life. They have more than force of treaties in themselves. They are obligations from the heart."

(Edmund Burke, 1796: 155)

Overlooked in the recent quest for 'cultural intelligence' have been the efforts of the 'Anglo-Saxon' settler colonial states to develop military capabilities to better understand culture and cultural factors of violence and conflict behaviour using anthropology and recruiting anthropologists. Interest in how cultural intelligence can be collected and used has increased in the 'Anglo-Saxon' settler colonial states, through formalised arrangements such as the America, Britain, Canada, Australia, and New Zealand (ABCA) Armies.

There is a growing awareness among ABCA Armies of the need to better understand the social and cultural environments (referred to as the 'Human Terrain') of potential and current conflict zones and areas of operations. A result of this evolving awareness is the trend among ABCA Armies to recruit and embed cultural and social anthropologists to work alongside military units. Global ethnographic surveillance is on the military agenda (Ferguson, 2012). ABCA Armies are reaching for the tools to culturally understand and manage transnational geopolitics of nation-against-state wars and intrastate internationalised armed conflicts as scenes of civil–military interventions and counterinsurgency where their strategic interests are at stake.

ABCA is little known to the public, and has been referred to as "the alliance you never heard of" (Betz, 2008: 1). ABCA grew out of the close cooperation among Anglo-Saxon allies during World War II, and evolved through the Korean War and the American war in Vietnam. ABCA represents the alliance of five armies, not based on a treaty, but on the Basic Standardisation Agreement between America, Britain, Canada, Australia, and New Zealand. ABCA originated in 1947, and included America, Britain, and Canada endeavouring to improve standardisation; with Australia joining in 1963, and New Zealand in 2006. Following the events of September 11 and conflicts in Iraq and Afghanistan and especially since 2004, the relationships between ABCA armies have been significantly renewed and refocused on interoperability; defined as "the ability of Alliance Forces...to train, exercise and operate effectively together in the execution of assigned missions and tasks" (ABCA, 2012). ABCA is also "about interoperability of the spirit and mind — the realm of *esprit de corps*" (Maginnis, 2005: 4).

Members perceive ABCA as an exclusive club based on military culture, common language, and common history, expressed as "an alliance of those actually doing the fighting and the dying" (Betz, 2008: 3). Members conceive of ABCA as an alliance that works because it is founded on the ability to communicate and trust, and rely on each other's judgement. Despite their significant geographic dispersal, it is the ABCA armies' common shared cultural affinities that bind the group. A shared Anglo-Saxon history and heritage, common-law legal system, and similar institutions of political and bureaucratic governance provides the foundational bond that unites the ABCA armies in interstate and intrastate armed conflict, stabilisation and peacekeeping operations (Durrell-Young, 2003).

ABCA Armies have shared hardships and victories, and have undergone transformation for combat interoperability that places them at the cutting-edge of force projection in the 21st century (Maginnis, 2005). ABCA is able to conduct joint and combined operations as a result of deliberate efforts to pursue high levels of war-fighting interoperability. The "intimate Anglo-Saxon connection appears to have been the needed basis for enduring well into the post-cold-war era" (Betz, 2008: 3). ABCA is more than just a mechanism for sharing technology and new capabilities; the group shares intellectual foundations, which enable the "free exchange of new ideas, concepts, and supporting data at almost all levels (strategic to tactical) that makes the relationship a powerful force in the diffusion of military innovation ideas about the nature of future warfare" (Durrell-Young, 2003: 95).

ABCA represents an exceptionally unique military relationship that has become stronger over time, despite differences between each country's perceptions of threat. Conflict in the 21st century is conceptualised variously as the problematic era of hybrid warfare, complex insurgency, and war among the people; as well as the emergence of the transnational, asymmetrical, and non-state actor enemies that requires land forces like ABCA to prevail (Betz, 2008: 3). Political military operations are force multipliers to fight and win, and ABCA incorporates lessons from ongoing combat and operational missions.

ABCA Armies are deployed to parts of the world very different from their own, the local language is rarely spoken or studied in their home country, and the culture is very different. Culture, defined as "the set of opinions, beliefs, values and customs that form the identity of a society" (ABCA, 2010: 1), and building trust are taken seriously by the ABCA Armies. The ABCA Armies are aware that other cultures have a perception of them and they are aware of not imposing their own culture. The implications of cultural issues for ABCA include (ABCA, 2010: 2):

- Self-awareness of culture shock;
- Cultural sensitivity for heeding local customs and developing trusting relationships between ABCA and Indigenous forces; and
- Opportunity to understand the Human Terrain.

Human Terrain System: ABCA Armies Operational and Tactical Tool of Counterinsurgency

The Human Terrain System (HTS) experimental counterinsurgency programme was created by the American Army between 2005 and 2006 for deployment to Iraq and Afghanistan. Controversially, in 2006, HTS began to 'embed' anthropologists and other social scientists with combat brigades in Iraq and Afghanistan, where they helped gather intelligence, referred to as gathering 'research', to improve knowledge of the local culture (Sluka, 2010). HTS offered a 'kinder and gentler' counterinsurgency designed to gain public support for two unpopular wars, but initially equivocated whether accumulated databases might be used to target suspected Iraqi or Afghan insurgents for abduction or assassination (Gonzales, 2008). The military had failed with predominately kinetic tactics, and Montgomery McFate was available at the right time to sell the military a cultural-centric counterinsurgency remedy (Sluka, 2010). It became increasingly popular in the American military to consider social, ethnographic, cultural, economic, and political elements in gathering intelligence, where force operated in order to turn around a failed occupation.

McFate called for human terrain focussed on social scientists with strong connections to the services and combatant command (McFate and Jackson, 2005). Anthropology was boldly declared to be the academic discipline "invented to support warfighting in the tribal zone" (McFate, 2005: 43). Major General Robert Scales noted the colonial British Army had immersed officers in the cultures of the Empire and endorsed the imperialist culture-centric approach for human terrain, which included postgraduate studies in human behaviour and cultural anthropology (Scales, 2004).

Human terrain contrasts with geophysical terrain in conventional state-versus-state warfare. In the 21st century, combatants fought population-centric wars for the control of people (Killen, 2007), and people in human terrain became geographical space to be conquered and human beings as territory to be captured (Gonzales, 2008). In recognition of the controversial terminology, the American Dialect Society named 'Human Terrain Team' the most euphemistic phrase of the year in 2007 (Sluka, 2010).

The HTS program became known as 'a CORDS for the 21st century' (Kipp *et al.*, 2006). In Vietnam, the Civil Operations and Revolutionary Development Support (CORDS) program was made operational in 1968. CORDS became one component of the counterinsurgency strategy, with the infamous Phoenix program as the other component. Intelligence was gathered to target tens of thousands of Vietnamese for 'neutralisation' (Valentine, 1990). CORDS were presented as a humanitarian project for winning hearts and minds, while Phoenix remained as the secret paramilitary arm. Wolf and Jorgenson (1971: 33) recalled a Thailand specialist's observation that "the old formula for successful counterinsurgency used to be 10 troops for every guerrilla…now the formula is 10 anthropologists for each guerrilla". For the decades since the Vietnam War, anthropologists have considered involvement in counterinsurgency as ethically 'taboo' (Sluka, 2010).

Montgomery McFate advocated anthropology as fundamentally one of applied state control, compared with Nancy Scheper-Hughes (1995) who supported "The Primacy of the Ethical", and called for the anthropology of resistance, critical reflection, and human liberation.

In the last two decades, American military forces have begun tasking anthropologists to conduct ethnographic research that informs military commander's contextual understanding of the 'Human Terrain' of the 'battle-space'. More controversially, this anthropological 'research' is sometimes utilised as a stream of intelligence to support targeting and, as a result, has been challenged ethically to do no harm, be transparent, and be based on voluntary informed consent (Gonzales, 2009). In 2007, the AAA formally opposed the HTS and denounced it as 'an unacceptable application of anthropological expertise'. HTS potentially harmed research participants, risked researchers in the field, and prevented informed consent, public dissemination of research results, and opportunities for future research by other academics (Sluka, 2010). It is estimated that 1% of American anthropologists have undertaken placement with the Human Terrain System, while 99% have not (Price, 2011).

BAE Systems made job announcements in 2007, and trained human terrain members in military and weapons training; the first team arrived in Afghanistan in February 2007, and others arrived in Iraq in mid-2007 (Gonzales, 2008). By 2009, HTS was seriously compromised because three social scientists had been killed in the field. McFate and the HTS leadership were blamed for inadequate training. Abruptly, the HTS program was removed from control of BAE Systems, and placed under Army control with substantial pay cuts.

Among the ABCA Armies, "HTS was both an operational and tactical tool of counterinsurgency that balanced between security and development tasks and between kinetic and non-kinetic effects. Intelligence, termed 'research', operated among the local population for 'cultural appreciation used in planning, execution and assessment of operations" (ABCA, 2011).

HTS was defined by the ABCA Armies as "the social, political, economic and infrastructural environment...in which soldiers operate", and it made use of "cultural, regional, and linguistic expertise to inform intelligence preparation of the environment." Human Terrain Teams provided "expeditionary teams to support military commanders" through direct engagement and investigated the sociocultural environment of the local population (ABCA, 2011: 2).

Knowledge of the human terrain could avert unnecessary cultural conflict; shape military operations, and enable future joint land combat

(ABCA, 2011: 3). Human terrain was rendered to a geographic map with demographic features and social features of kinship, ethnicity, religion, and physical features of ideological significance. Human Terrain provided ABCA commanders with cultural understanding considered equivalent to military threat and geospatial factors (ABCA, 2011).

The five ABCA Armies were not adequately resourced to conduct human terrain analysis. There were significant interoperability gaps between ABCA Armies that included the lack of standard human terrain methodology, the lack of social science reach back capability, and the inconsistent use of social science methods (ABCA, 2011). ABCA Armies recognised that "social scientists and anthropologists were able to measure social demographics in a way that was beneficial to the military commander" and that there "may be certain legal, ethical, and security considerations to the collection of some elements of human terrain information". Moreover, Human Terrain Teams consisted of civilians that "were constrained by complex moral and legal CAVEATS with regard to the collection and use of human terrain data" (ABCA, 2010: 8).

Deployed American Army Human Terrain Teams delivered "cultural advice to commanders." Human Terrain Teams were "led by a military officer and included 'embedded' expert social scientists." American Human Terrain Analysis Teams and Human Terrain Teams conducted field 'research' among the local population for cultural appreciation used in planning, execution, and assessment of operations (ABCA, 2010).

The British Army delivered cultural analysis to commanders through employing Cultural Advisors (CULADS) from the Defence Cultural Specialist Unit (ABCA, 2011: 7). Other ABCA Armies were establishing a Human Terrain System (HTS) capability and a sociocultural capacity will be a future expectation.

The New Zealand Army considered the role of HTS as providing cultural awareness and improving the conflict resolution of missions (Parkinson, 2013). ABCA doctrine stressed the primacy of the host state in stability operations. Understanding the culture of the host may improve security of the New Zealand Army personnel, but the capability cannot simply be acquired in a short deployment briefing or training session (Parkinson, 2013). A HTS capability in the New Zealand Army could be a tool for the resolution of conflicts in complex warfare that required a "balance between security and development tasks and between kinetic and non-kinetic effects" (Parkinson, 2013).

The future of HTS is unclear. The ABCA Armies acknowledged the "relationship with intelligence and targeting" and the "ethical opposition to militarising anthropological–ethnographic approaches". The ABCA Armies debated whether HTS should be continued and be "independent of, or integrated with, an intelligence function" (ABCA, 2011). Former HTS member Zenia Helbig exposed that the American program was grossly incompetent and desperate to hire in the categories of 'academic', 'social science', 'regional expert' or 'PhD' (Gonzales, 2008). Addressing critical anthropology, Gonzales (2008: 26) maintained that: "to the extent that the HTS might be employed to collect intelligence or target suspected enemies for assassination, the program deserves elimination."

Settler Colonialism

The states associated with the ABCA Armies, America, Britain, Canada, Australia, and New Zealand share the legacy of Anglo-Saxon settler colonialism, the history of militarised anthropology, and the first nation-versus-state armed conflicts. The study of settler culture is central to anthropological understanding of colonialism in the ABCA Army countries. Settler colonialism followed similar patterns in America, Canada, Australia, and New Zealand, with the occupation of sparsely populated new lands by British immigrants and the destruction or displacement of local Indigenous peoples.

Settler colonialism is based on the logic of elimination for the expropriation of Indigenous land (Wolfe, 2006). Colonial settlers dealt with Indigenous peoples through resistance, containment, appropriation, assimilation or attempted destruction. Settler colonialism not only played a vital part in constructing the foundational myths and narratives of settler colonialism in the past, but also in challenging and transforming public discourse in these countries today (Hodge, 2008). Past settler colonialism cannot be demarcated from colonial struggles in the present (Thomas, 1994).

The world is in a permanent state of exception of conflict with governmentality on the borderline between legality and force. There is a crisis in the order of state borders and an intensification of colonial military intervention (Hage, 2016: 1). Globally, there are two types of borders; the obvious is the state border that separates different states, and the less obvious is a nation and a state border that separates two realities that coexist within the same global space (Hage, 2016: 6).

There is a globalisation of the settler colonial ethos. The settler colonial societies of America, Canada, Australia, and New Zealand have, for the most part, defeated anticolonial resistance, but settler colonial societies are always geared toward conflict, even though they are not actually at war. In settler colonial societies, resistance of the colonised is delegitimised because they cannot afford to have them depicted as a warring party of equal status. Settler colonial societies have exemplified a permanent state of exception well prior to becoming pervasive in the West (Hage, 2016: 3). Settler colonialism is a structure, not an event; invasion is a structural ongoing process, not some historical event; and the aim is to eliminate native nations and displace them from the land (Wolfe, 2006).

There were four types of British colonialism that exhibited the following geographic and temporal pattern:

> "The British first established settler and directly ruled plantation colonies in the Americas and Australasia, then they colonised Asian territories through direct and hybrid forms of rule, and finally they colonised sub-Saharan Africa, Borneo, and a few Pacific Islands through indirect and hybrid forms of rule"
>
> (Lange, Mahoney and Hau, 2006: 1,427).

Most settler colonialism occurred after the mid-18th century in less complex pre-colonial regions occupied by hunter–gatherers and simple agriculturalists, when Britain advocated free trade and viewed the state as a tool for law and order (see Table 1.1). Where Britain pursued extensive settler colonialism in the Americas and Australasia, permanent settlers transplanted institutions without preserving pre-colonial arrangements.

The British first established settler colonies in the future America and Canada. A century later, Britain established settler colonies in Australia (1788) and New Zealand (1840). Sparsely populated pre-colonial societies were decimated by disease and warfare, and removed for the introduction of little Great Britain's (see Table 1.1).

Table 1.1: Timing of British Settler Colonialism

British Colonies	Onset of Colonialism	Conclusion of Colonialism
America	1607	1783
Canada	1610/1763	1867
Australia	1788	1901
New Zealand	1840	1907

Source: Lange, Mahoney and Hau (2006).

Table 1.2: Levels of Pre-colonial Development and British Settler Colonialism

Country	Level of Pre-colonial Development	Level of Colonialism	Pre-Colonial Population Density (persons per km^2)	Settler Population at End of Colonialism (% total)
America	Low	High	0.09	81.2
Canada	Low	High	0.02	96.8
Australia	Low	High	0.03	98.7
New Zealand	Low	High	0.37	94.7

Source: Lange, Mahoney and Hau (2006).

The British pursued significantly higher levels of colonialism, and settled more extensively in pre-colonial regions with less people and less institutional complexity. Pre-colonial levels of development, population density, and percentage of total settler population at the end of the colonial period are shown in Table 1.2.

Cash crops and slavery transformed the American South from a settler colony of small farmers to a plantation colony, with settlers directly ruling over imported forced labour, and slaves accounted for nearly 20% of the population at the end of colonialism. In America, Canada, Australia, and New Zealand, British-based settler colonialism left behind a functioning legal system underpinned by property rights capable of sustaining capitalist development. Conquered Indigenous peoples were uprooted and marginalised, and cultural stratification promoted by settler colonisers contributed to pervasive social inequalities (Lange, Mahoney and Hua, 2006).

The Indigenous peoples of America include the Native Americans, the Inuits, and the Hawaiians; the percent of the Indigenous population from

Table 1.3: Estimated Indigenous Population in America, Canada, Australia, and New Zealand

Population	America	Canada	Australia	New Zealand
Population Size (Census Year)	5,200,00 (2011)	1,400,685 (2012)	669,900 (2011)	598,065 (2013)
Population (% total)	1.7%	4.3%	3.0%	14.9%

Source: Norris, Tina; Paula Vines; Elizabeth Hoeffel, 2012; Statistics Canada, 2012; Australian Bureau of Statistics, 2011; Statistics New Zealand, 2013.

the end of colonialism to present day with the end of slavery is only 1.7%. The Indigenous peoples of Canada include the First Nations, the Metis, and the Inuit; the percentage of the Indigenous population from the end of colonialism to present day increased minimally from 3.2% to 4.3%. The Indigenous peoples of Australia include the Aboriginals and the Torres Strait Islanders; the percentage of the Indigenous population from the end of colonialism to present day increased minimally from 1.3% to 3%. The Maori are the Indigenous people of New Zealand; the percentage of the Indigenous population from the end of colonialism to present day nearly tripled from 5.3% to 14.9% (see Table 1.3).

Militarised Anthropology

Critical analysis of militarised anthropology starts with the 19th century settler colonial period, when evolutionary anthropologists were a central part of settler colonial intelligence. Ethnography in the early 20th century is explored as a settler colonial instrument for government planning. Militarised anthropological intelligence in the ABCA Armies during World War II is examined. With the emergence of the cold war and the demise of the colonial empire, anthropology ethically rejected militarised anthropology, and shifted the discipline away from being a tool of domination. By the end of the 20th century, there was a malaise between materialists and mentalists in the sociopolitical status of anthropology. The mentalists in anthropology began turning away from studying Indigenous peoples and did not engage with the internationalisation of native nations.

British colonial military intelligence deployed hard-nosed anthropologists, such as the flamboyant Richard Francis Burton (Kennedy, 2005), and many 19th century evolutionist anthropologists who were amateurs and had served in the military. In the early 20th century, there was a move to an anthropology more suited to colonial administrative needs. Anthropologists produced some of the first ethnographies of peoples recently placed under colonial rule in the British Empire; ethnographies that would again inform the understanding of culture and violence in recent nation-against-state conflicts, like those in Sudan. The cultural history of the anthropological method and the political tasks it performed (Fabian, 1983) suggests that professional ethnography was regarded as a specific offshoot of a wider field of colonial intelligence (Pels, 1997).

British anthropologists in World War II directed their fieldwork skills at people within the colonial boundaries of the Empire. War interests conflated with the interests of colonialism as anthropologist administered or defended outposts of the empire (Price, 2008). Anthropologists in the settler colonial states were involved in military intelligence in World War II, and America and Australia were also involved in counterinsurgency in the Vietnam War.

Asad's *Anthropology and the Colonial Encounter* (1973) had a counterpart in America with the appearance of *Reinventing Anthropology*, edited by Hymes (1969), that was similarly critical of anthropology's history and future (Silverman, 2005). If British anthropology was concerned with the role of colonialism in former and current colonies, the counterpart for American, Canadian, Australian, and New Zealand was the settler colonial relationship to Indigenous nations.

Nation Against State Armed Conflict Among the People

By the late 20th century, anthropology was disengaging from research with Indigenous peoples and Indigenous peoples were rejecting anthropologists. Anthropologists were not present for the United Nations (UN) Declaration on the Rights of Indigenous Peoples. It was a critical period of Indigenous activism under settler colonialism; militant Indigenous peoples claimed a

Fourth World. Globally, the most prevalent type of conflict pitted Fourth World nation against state. A nation-based analysis of contemporary geopolitics demonstrates the prevalence of intrastate, rather than interstate, war. The new type of armed conflict among the people by the early 21st century is defined as intrastate internationalised war.

The United Nations (UN) Working Group on Indigenous Populations (WGIP) established in 1982 by a decision of the UN Economic and Social Council sharply focuses on the issues of autonomy, self-management, and self-determination, and serves to move Indigenous nations from domestic jurisdiction to international agendas. The first 30 years of the WGIP escaped anthropological attention; yet, it is the only global institution in which Indigenous identity has been discussed for decades (Muehlebach, 2001). Indigenous delegates travel to Geneva to comment on national and international developments, and to voice their opinion on legal standards for protection of their rights. The WGIP represents a "unique exercise in international affairs" (Burger, 1994: 90), that is "an exceptional UN forum in this regard" (Lam, 1992: 617), as well as a vital node in the global "indigeno-scape" (Beckett, 1996). The WGIP makes Indigenous difference its dictum (Muehlebach, 2001) and, although a marginal site of political experience, has potentially revolutionary implications (Wilmer, 1993).

In the course of their emergence on the global political scene, Indigenous delegates in the WGIP have insisted on the inseparability of ecology and indigeneity. Place is infused with culture, and Indigenous cultural politics are a politics of land and a politics of rights to land. Therefore, struggles for and about land are also struggles about identity and culture. Indigenous ecological culture maps moralities onto places, and it is the only way they have of gaining (or retaining) access as nations to lands capable of nurturing their cultures, and a resource base capable of supporting their self-determination (Hipwell, 1997).

The ecopolitical discourse of the veteran delegates to the WGIP predominantly from North, Middle, and South America, as well as Australia and New Zealand, continued with the presence of Asian and African delegates starting in the 1990s. The Asian and African newcomers to the WGIP embraced the politics of morality, and vigorously took up the ecopolitical discourse. The newcomers look back on different histories of colonialism from the settler colonialism of America, Canada, Australia, and

New Zealand, and have aligned themselves with the aim of taking social control of their territory as a precondition for survival and strengthening biocultural diversity. Only 30 Indigenous and non-Indigenous participants attended when the WGIP was established in 1982. By 1999, the WGIP was attended by more than 1,000 Indigenous nation representatives from all five continents (Muehlebach, 2001).

The basic neoliberal model of equal rights and freedoms does not allow for group rights to be claimed within state structures, and since most states are formed over unconsenting nations, recognition of them as a people would jeopardise state territorial claims. In 1995, the Confederacy Treaty of Six First Nations in Canada stated that Indigenous peoples are distinct nations who have the right to be distinct, but not necessarily separate from state society (Muehlebach, 2001). The Mohawk nation's concept of 'Canada' is not that of a state at all, but rather a legal–political framework for cooperation among nations (Alfred, 1995). Concepts of self-determination, sovereignty, and the future of state structures are being questioned.

To further indigenous nation self-determination, the WGIP provided a draft declaration on the rights of Indigenous peoples in 1994. The process moved slowly because states were concerned with the core provisions of Indigenous nations' right to self-determination and of control over natural resources existing on Indigenous people's lands. There was a constant struggle over the role of Chairperson–Rapporteur Chavez during the protracted draft declaration debate; he was found by the Indigenous delegates to be inconsistent and to extend excessive weight to the objections of the settler colonial states of Canada, Australia, New Zealand, and the US (the CANZUS group) in seeking consensus on the text. Indigenous delegates found the CANZUS states to be particularly obstructionist to provisions relating to rights to self-determination, lands, territories, and resources. The notion of consensus was a continuing problem over the protracted years of negotiating the draft declaration through the UN. The settler colonial states of the CANZUS group interjected and objected the most; even the sole objection of the US was evidence of non-consensus for the Chairperson (Davis, 2008).

The draft declaration was approved unanimously in 1994 by the Sub-Commission on Prevention and Discrimination and Protection of

Minorities, and moved up the UN ladder to be debated in the Human Rights Commission in 1995. In July 2000, the General Assembly voted for the establishment of a permanent forum on Indigenous issues as a subsidiary organ and advisory body to the UN Economic and Social Council (Meuhlebach, 2001). The UN Permanent Forum on Indigenous Issues (PFII) was established on 28 July 2000 "to discuss indigenous issues within the mandate of the Council relating to economic and social development, culture, the environment, education, health and human rights." The Declaration on the Rights of Indigenous Peoples was adopted by the General Assembly on 13 September 2007 by a majority of 144 states in favour. Eleven abstentions and four votes against that came from the CANZUS settler colonial states of Canada, Australia, New Zealand, and the US; they later reversed their position and begrudgingly endorsed the Declaration (PFII, 2007). The embryonic participatory democracy applied at the WGIP and the PFII continues to shape the UN and change the future of international law and politics today (Meuhlebach, 2001).

Research

Research Problem

How has the interrelationship between civil–military operations, settler colonialism, militarised anthropology, and internationalised nations influenced the use of cultural intelligence in the Anglo-Saxon ABCA Armies?

This book represents a timely investigation into a number of important issues regarding how the ABCA Armies have attempted to understand the cultural environment of civil–military intervention zones. It draws on the expertise of anthropologists, highlights the ways culture 'is done' by ABCA Armies, and discusses the challenges and problems that currently exist with respect to data analysis and ethical acceptability.

Ethnography

For the purpose of evaluating fieldwork data, this research uses a combination of ethnography and content analysis. The ethnographic research seeks to understand the perspectives of current ABCA Army anthropology or social science practitioners in civil–military roles *as they see it*; it attempts to represent the ideas and behaviours of practitioners as accurately, precisely, and organically as possible. Doing so recognised that the practitioners stated claims and beliefs as dimensions that constitute parts of their lived reality (i.e., their mission and organisational influences). The research treats the ABCA Army practitioner's knowledge, language, and practices seriously, because these dimensions of their stories provide insights into their knowledge of their task, how they derived this knowledge, and the ways this knowledge affects how they see themselves and their role within an organisation and its strategy. The ethnographic approach enables a deeper understanding of the motivations and behaviours of anthropologists and other social scientists in the ABCA Armies engaged in civil–military operations. Through firsthand discussions with practitioners, they can be seen as real persons in their everyday environment, which provides insight into how views and motivations of practitioners facilitate or impede the realisation of organisations strategic goals.

Content Analysis

A practitioner's view of their own work 'as they make sense' of things', is known as the emic (insider) approach in anthropology. Content analysis manages research, and provides an effective technique for sorting, classifying, querying, and analysing the large volumes of rich descriptive text produced through ethnographic interviews. A manually applied content analysis was used to evaluate the content of text and written communication. Content analysis linked statements from ABCA interviewees to the following themes:

- Deployment Cultural Knowledge,
- Cultural Research in Conflict among the People,
- Anthropology and Traditional Intelligence Analysis,
- Ethical Challenges of Anthropological Research,
- Cultural Comparisons between the ABCA Armies and;
- Human Terrain System:

Case Study Analysis

There are two detailed case study analyses of civil–military interventions that examine the relationships between cultural intelligence, militarised anthropology, settler colonialism, and native nations in the ABCA Anglo-Saxon armies of Australia and New Zealand. Case study analysis enabled the researcher to 'make sense' of the perceptions of practitioner's 'as it is' etic (outsider) perspective. Organising ethnographic interviews around content analysis helped illuminate any contradictions that may exist between statements (emic) and actual behaviour (etic).

Grant and Affiliations

Dr Scott Flower, Senior Researcher, and Dr David Hyndman received a research grant in 2012–2013 in support for their project titled "Anthropology, Counterinsurgency and Civil–Military Relations for Stabilisation, Peace-building and Conflict Prevention" from the Australian Civil–Military Centre. The project was located in the multidisciplinary School of Business, University of New South Wales, Canberra, and was hosted by Professor Satish Chand's Fragile States Research Program, and by Dr Nelia Hyndman-Rizk's cross-cultural communication and cultural competency research. Ethical clearances were obtained from the University of New South Wales, Canberra, and the Australian Defence Force.

Conclusion

Civil–Military Armed Conflict and Disaster Management and Interventionism

As military campaigns shifted away from war between states to civil–military occupations of regions identified as "tribal" and "Indigenous", the ABCA Armies sought anthropological knowledge to understand the shifting characteristics of enemies and inform engagement with such adversaries (Price, 2011: 3). Civil–military armed conflict prevention and peacemaking is ideally followed by peacekeeping and peacebuilding. Defence predominates in the armed conflict phase, with multi-agency, whole of government coordination occurring in the post-ceasefire and peace phases. Internationalised intrastate armed conflicts and disasters in the early 21st century have become embedded in the same global logic of interventionism, which is based on the temporality of emergency and the conflation of military and humanitarian operations used to justify a state of exception (Fassin and Pandolfi, 2010). The urgency of the situation and the danger to victims from war and disaster justify the exception of intervention.

ABCA

Interest in how cultural intelligence can be collected and used has increased in the 'Anglo-Saxon' settler colonial states through formalised arrangements such as the America, Britain, Canada, Australia, and New Zealand (ABCA) Armies. ABCA, referred to as "the alliance you never heard of", is little known to the public, and grew out of the close cooperation among Anglo-Saxon allies during World War II. Anglo-Saxon history and heritage, common-law legal system, and similar institutions of political and bureaucratic governance provide the foundational bond that unites the ABCA armies in interstate and intrastate armed conflict and civil–military interventions.

Human Terrain System: ABCA Armies Operational and Tactical Tool of Counterinsurgency

Among the ABCA Armies, "HTS was both an operational and tactical tool of counterinsurgency" that balanced between security and development tasks and between kinetic and non-kinetic effects. Intelligence, termed 'research', operated among the local population for "cultural appreciation used in planning, execution and assessment of operations" (ABCA, 2011).

The Human Terrain System (HTS) experimental counterinsurgency programme was created by the American Army between 2005 and 2006 for deployment to Iraq and Afghanistan. 'Embedded anthropologists' helped gather intelligence, referred to as gathering 'research', to improve knowledge of local culture (Sluka, 2010). McFate (2005: 43) boldly declared Anthropology to be the academic discipline "invented to support warfighting in the tribal zone". The HTS program became known as "a

CORDS for the 21st century" (Kipp *et al.*, 2006). In Vietnam, the Civil Operations and Revolutionary Development Support (CORDS) program was made operational in 1968. CORDS became one component of the counterinsurgency strategy, and the infamous Phoenix program as the other component, which gathered intelligence to target tens of thousands of Vietnamese for "neutralisation" (Valentine, 1990). Controversially, anthropological 'research' is sometimes utilised as a stream of intelligence to support targeting, and as a result, has been challenged ethically to do no harm, be transparent, and be based on voluntary informed consent (Gonzales, 2009). In 2007, the American Anthropological Association (AAA) formally opposed the HTS and denounced it as "an unacceptable application of anthropological expertise".

Deployed American Army Human Terrain Teams delivered "cultural advice to commanders". Human Terrain Teams were "led by a military officer and included 'embedded' expert social scientists". American Human Terrain Analysis Teams and Human Terrain Teams conducted field 'research' among the local population for cultural appreciation used in planning, execution and assessment of operations' (ABCA, 2010).

ABCA Armies recognised that although 'social scientists and anthropologists were able to measure social demographics in a way that was beneficial to the military commander' it was contentious, because of the social science ethical opposition to militarising anthropology and to the relationship with intelligence and targeting (Parkinson, 2013). Thus, it is debateable within ABCA Armies whether HTS should be independent of or integrated with an intelligence function. Gonzales (2008: 26) maintained that: "to the extent that the HTS might be employed to collect intelligence or target suspected enemies for assassination, the program deserves elimination".

Settler Colonialism

The ABCA states share the legacy of Anglo-Saxon settler colonialism, the history of militarised anthropology, and the international geopolitics of nation against state conflicts. Globally, there are two types of borders; the obvious is the state border that separates different states, and the less obvious is a nation and a state border that separates two realities that coexist within the same global space. Settler colonial invasion is a structural ongoing process, not some historical event, and the aim is to eliminate native nations and displace them from the land.

Militarised Anthropology

In the 19th century settler colonial period, evolutionary anthropologists were a central part of settler colonial intelligence. Ethnography in the early 20th century was a settler colonial instrument for government planning. Militarised anthropological intelligence in the ABCA Armies flourished during World War II. With the emergence of the cold war and the demise of colonial empire, anthropology ethically rejected militarised anthropology and shifted the discipline away from being a tool of domination.

Nation Against State Armed Conflict Among the People

The United Nations Working Group on Indigenous Populations (WGIP), established in 1982, sharply focuses the issues of Indigenous autonomy, self-management, and self-determination, and served to move nations from domestic jurisdiction to international agendas. The first 30 years of the WGIP escaped anthropological attention, yet it was the only global institution in which Indigenous identity and geopolitics has been discussed for decades. The emergence of intrastate wars of the 21st century involved armed conflict among the people, which consisted of internationalised nations whose claim for equal rights and freedoms did not allow for group rights to be claimed within state structures, and since most states have formed over unconsenting nations, recognition of them as a people would jeopardise state territorial claims.

CHAPTER 2

19th Century Evolutionary Anthropology as Colonial Intelligence

Introduction

America

The treaty was a unique Indigenous legacy, and in 1831, the US Supreme Court created the concepts of wardship and domestic dependent nationhood. Powell professionalised the study of Indigenous nations within an evolutionary interpretive framework. Powell and the ethnologists of the Bureau of American Ethnology carried out fieldwork on the militarised frontier. The most important 19th century lawyer and gentleman anthropological scholar was Lewis Henry Morgan.

Britain

There is political and moral complicity between anthropology and the colonial enterprise, and there are obvious connections between British evolutionism and the establishment of the British Empire. In 1898, Haddon launched a second Torres Strait expedition with anthropologists, psychologists, and sociologists, which represented a turning point in

British anthropology. Scholarship was transformed through gaining information directly from local research informants. Particular local cultures, rather than culture generally, became the object of anthropological research. Some of the first ethnographies appeared of peoples recently placed under colonial rule in the British Empire, ethnographies that would again inform understanding of culture and violence in the intrastate nation-against-state armed conflicts, like those in Sudan.

Canada

The Canadian Army, the North-West Mounted Police, the then Royal Canadian Mounted Police, and the Department of Indian Affairs implemented an eliminationist–assimilationist policy by destroying Indigenous political and economic systems, social organisations, and religions. By the mid-1880s, the Department of Indian Affairs had an important place in government, and Canadian anthropology was oriented to salvage ethnography that attempted to reconstruct cultures that were destined to assimilate or disappear.

Australia

An assimilation policy was designed to eliminate Aborigines through 'breeding them white'. The assimilation legislation continued the logic of elimination, taking the children away removed an obstacle to state legitimisation. Thus, the projects of ethnography and ethnocide informed evolutionary anthropology and settler colonialism. *Terra nullius* was the rationalisation, and greed for land was the motive for settler colonial invasion.

New Zealand

The phase of evolutionary anthropology in New Zealand was the period of the enthusiastic amateur, when the researchers of the Maori were largely self-trained. The 19th century was the beginnings of Maori participation as anthropological subjects as well as analysts of their own culture. The New Zealand Wars were followed by the Waitangi Treaty in 1840, and from 1845–1872, Maori land was sold to and confiscated by the settler colonial population. The two versions of the Waitangi Treaty, one in English and one in Maori, are not identical, which has led to protracted problems of interpretation.

America: 19th Century Evolutionary Anthropology, Settler Colonialism, and Wardship of Indigenous Nations

Techniques of settling America spanned the 17th, 18th, and 19th centuries, and were complementary implementations of the settler colonial logic of elimination. The treaty was a unique Indigenous legacy that has not been extended to any other social group in the US. Constitutionally, the status of Indigenous nations was established in the 1831 US Supreme Court case of *Cherokee v. Georgia* that created the concepts of wardship and domestic dependent nationhood, which provided an inferior form of Indigenous title that was extinguishable at will by the discovering sovereign (Wolfe, 2011). Post-frontier settler colonial strategies incorporated Indigenous peoples into US society. With the passing of the frontier, American Indigenous affairs shifted from international relations establishing treaties with Indigenous people to a depoliticised domestic administration. Indigenous occupancy was detached from title; "property starts where Indianness stops" (Wolfe, 2011: 15).

Indigenous removal was predicated on the availability of unclaimed space for relocation of those dispossessed. President Jefferson came up with the idea of an Indian Territory for the removal of Indigenous peoples, and the purchase of the Louisiana Purchase provided the geographical feasibility. Jefferson envisioned the reciprocal exchange of land for civilisation. The Louisiana Purchase forged a fateful union between treaties and removal, whereby "the extension of the slave-plantation economy in Georgia, Tennessee, Arkansas, Louisiana, Mississippi, Alabama, and the Florida panhandle was conditional upon Indian removal" (Wolfe, 2011: 17). Removal required the frontier existence of US territory unclaimed by settlers. Between 1853 and 1856, there were over 50 negotiated treaties and the majority provided for allotment. Removal treaties allowed for allotments to certain Indigenous members to become agriculturalists on individually owned parcels of land. Although long established as agriculturalists, Indigenous peoples were regarded as wandering savages, and therefore "nomadism naturalised removal" (Wolfe, 2011: 18). Allotments provided a way for White traders to recover debt incurred by Indigenous individuals with the assumption that allottees would sell their plots. The alternatives posed by President Jackson in 1817 included remaining Indigenous peoples undergoing removal or untraditionally remaining on former land on individual allotments; either way, Indigenous people lost their land. The choice from a Chickasaw treaty negotiator's perspective was to stay behind, lose their name and language, and become White, or cross the Mississippi and lose their homeland (Wolfe, 2011).

Subsequently, the Civil War intensified the militarisation of America, including bringing "guns into the home, making them part of the domestic environment and an unquestioned member of the American family" (Bellesiles, 1966: 455). Indigenous nations of the Great Plains were rapidly conquered and relegated to reservations, to enable the westward expansion of settlers.

The post-Darwinian era generally followed evolutionary interpretations in America (Silverman, 2005). The most important 19th century lawyer and gentleman scholar was Lewis Henry Morgan. Morgan represented the Seneca nation in a land dispute, and subsequently developed an interest in Iroquois kinship (Morgan, 1851) and an ongoing comparative interest in kinship systems (Morgan, 1870). From his interest in kinship, Morgan developed his broader theory of social evolution that was published in *Ancient Society* (1877).

Westward expansion of settler colonialism stimulated practical as well as intellectual motives for gaining cultural intelligence about the Indigenous nations. John Wesley Powell emerged as the foremost compiler of Indigenous languages and customs. He was first appointed as Head of the US Geological Survey, and then in 1879, he became Head of the newly created Bureau of American Ethnology. Powell professionalised the study of Indigenous nations within an evolutionary interpretive framework (Silverman, 2005). Powell and the ethnologists of the bureau carried out fieldwork on the militarised frontier.

With the passing of the frontier, focus shifted to the reduction of Indigenous nations as Indigenous nations, rather than a geographic displacement of Indigenous nations. The passing of the frontier inaugurated a shift in techniques of eliminating Indigenous nations:

> "[…] on 3 March 1871, when Congress resolved that: 'No Indian nation or tribe within the territory of the United States shall be acknowledged or recognised as an independent nation, tribe, or power with whom the United States may contract by treaty'. The era of treaty-making with Indian tribes was formally over…Through being rendered internal; the Indian problem was discursively reconstituted as administrative rather than political."
>
> (Wolfe, 2011: 33)

Anthropology became institutionalised in museums as well as government agencies. By the mid-19th century, the National Museum of the Smithsonian, the Peabody Museum at Harvard, and the American Museum of Natural History in New York became established, and they each developed archaeological and ethnological divisions to gather and curate collections. From these institutions, a Washington/Cambridge axis formed in opposition to Boas at Columbia and the Boasians:

> "[…] division was theoretical, counterpoising evolutionary to historicist models, racialist to cultural determinism, and fixed types of plasticity; it was a cultural divergence, with predominately old-American WASPs on the one side and the immigrant, often Jewish, Boasians on the other; and it often corresponded to political differences around the issue of immigration policy, race relations, nationalism and isolationism during World War I, American Indian separatism and assimilationism, and other matters."
>
> (Silverman, 2005: 261)

Britain: 19th Century Evolutionary Anthropology as Colonial Military Practice

Britain's colonial expansion in the 19th century led to scholarly and public global knowledge of geography, zoology, and botany. However, there was initially little serious attention given to the lives of 'savages'. The campaign by non-conformist and Quaker activists against African slavery was achieved in 1833, and they subsequently formed the Aboriginal Protection Society that compiled and systematised information about 'uncivilised tribes' and fostered the growth of an anthropological perspective (Stocking, 1971).

A break between evangelists and scholars led to the establishment of the Ethnological Society of London in 1844, which combined medical and linguistic approaches to trace the unity of humankind. Those that traced several origins of human races and those tracing a single origin split the Ethnological Society. Those that favoured slavery and natural aristocracy and opposed the humanitarian ethnologists and Darwinians formed the Anthropological Society in 1863 (Feuchtwang, 1973). Richard Francis Burton co-founded the Anthropological Society of London and the journal *Anthropologia* (Kennedy, 2005). By contrast, the Ethnological Society of London maintained a liberal political orientation (Feuchtwang, 1973). Under the leadership of Thomas Huxley, there was a successful alliance between the two societies, and they created the Royal Anthropological Institute in 1871 that postulated Darwinian evolution (Barth, 2005).

Edward Tylor (1832–1917) received a modest life pension from his Quaker father and started attending meetings of the Ethnological Society in 1862 with other archaeologists and ethnographers. Tylor was fascinated by the parallels between unearthed European stone tools and the tools of contemporary 'savages'; the defining topic for the early discipline of anthropology became a speculation on the resemblance between contemporary 'savages' and ancient primitive humanity. Tylor formulated the concept of the 'psychic unity of man', and published his influential *Primitive Culture* (1871). The humanitarian commitment to the equality and moral value of all humankind introduced relativism to anthropology that would come to fruition in the practices of participant observation fieldwork (Barth, 2005).

Tylor brought order to the analysis of culture through his concept of 'survivals'; interpreted to provide evidence of evolutionary stages. The evolution of religion was Tylor's main interest, which was presented as the product of people's efforts to understand the world rather than from divine revelation. Animism was conceptualised as the earliest and most basic form of religion that culturally evolved to monotheistic religions.

Evolutionary anthropology speculations were based on written sources like that of classic and historical scholars; rather than direct field observations and the explanations remained trivial. However, the development of anthropology benefited from the addition of such descriptive terminology as animism, exogamy, matriliny, totemism, and taboo. Tylor was elected as Fellow of the Royal Society and appointed Professor at Oxford in 1896, but he never developed significant relationships with students (Barth, 2005).

The zoologist Alfred Haddon (1855–1940) contributed to the next enhancement of anthropological data. He investigated coral reef formation in the Torres Strait in 1888, and subsequently published in zoology and anthropology. In 1898, Haddon launched a second Torres Strait expedition with anthropologists, psychologists, and sociologists, which represented a turning point in British anthropology. Scholarship was transformed through gaining information directly from local research informants. Particular local cultures, rather than culture generally, became the object of anthropological research. River's genealogical methodology was developed for mapping kinship relations. W.H.R. Rivers (1864–1922) and Charles Seligman (1873–1940) trained in the Torres Strait and inspired the next generation of British anthropologists (Barth, 2005).

Rivers worked in South India in 1901 and wrote *The Todas* (1906), regarded as an early exemplary ethnography based on intensive field methodology. Rivers retuned to Melanesia in 1908 and 1914, where his star pupil was Malinowski, who worked in Mailu in the Gulf of Papua in 1914 and in the Trobriand Islands from 1915–1918. Rivers' conceptual work on social organisation endured and established the foundation for the work of several generations of British anthropologists. Not so enduring to the discipline was Rivers' conversion to diffusionism in 1914; the next generation under Radcliffe-Brown effectively dismissed all diffusionist speculation and evolutionist conjectures from anthropology (Barth, 2005).

Seligman returned to Melanesia in 1903 and produced the documentary work *The Melanesians of British New Guinea* (1910). With his anthropologist wife Brenda, Seligman conducted ethnographic research from 1907–1908 with the Veddas in present-day Sri Lanka (Seligman and Seligman, 1911). The husband and wife anthropology team then made three expeditions to central and southern Sudan, and published (Seligman and Seligman, 1932) on the cultures of the Arabic, Nuba, and Nilotic peoples (Barth, 2005). Rivers and Seligman produced some of the first ethnographies of peoples recently placed under colonial rule in the British Empire, ethnographies that would again inform understanding of culture and violence in Indigenous nation against state conflicts, like those in Sudan.

Canada: Anthropology and Settler Colonial Accession of Indigenous Land

France sent the first large number of settler colonists in the 17th century, but subsequently, the collection of territories and colonies now comprising the Dominion of Canada became ruled by the British until full independence was attained by the former British settler colonists in the 20th century. British and French conflicts escalated, with settlers from both colonies forming alliances of friendship with First Nations people and treaties to secure trade routes for the lucrative fur trade. The 1763 Treaty of Paris ended the Seven Years War and organised the governments of Britain's acquisitions in North America (Behrendt, 2009).

The new provinces of Upper Canada and New Brunswick were created after the American Revolution. Later in 1841, Upper and Lower Canada were united to form the Province of Canada. These new provinces with the original colonies of Quebec and Nova Scotia entered Confederation in 1867. Prior to Confederation, the purchase of First Nation land by treaty primarily occurred in Ontario. Manitoba was created in 1870, and union with British Columbia in 1871 was contingent on completion of a transcontinental railway, which facilitated new treaty negotiations with First Nations. Settler colonist governments signed 11 numbered treaties that acquired First Nation title in exchange for promises of reservations, small annuities, and rights to hunting, fishing, and trapping (Behrendt, 2009).

Canadian society engages in colonial action against Indigenous peoples whose claim to land and self-determination continue to undermine legitimacy of state hegemony. Settler colonialism is inherently eliminatory and the primary motivation for elimination is access to territory (Wolfe, 2006). The logic of elimination and the extinguishment of Indigenous and treaty rights have informed federal policy since Confederation in 1867. Settler colonialism's project "was, and still is, to lay waste a people and destroy their culture in order to undermine the integrity of their existence and appropriate their riches...it is pursued through total war" (Stevenson, 1992: 28). The federal government adopted eliminationist Indigenous policy objectives of protection, civilisation, and assimilation through containing Indigenous peoples on reserves, and bureaucratising them through churches and the civil service (Green, 1995).

The use of the settler colonial term 'Indian' bears no relation to what Indigenous peoples call themselves, implies a false unity among disparate nations, and provides linguistic plausibility for a homogeneous eliminationist policy adopted by Canada towards Indigenous peoples. Settler colonial land theft was legitimised by constructing evolutionist paradigms of deficient Indigenous social, political, and cultural development that was incapable of holding sovereignty or resisting modernising colonial domination. Settler colonial law used the fiction of "discovery" to appropriate Indigenous land, and of *terra incognita* to enable a sovereign to claim underlying title to unknown lands. This land becomes 'settled' by 'settlers' who import the colonial law (Green, 1995).

Canadian settler society pits settler and Indigenous peoples against one another, which benefits the government and corporate elites at the expense of individual and collective autonomy (Barker, 2009). Canada colonises the 'aboriginal' as a cooperative comprador class because the colonial needs the 'native' in order to remain privileged:

> "Aboriginalism, with its roots in this dichotomising essentialism, plays the perfect foil to the Euroamerican mentality. Settlers can remain who and what they are, and injustice can be reconciled by the mere allowance of the Other to become one of Us. What higher reward or better future is there than to be fully recognised as achieving the status of a European."
>
> (Alfred, 2005: 135)

Indigenous peoples in Canada are those peoples whose societies predate colonisation, have a complex relationship to the land, and remain active targets of colonialism:

> "Indigenousness is an identity constructed, shaped and lived in the politicised context of contemporary colonialism. The communities,

clans, nations and tribes we call Indigenous peoples are just that: Indigenous to the lands they inhabit, in contrast to and in contention with the colonial societies and states that have spread out from Europe and other centres of empire. It is this oppositional, place-based existence, along with the consciousness of being in a struggle against the dispossessing and demeaning facts of the colonization by foreign peoples that fundamentally distinguishes Indigenous peoples from other peoples of the world."

(Alfred and Corntassel, 2005: 597)

The new 1867 state of Canada was dependent upon land; the National Policy consisted of building a transcontinental railway, a protective tariff on imports, and western settlement. Settlers of approved White immigrant stock populated the land controlled by Indigenous nations, including the Metis, and provided labour for natural resources, and a market for eastern goods. The consortium building the railroad was given Indigenous land as a right-of-way and payment for their effort, with settlers given Indigenous land to homestead. Acquiring land for unobstructed railway construction, natural resource exploitation, and settlement was accomplished through the colonial treaty-making endeavour, the reserve system administered under the Indian Acts, the military conquests, and the dispersal of the Metis. This policy was only pursued where settler colonial and Indigenous interests collided. Indigenous nations of no immediate concern were mostly ignored (Green, 1995).

It was expected that implementing the National Policy would eliminate culturally distinct Indigenous nations and assimilate them into settler colonial society. The eliminationist–assimilationist policy was implemented by the army, the North-West Mounted Police, the then Royal Canadian Mounted Police, and the Department of Indian Affairs, by destroying Indigenous political and economic systems, social organisations, and religions (Manual and Posuns, 1974). The conclusions of Treaties One and Two declared that "eventually on the 3rd of August 1871, a treaty was concluded, its principal features being the relinquishment to Her Majesty of the Indian title" (Morris, 1971: 224). Treaty commitments to First Nation harvesting rights were abandoned by the Canadian government. Provincial encroachment on treaty rights was not even provided for in the

Indian Act until 1951. Treaty rights were insecure and indigenous rights were essentially non-existent (Behrendt, 2009). Contrary to settler colonial legal assertions that Indigenous title was not landholding proper and was merely personal and usufructory in nature, Indigenous nations insisted that their title be recognised.

Colonial missionary anthropology in Canada dates back 300 years to the 17th century, in what was then the Domain of Canada, with the oldest ethnographic records of the First Nation peoples written by the Jesuit missionaries Fathers Le Clercq, Le Jeune, and Sagard (Darnell, 1998). The period of pre-professional amateur evolutionary anthropology occurred in the late 19th century. Edward Tylor, the founder of evolutionary anthropology in Britain, addressed the British Association for the Advancement of Science in Toronto in 1884. Tylor, grounded in British colonialism, advocated that because of its distinct colonial history, Canada would be able to retain stronger connections to British anthropology than the Americans. Tylor drew international attention to the importance of Canadian anthropological data and emphasised that First Nation questions in Canada were more immediate and pressing than in the United States (Darnell, 1998). Significantly, the committee on the North-western Tribes of Canada carried out a strike against the 1884 meeting of the British Association for the Advancement of Science (Hancock, 2006).

Anthropologists' treatment of the management of Indigenous nation-state relations in the late 19th century reflected the prominent place of managing Indigenous affairs in government. By the mid-1880s, the Department of Indian Affairs had an important place in government and was near the epicentre of national political concerns. In contrast, anthropology was just beginning to establish an institutional and professional presence in Canada (Dyck, 2006). Precursors of professional anthropology included George Dawson, who directed the Geological Survey of Canada and provided an incipient framework for ethnology. Hale was an ethnologist and linguist for the Wilkes Exploring Expedition in the United States, who returned to his native Canada in the 1880s, and worked with a committee of Iroquois chiefs on a history of the Six Nations Confederacy (Darnell, 1998).

Canadian anthropology was oriented to salvage ethnography that attempted to reconstruct cultures that were destined to assimilate or disappear. There was shared settler colonial discourse in anthropology and Canadian society that traditional lifeways of Indigenous people were irrelevant to life in the late 19th to early 20th century. Explaining the present situation of Indigenous peoples in terms of culture loss and inevitable assimilation was the effect of Canada's settler colonial legacy. Settler colonial relations reaffirmed evolutionist discourse that presumed innate settler superiority and relegated Indigenous people as savage, rudimentary, and inferior. Settler colonial intervention to transform and assimilate Indigenous people naturalised their oppression and marginalisation (Buchanan, 2006).

By the early 20th century, the Anthropology Division of the National Museum was the main focus of anthropological research in salvage ethnography. The perceived Indian problem was the refusal of Indigenous people to assimilate and abandon their cultures. First Nations and settler colonists initially cooperated but by Confederation, the pattern was displacement and assimilation that eroded Indigenous political and cultural autonomy. Indigenous people went from allies and trading partners to impeding settlement and being a nuisance to be managed. Relations between the settler population and First Nations were codified in the Indian Act that authorised the Canadian government to regulate most aspects of Indigenous life. The complex of legislation and moral regulation, known as the Bible and plough policy, sought to raise savages up the scale of civilisation. Indigenous people needed to forsake the supposedly primitive ways in order to achieve evolutionary cultural advancement (Buchanan, 2006).

Australia: Anthropology and Settler Colonial Frontier Wars

There is political and moral complicity between anthropology and the colonial enterprise, and there are obvious connections between British evolutionism and the establishment of the British Empire (Fabian, 1983). Evolutionary anthropology collapsed time and space, to leave Europe and travel in space was to travel back in time (Fabian, 1983). Ethnographers in the 19th century was obsessed with origins, and they used ethnography to recreate prehistory. Social evolutionists attempted to penetrate furthest back in prehistory. Morgan through kinship systems and Tylor through cultural survivals attempted to recover the primal, established in terms of distance from the modern. Societies were significant not for themselves but for the light they could shed on the past. Purity of the Indigenous Other was based on the extent they remained uncontacted, which made ethnography contradictory, because data was jeopardised in the gathering (Wolfe, 1994).

Spencer and Gillen's (1899: 265) allegation that the Arunta did not realise that conception was the result of sexual intercourse categorised the Arunta as the ultimate in living savagery, and was the high point in Australian evolutionist ethnography. Spencer became the unrivalled authority on Aboriginal matters, while participating in Australian government policy to eliminate Aboriginal people. In 1911, Spencer was appointed Chief Protector of Aborigines in the Northern Territory, and recommended removal of half-caste children. The recommendation reinforced the abduction of Aboriginal children as a central state-forming strategy. Evolutionist ethnography was predicated on the extreme inferiority of the colonised, which legitimated their oppression. An assimilation policy was designed to eliminate Aborigines through 'breeding them White'; thus, the projects of ethnography and ethnocide informed evolutionary anthropology and settler colonialism (Wolfe, 1994).

In terms of evolutionary anthropological theory, British evolutionists were concerned that the theory of mother-right had immediate links to domestic sexual politics. Women lacked rights to marital property, and in divorce, they did not have rights to their children. Themes in Aboriginal ethnography of primal promiscuity, uncertain paternity, subordination of maternal descent, and the primacy of patriarchal property were refractions of Victorian sexual politics (Wolfe, 1994).

In the first 50 years of British colonisation from 1788–1838, frontier armed conflict was characterised by a new form of Aboriginal warfare concentrated on raiding crops, animals, and farmhouses; goods and foodstuffs were taken when useful and destroyed when they were not. When the terrain assisted them, the Aborigines were able to temporarily stop settler occupation of their land. Fighting was carried out by soldiers and settlers on the British settler colonial side. Although the British Army arrived with experience of colonial warfare elsewhere in the Empire, they found it difficult to operate on the frontier. Initially, Aboriginal tactics overcame British muskets and Aboriginal warriors evaded pursuing British soldiers, but after 1825, soldiers were provided with horses and the mobility to track and attack. After the last major British Army deployment in 1838, fighting was left to settlers and civilian police, and the frontier became more violent (Connor, 2005).

Australian settler colonialism was part of the British project of global colonisation. Although Phillips was instructed to engage in friendly commerce, it was not long before the Aborigines were shot, a pattern repeated across the continent for the next century and a half. Colonising was based on the doctrine of *terra nullius* rather than upon any acknowledgement of Indigenous land rights, and Aboriginal defence of their property was actually seen as an incursion of the settler entitlement to occupy the land. *Terra nullius* was the rationalisation, and greed for land was the motive for colonial invasion. Settler colonialism was not premised on extracting surplus value from Indigenous labour, but upon displacing Indigenous peoples from and replacing them on the land. Imported labour to add value to the land mostly came from British and Irish convicts and the blackbirding of Melanesians for the sugarcane fields. The cultural logic was one of elimination, whereby economic use of the colonised land was primarily for pastoral settlement with an exclusive requirement for territory. The violence and conflict established by the First Fleet was not wanton but systemic to settler colonialism (Wolfe, 1994).

Aboriginal Indigenous nations with subsistence economies and part-time warriors encountered the British state with a population of more than 10 million and an industrialising economy that employed professional soldiers. The invasion and settlement of Indigenous Australia was a manifestation of British imperial expansion worldwide. Fighting on the frontier was on a smaller scale than comparable conflicts such as the New Zealand wars. Aborigines were non-hierarchical, and each Aboriginal nation fought the British on their own. Aborigines had a spear tradition and did not possess or use firearms on the frontier; they held the advantage through superior bushcraft and tactics, and not from superior weaponry. Aborigines, unlike the Maori, lacked the bargaining power to force the British into trading for firearms. Trade between the British and Indigenous peoples in other settler colonies led to the widespread adoption of firearms; the Maori in New Zealand traded foodstuffs, greenstone, timber, and flax for muskets, while Indigenous nations in America traded wampum (shell money) and beaver pelts (Connor, 2005).

Aboriginal warfare tactics on the frontier retarded settlers in certain areas but could not prevent settler colonial encroachment over the whole frontier. Few Indigenous peoples anywhere in the world were able to defeat the British and to force them to retreat. Even the large Iroquois nation in North America with agriculture, metal-working, and an arsenal of firearms was eventually defeated by settlers. Settlers fought for themselves and became better equipped with guns and horses, and fighting continued on the frontier until 1928. Frontier wars contributed to sweeping away Aboriginal sovereignty and replacing it with settler colonial institutions and culture. Victory was so overwhelming, it continues to determine the relationship between descendants of the victors and descendants of the defeated (Connor, 2005).

Indigenous mortality in the initial phase of land seizure was the result of homicide, sexual abuse, disease, and starvation. According to the former anthropologist, government official, and settler Edward Curr (1886: 100), "the meeting of the Aboriginal tribes of Australia and the White pioneer, results as a rule in war, which lasts from six months to ten years." The effectiveness of Aboriginal resistance was severely reduced by differences in firepower and introduced diseases (Crosby, 1986). Aboriginal troopers and police, recruited by settlers to attack their Indigenous enemies (Rosser, 1991; Fels, 1988), fought the colonised at the same time they colonised themselves (Pels, 1997). As the war frontier moved across Australia, the repeated pattern was one of a decimated, but mostly pacified, surviving Aboriginal population (Wolfe, 1994).

Survivors were gathered at missions, stations, and reservations, which advanced the evacuation of Aboriginal land, making it available for pastoral settlement. In addition to their tangible decimation, the evolutionists presumed the Aboriginal population was dying out through weakened selection that rendered them unfit to continue in the present or distant future (Stanner, 1938; Fabian, 1983). Aboriginal women kept house for the pastoralists who took advantage of their sexual services to breed their own labour (Huggins, 1988), but the exploitation of Aboriginal labour was subordinate to the takeover of territory. However, the sexual element of the colonial invasion contradicted the logic of elimination.

Only settlers could expand, the problem of miscegenation was absorption into the settler category. The half-caste menace threatened the colonial basis of citizenship and geography. The response of the assimilation policy separated Aboriginal people of mixed race from their natal kin and those of mixed descent were to be accounted as White settler. Assimilation legislation continued the logic of elimination, taking the children away removed an obstacle to state legitimisation (Wolfe, 1994).

New Zealand: 19th Century Anthropology and Settler Colonial Maori Wars

Anthropology in New Zealand has three divisions. The first anthropological interest in the Maori began in the 19th century, and appeared in diaries, journals, and records. This second phase of anthropology in New Zealand provided unscientific accounts of travels, animals, and plants, as well as customs of the Maori (Beaglehole, 1938). Scholarly interests in the newly-subjugated Maori followed missionary and settler colonial expansion. The third phase of evolutionary anthropology in 19th century New Zealand was closely intertwined with settler colonisers forming a majority settler population, and with Indigenous experience one of continuous and ongoing processes of colonisation.

Captain James Cook sighted New Zealand in 1769 and mapped the entire coastline by the beginning of 1770. In 1833, James Busby arrived in the Bay of Islands as the appointed British Resident, with instructions from Governor Richard Bourke of New South Wales to protect 'well-disposed settlers and traders' and prevent 'outrages' by settler colonists against the Maori. Busby gathered a confederation of chiefs in 1834 to choose a flag for New Zealand-built trading ships. In 1835, Busby drew up a New Zealand Declaration of Independence that assigned sovereign power and authority with the Maori hereditary chiefs (Behrendt, 2009).

The Musket Wars were a series of more than 500 Maori armed conflicts from 1807 to 1842. At least 20,000 Maori died in these conflicts, and an additional 30,000 were enslaved or forced to migrate. It is estimated that more than half of all Maori tribes (*iwi*) suffered population loss through battle casualties, enslavement, and cannibalism, and that eight *iwi* were wiped out (Crosby, 1999).

The phase of evolutionary anthropology in New Zealand was the period of the enthusiastic amateur, when the students of the Maori were largely self-trained (Beaglehole, 1938). Shortland has been described as "the first anthropologist of the Maori" (Anderson, 1990: 397). The amateur anthropologists like Southland were preoccupied with mapping out the evolutionary stages of progress and the determination of origins. The Maori were positioned higher on the socio-evolutionary scale than Aboriginal people because they had agriculture (Beaglehole, 1938).

Edward Shortland was born and completed his medical studies in England before migrating to New Zealand in 1841 (Byrnes, 1994). Shortland's southern ethnographic expedition from 1843–1844 was an exercise in colonial administration, and involved the collaborative role of the Maori in scientific and exploratory discourse in the construction of a new settler colonial cultural space. The published account appeared in 1851 as The *Southern Districts of New Zealand*. Shortland viewed the country as becoming a Britain of the South. As a traveller, ethnographer, and cultural mediator, Shortland described the southern regions as a new cultural landscape, itself comparable to the southern coasts of Devon and Cornwall. By encoding places on a map, Southland laid the foundation for further extension of settler colonial hegemony (Byrnes, 1994).

Travel in the service of the Colonial government became a rudimentary ethnography. Above all, the *Southern Districts* was an anthropological text, "the seminal work of South Island Maori history and ethnography" (Anderson, 1990: 396). Shortland applied an evolutionist definition of culture to his observation of the Maori:

> "[…] the natives of New Zealand differ essentially from those of all other of our Australian colonies. They are comparatively more numerous; they are given to agricultural pursuits; and have been found to learn, and readily adopt, the more civilized practices of Europeans; at the same time that their bodily and mental organisation is generally considered not inferior to our own."
>
> (Shortland, 1851: vi)

Shortland (1851: 77) was eager to engage with the wider debates of evolutionist anthropology and he argued that "there is no sufficient reason to anticipate the extinction of the Maori race, except by the possible means of its becoming blended with European stock. This, too, is an event, the accomplishment of which must be very remote under any circumstances."

The 19th century was the beginnings of Maori participation as anthropological subjects as well as analysts of their own culture. Governor George Grey, recognised by Stocking (1987) as a perceptive ethnographer of his day, was tutored by Maori chiefs and priests (*tohunga*) that included Te Rangikaheke, who contributed 800 pages of Maori cosmologies (Henare, 2007: 94). Elsdon Best, another 19th century pioneer of Maori ethnography, developed similar relationships with Maori elders (*kaumatua*), including Ranapiri who wrote letters in response to Best's ethnographic enquires. Ranapiri famously explained the Maori concept of breath of life (*hau*), described by Mauss as the spirit of the gift. Anthropology in the 19th century was characterised by enduring and often close relationships between mainly British analysts and their knowledgeable Maori researchers (Henare, 2007: 95).

William Hobson was appointed consul by the British government in 1839 and instructed to obtain sovereignty with the consent of a 'sufficient number' of Maori chiefs. The Treaty of Waitangi was signed on 6 February 1840 by 40 chiefs and, by September, an additional 500 chiefs had signed. In the two versions of the Treaty, one in English and one in Maori, the texts are not identical, and this has led to protracted problems of interpretation (Behrendt, 2009). Under the terms of the Treaty of Waitangi, the Maori could only sell their land to the Crown. Settler dominance became naturalised, and British appointed governors and later settler governments acted as though the Waitangi Treaty granted them sovereignty over the Maori as a subject people. Settlers drew political and constitutional justification from an English treaty draft whereby the British gained sovereignty. Maori land was confiscated and alienated through the courts. The settler colonial logic was elimination of the native (Wolfe, 2006). Settler colonialism was manifested in assimilation policies for education, health, and social service that economically dispossessed the Maori, who have struggled to maintain their land rights and cultural institutions (Huygens, 2011).

The New Zealand Wars followed the Waitangi Treaty between 1845–1872 over Maori land being sold to and confiscated by the settler colonial population (Belich, 1986). Huge areas of North Island had been depopulated and repopulated with new *iwi* following the Musket Wars.

The wars were four-sided conflicts. The Maori fought on both sides of the wars. Although they were allies only while fighting, the Maori warriors fought the colonised while at the same time they colonised themselves. The Pakeha colonists had imperial troops (mostly from India and Afghanistan) supplied and paid for by Britain and settler militias answerable to the New Zealand government. Typically, the Maori would build a fortified *pa* and the British soldiers would attack, but such frontal attacks were costly. Later, the British troops neutralised the *pa* through destroying the surrounding Maori economic base. More than 16,000 square kilometres of land were confiscated from "loyal" and "rebel" Maori alike under the New Zealand Settlements Act of 1863 (Belich, 1986).

Conclusion

America

In 1831, the US Supreme Court created the concepts of wardship and domestic dependent nationhood. Powell and the ethnologists of the Bureau of American Ethnology carried out fieldwork on the militarised frontier.

Britain

There is political and moral complicity between anthropology and the colonial enterprise, and there are obvious connections between British 19th century evolutionism and the establishment of the British Empire. In 1898, Haddon launched a second Torres Strait expedition. Particular local cultures, rather than culture generally, became the object of anthropological research. The ethnographies that appeared of peoples recently placed under colonial rule in the British Empire would later inform understanding of intrastate armed conflict among the people.

Canada

The eliminationist-assimilationist policy in Canada was responsible for destroying Indigenous political and economic systems, social organisations, and religions. By the 1880s, the Department of Indian Affairs became oriented to salvage ethnography.

Australia

The assimilation policy was designed to eliminate Aborigines through 'breeding them white'. Ethnography informed evolutionary anthropology and settler colonialism; *terra nullius* was the rationalisation and greed for land was the motive for the colonial settler.

New Zealand

The 19th century was the beginnings of Maori participation as anthropological subjects as well as analysts of their own culture. The Waitangi Treaty was in 1840, and from 1845–1872, Maori land was sold to and confiscated by the settler colonial population.

CHAPTER 3

Early 20th Century Ethnography as Colonial Instrument for Government Planning

Introduction

America

The commitment of Indigenous nations to collective ownership was a major obstacle to assimilation. The settler objective shifted to imposing Western style governance on Indigenous nations to eliminate them as Indigenous institutions. Professor Boas promoted historical particularism as an alternative to evolutionism and assigned greatest importance to salvage ethnography. Professor Boas published "Scientists as Spies" in *The Nation* in 1919, as an ethical critique of unnamed people who used the cover of anthropological research to work as World War I government agents. Half of the anthropologists in the 1930s and 1940s worked with the Applied Anthropology Unit at the Bureau of Indian Affairs and the Community Analyst Program under the War Relocation Authority.

Britain

The British Empire colonial policy in the 1930s imposed indirect governance to allay colonial-nationalist sentiment in the colonies. To avoid colonial struggles around race conflict and indigenous revolt, Professor Malinowski advocated a colonial strategy based on anthropological knowledge to achieve desired evolutionary progress inexpensively and with minimal violence. The move to social anthropology theory and fieldwork methods was more suited to colonial administrative need.

Canada

Settler colonial intervention to transform and assimilate Indigenous people naturalised their oppression and marginalisation. The National Museum in Ottawa held a dominant position in anthropological research in Canada prior to World War II. Anthropology shared a settler colonial discourse that traditional lifeways of Indigenous people were irrelevant to life in the 20th century.

Australia

Professor A.R. Radcliffe-Brown established the Department of Anthropology at the University of Sydney in 1925, followed by Professor A.P. Elkin from 1933–1956. Australian anthropology was exclusively associated with the University of Sydney until after World War II. Applied anthropology aided government control, development, and advancement of Aboriginal peoples, and the Sydney department trained administrators and missionaries for Australia's overseas colonies.

New Zealand

Peter Buck (Te Rangi Hiroa) was a Maori medical doctor and anthropologist who became director of the Bishop Museum in Hawaii. When World War I broke out, Buck with other Maori MPs, recruited a volunteer Maori contingent; after fighting in Gallipoli, Buck was promoted to second-in-command of the Maori Battalion. Best and the Maori anthropologists, Ngata and Buck, pioneered the Dominion Museum field-based anthropology. New Zealand was responsible for administering over 144,000 Maoris and other Polynesians in mandates, and dependencies in the Pacific and Maori social life was considered still worth studying.

America: Post-Frontier Settler Colonialism, Salvage Ethnography, and Anthropologists as Spies

Various techniques of assimilation came to dominate Indigenous policy in America. The post-frontier assimilation campaign featured allotments, which split up Indigenous land into individually-owned plots that Indigenous owners could transfer to White settlers, and blood quanta that in combination destroyed Indigenous self-governance and the break-up of Indigenous lands (Wolfe, 2011).

The overriding concern of settler colonialism was territorial acquisition through removal to separate Indigenous nations from their land and allotment that assigned Indigenous individuals to their own parcels of land. In a 1901 message to Congress, President Roosevelt found in the *General Allotment Act* "a mighty pulverising engine to break up the tribal mass" (Wolfe, 2011: 27). With westward expansion, there was a limit on removal and reservation, but not so with allotment. The key element of allotment was individuality; allotment was designed to strip Indigenous individuals of land and identity, assimilate Indigenous individuals, and eliminate them collectively; "elimination was inherently chronological — whether dead, removed or assimilated, Indians would pass into memory" (Wolfe, 2011: 23).

Indigenous individuals were relied on to sell their private plots and, in the process, cease being Indigenous. As Indigenous individuals assimilated into settler society through allotments, the Indigenous nation ceased to obstruct settler access to Indigenous homeland. The problem for the settler state was that assimilating individual members would not make the collectively held Indigenous nation available to the settler. The impediment to assimilating Indigenous nations was that they were collective groupings discordant with settler society that were constituted around private property. The commitment of Indigenous nations to collective ownership was a major obstacle to assimilation, "Indians were the original communist menace" (Wolfe, 2011: 26).

In 1883, Boas went as a geographer to study Inuit on Baffin Island, and returned as an anthropologist. Later, he conducted field trips to the northwest coast of North America. Boas established an intuitional base at Columbia University, where he shifted the concept of culture from a synonym for civilisation as used by the evolutionists to the plural sense of learned human behaviour, and promoted historical particularism as an alternative to evolutionism (Silverman, 2005). Boas assigned greatest importance to salvage ethnography that:

> "[…] made the empirical study of what were thought to be the rapidly disappearing native cultures the priority for anthropology; fieldwork was key to such study, although that generally meant the debriefing of elders and the recording of texts rather than the participant observation of later ethnography. It saw the four subfields of anthropology as complementary means for the study and historical reconstruction of nonliterate cultures."
>
> (Silverman, 2005: 261)

Boas published "Scientists as Spies" in *The Nation* in 1919 as an ethical critique of unnamed people who used the cover of anthropological research to work as World War I government agents. Boas "had in mind the Carnegie archaeologists. The Washington-Cambridge alliance used the letter to have Boas censured by the AAA and removed from several key positions. His excommunication, however, did not last long" (Silverman, 2005: 264–265). Boas was a lifelong pacifist and opposed American involvement in World War I; his "belief in the existence of pure science independent of the corrupting influence of a militarized and politicized nation-state fuelled his attack more than his disapproval of American participation in the war" (Price, 2008: 12). The critique from Boas set the stage for the ethical struggles that would follow over World War II and the Vietnam War.

Under the New Deal reforms of President Roosevelt, the allotment system was formally discontinued. The Commissioner of Indian Affairs, John Collier, advanced the principle of Indigenous nation self-government: "the 1934 *Indian Reorganisation Act* put an end to the catastrophic process of tribal allotment and returned surplus tribal lands that had yet to be sold off" (Wolfe, 2011: 34–35). The sale of Indigenous assets to outsiders was also curtailed. Although the campaign to assimilate Indigenous individuals was abandoned, those with allotments opposed surrendering back to the collectively of the Indigenous nation. The Bureau of Indian Affairs (BIA) model constitutions included elections and blood quantum-based membership. The settler objective of assimilation shifted from creating individuals as property owners to eliminating them as Indigenous people, and to imposing Western style governance on Indigenous nations to eliminate them as Indigenous institutions:

"Prior to the Indian Reorganization Act, tribes were presented with certain kinds of decisions and they were believed to possess inherent powers to control their domestic affairs. After the Indian Reorganization Act, the Secretary of the Interior was allowed to approve or disapprove the actions of a tribal government in almost every field."

(Deloria, 1989: 213)

By the time Boas retired in 1936, his third generation of students had become more politically engaged, as reflected in their research on actual historical and economic contact experiences of Indigenous nations. This group included:

"Oscar Lewis, who wrote on the effects of the fur trade on Blackfoot culture (1942); Bernard Mishkin, who analysed rank and warfare in Plains Indian culture (1940); Jane Richardson, who studied law and status among the Kiowa (1940); and Alexander Lesser, whose study of culture change as revealed in the Pawnee Ghost Dane hand game (1933) has become a classic."

(Silverman, 2005: 270)

Depression-era New Deal programs offered support for ethnographic studies. During the 1930s until the end of World War II, most anthropological research was under government, rather than academic, auspices. With passage of the Indian Reorganization Act in 1934, many anthropologists and archaeologists were employed in the Indian service, and anthropologists conducted ethnographic studies of race relations and of rural communities (Silverman, 2005). There were two big applied anthropology programs of the 1930s and 1940s; the Applied Anthropology Unit (AAU) at the BIA under the Indian New Deal, and the community analyst program under the War Relocation Authority's efforts to administer wartime Japanese–American internment camps:

> "These programs exemplify many of the hazards that anthropologists have so far failed to adequately address in working under conditions in which their goals, methods, and access are determined by outside political actors, rather than scientific exigency, or the needs of the peoples with whom anthropologists work."
>
> (Wax, 2010: 156)

Although the Commissioner of Indian Affairs John Collier was anti-assimilationist and halted the division of reservations into individually owned plots of land, he faulted Indigenous nations for their failure to maintain a utopian precontact state in the face of settler colonialism. By comparison, BIA bureaucrats advanced rapid assimilation as best for Indigenous peoples, and viewed resistance to allotments and blood quantum as failure within Indigenous nations. The AAU anthropologists were caught between intra-agency differences, and were often accused by both sides for obstructing the efforts of the BIA and failing in the main goal of crafting Indigenous nation constitutions that reflected beliefs and practices (Wax, 2010). In attempting instead to convince unresponsive Indigenous communities to accept one-size-fits-all constitutions drafted by BIA lawyers, the anthropologists were facilitating the settler colonial logic of elimination.

By the 1890s, discourse on culture, biology, and territoriality began to coalesce around the assimilationist policy of blood quota as a technique of elimination. Hybridity had furnished a means to fragment the Indigenous nation under the allotment regime, but under the act, mixed-bloodedness lacked implication for Indigenous nation membership (Wolfe, 2011). Prior to the act in April 1934, President Roosevelt signed Executive Order 6676 that specified a quarter-degree blood requirement for employment with the BIA. Subsequently, Section 19 of the act provided that:

> "The term 'Indian' as used in this Act shall include all persons of Indian descent who are members of any recognized Indian tribe now under

Federal jurisdiction, and all persons who are descendants of such members who were, on June 1, 1934, residing within the present boundaries of any reservation, and shall further include all other persons of one-half or more Indian blood."

(Indian Reorganisation (Wheeler-Howard) Act, s. 19)

Mixed-bloodedness ceased to operate within Indigenous nations confined to the reservations and came to focus on Indigenousness that prevailed off the reservation: "blood-quantum discourse was now aimed primarily at people living *off* the reservation, the 'all other persons' who were not 'of one-half or more Indian blood'. Those Indigenous people off the reservation could be Black or White but not Red, which intensified race in White settler space" (Wolfe, 2011: 37).

Indigenous nations under the post-frontier Indian Reorganization Act in the New Deal US were depoliticised from international to national relations, but they continued to endure as colonised peoples. Internationally, it was the era that British Empire colonial policy was imposing indirect governance to allay colonial-nationalist sentiment in the colonies. Indirect rule of the British colonies was not to foster independence, but to postpone it indefinitely (Wolfe, 2011).

Britain: Social Anthropology as Ethnography for Colonial Administration

Bronislaw Malinowski (1884–1942), in his *Argonauts of the Western Pacific* (1922), thrust the British anthropology tradition into social anthropology based on a new kind of ethnographic data. Incorporating lessons on the primacy of local context and recording all aspects of local life from the Torres Strait expedition, Malinowski called for participation and local language facility "to grasp the native's point of view, his relation to life, to realise his vision of his world" (Malinowski, 1922: 25). Malinowski conceived of functionalism to perceive of each local culture as constituting an integrated, complex mechanism (Barth, 2005). He wrote vivid ethnographies that were widely read by intellectuals and colonial administrators.

Malinowski established a footing in the London School of Economics, and his seminars and supervision provided the anthropological excitement in Britain through the 1920s and 1930s. Students under Malinowski shifted from Melanesian to Africanist ethnographic materials, with considerable fieldwork grants provided by the Rockefeller Foundation. Malinowski took his sabbatical leave to Yale University in 1938, where he chose to wait out World War II and he died there in 1942; "suddenly the magic of Malinowski was no longer around" (Barth, 2005: 28). Radcliffe-Brown filled the void when he took up the chair of anthropology at Oxford in 1937.

Alfred Reginald Radcliffe-Brown (1881–1955) published *The Andaman Islanders* in 1922, which, with Malinowski's *Argonauts of the Western Pacific* (1922), established new ethnographic data that dismissed evolutionary anthropology and laid the foundation for British social anthropology. Radcliffe-Brown subsequently engaged in fieldwork in 1911–1912 with Aboriginal peoples in northwest Australia and published the influential paper *The Social Organisation of Australian Tribes* (1930–1931).

To avoid colonial struggles around race conflict and indigenous revolt, Malinowski (1929) advocated a colonial strategy based on anthropological knowledge to achieve desired evolutionary progress inexpensively and with minimal violence. Anthropological theories and fieldwork methods for the holistic study of culture contact predominately served as instruments of governmental planning (Malinowski in Mair, 1938).

While Malinowski held a position in London, Radcliffe-Brown established chairs in Cape Town (1920–1925) and Sydney (1925–1931), where he engaged in training administers of the natives and conducted projects in applied anthropology (Feuchtwang, 1973: 83):

> "Radcliffe-Brown also played a prominent role in the broader field of politics. He was known as Anarchy Brown in his college days for his enthusiasm for P'etr Kropotkin, and his radical anticolonial views had driven him from South Africa and led to conflicts with the establishment in Australia, which motivated his move to Chicago in 1931."
>
> (Barth, 2005: 27)

After the move to Chicago (1931–1937), Radcliffe-Brown finally established a professorship at Oxford (1937–1946).

The social anthropology of Malinowski and Radcliffe-Brown represented a wholesale break with the philological, evolutionist, racist, and diffusionist anthropology offered in Britain until the 1920s, and a move to an anthropology more suited to colonial administrative needs (Feuchtwang, 1973: 83–84). It was post-war before anthropology assumed a more prominent place in British academia; it was Radcliffe-Brown's important essay compilation, *Structure and Function in Primitive Society* (1952), that served to establish the principles of British social anthropology (Barth, 2005).

Canada: Salvage Ethnography and Settler Colonialism

Franz Boas, the major figure to professionalise American anthropology, conducted his fieldwork in Canada in the early 1880s on Baffin Island and later on in the Northwest Coast; he remained closely involved in Indigenous issues in Canada. Although Boas's institutional base remained in America, he dramatically influenced the professional development of anthropology in Canada through his recommendation of his former student Edward Sapir, who took up the first director of the Anthropology Division of the Geographical Survey of Canada in 1910. Sapir's tenure in the Anthropology Division, which was located in the National Museum in Ottawa, continued until 1925 when he left Canada for the University of Chicago. The museum held a dominant position in anthropological research in Canada prior to World War II (Darnell, 1998; Hancock, 2006). Anthropological publications from this period made few comments about the ongoing administration of Indigenous affairs. These Indigenous matters were not identified as part of anthropology's formal intellectual undertaking. The museum era ethnographies were products of salvage ethnography and pre-contact ethnological reconstruction (Dyck, 2006).

Prior to World War II, Canadian anthropology was oriented to salvage ethnography that attempted to reconstruct cultures that were destined to be assimilated or disappear. There was shared settler colonial discourse in anthropology and Canadian society that traditional lifeways of Indigenous people were irrelevant to life in the 20th century. Explaining the present situation of Indigenous peoples in terms of culture loss and inevitable assimilation was the effect of Canada's settler colonial legacy. Settler colonial relations reaffirmed evolutionist discourse that presumed innate settler superiority and relegated Indigenous people as savage, rudimentary, and inferior. Settler colonial intervention to transform and assimilate Indigenous people naturalised their oppression and marginalisation (Buchanan, 2006).

Australia: Applied Anthropology in Aiding Government Control of Aboriginal Peoples and the Colonial Enterprise

Australian anthropology engaged in applied anthropology for colonial administration and in salvage anthropology in response to Australia's position as a settler dispossessing state and as a colonial ruler of Papua New Guinea. Professor A.R. Radcliffe-Brown established the Department of Anthropology at the University of Sydney in 1925, followed by Professor Raymond Firth in 1931–1932, and Professor A.P. Elkin from 1933–1956 (Gray, 2005; 2006). Australian anthropology was exclusively associated with the University of Sydney until after World War II, when the Australian National University was established in 1946. During this time, anthropology lacked variety and debate, and anthropologists tended to be utterly passive in their public criticism of the treatment of Aborigines. Australian academic anthropology culture then was intolerant and censorious, closely associated with government, and uncritical of Aboriginal policy and practice. The emphasis was on applied anthropology in aiding government control, development, and advancement of Aboriginal peoples and the colonial enterprise, and the Sydney department trained administrators and missionaries for Australia's overseas colonies. Indigenous peoples were considered a problem in need of change which appealed to government and agents of colonialism, rather than the colonisers and their interaction with Indigenous peoples requiring change (Gray, 2006).

Ralph Piddington (1906–1974) was a University of Sydney student, and had completed master's degrees in Anthropology and Psychology in the late 1920s. In 1930 and 1931, he undertook anthropological research in North West Australia. He made public criticism of the treatment of Aborigines at La Grange Bay, for which he was silenced and punished by A.P. Elkin, Professor of Anthropology at Sydney University and Chair of the Australian National Research Council Committee for Anthropological Research, and by A.O. Neville, Chief Protector of Aborigines in Western Australia (Gray, 1994).

Piddington started his PhD in 1932 at the London School of Economics and completed in 1938. He never returned to Australia as an academic, but in 1944, he worked in the Australian Army's Directorate of Research and Civil Affairs, and in 1945, moved to the School of Civil Affairs, which later became the Australian School of Pacific Administration. In 1946, he took up a Readership in Social Anthropology in the University of Edinburgh. In 1949, he became foundation Professor of Anthropology at the University of New Zealand (Auckland), which he held until retirement in 1972 (Gray, 1994).

Piddington in January 1932 published "Aborigines on Cattle Stations are in Slavery" in *The World* and later, in July 1932, *The World* further reported Piddington's significant allegations of sexual violation of Aboriginal women, beatings of Aboriginal men and women, provisioning of alcohol to Aborigines, and misappropriation of government rations (Gray, 1994). The response to Paddington's criticism was considered to be a "major incident concerned with academic freedom and civil rights" Mulvaney (1988: 221). Neville took Piddington's observations as a personal attack and accused Piddington of misconduct. The ANRC asked Piddington to explain, but he refused to withdraw his statements. Elkin, as chair of the Committee for Anthropological Research, vetted research funds on behalf of the ANRC and the Rockefeller Foundation, while assuring government authorities that the research worker would not cause trouble with Whites or Aborigines (Gray, 1994). Raymond Firth, acting Professor of Anthropology at the University of Sydney, found that Elkin overly mollified government sensitivities. In 1946, Elkin, subsequently as chairman to the Committee for Anthropological Research, rejected Piddington's application to investigate how the war affected the natives of New Guinea (Gray, 1994). Piddington never again worked again in an Australian academic institution.

New Zealand: Maori Field-based Ethnography and the Colonial Division of Anthropology Research in the Pacific

The incentive for the third phase of 'modern' colonial research in anthropology in New Zealand came from the First Pan-Pacific Science Conference held in Honolulu in 1920. The following gentlemen's agreement was reached:

> "It is suggested — (i) That Australian ethnology be the special concern of Australia. (ii) That Australia should more particularly investigate Papua, The Mandated Territory of New Guinea, and Melanesia, but Great Britain and France should assist in this work. (iii) That the investigation of the Maoris be the special province of New Zealand. The rest of Polynesia may be regarded as pre-eminently the field for American research, with the co-operation of France and New Zealand. (iv) That the study of Micronesia be the particular province of Japan and America."
>
> (Australian National Research Council, 1923: 43)

Beaglehole (1938), psychologist and anthropologist at Wellington, acknowledged the contribution to modern anthropology by Te Rangi Hiroa for material culture research, and by Raymond Firth for his research on Maori economics, but noted that both anthropologists went on to work in wider fields. Te Rangi Hiroa (also known as Peter Buck) argued for a Micronesian dispersal into Polynesia.

In the early 20th century, Maori leader and anthropologist Ngata exhorted young Maori to learn the new ways while retaining the culture of their ancestors (Henare, 2007: 97). Ngata supported ethnographic field expeditions to different parts of the North Island, which was inspired by the Cambridge Torres Strait expedition and encouraged by Rivers on his 1915 visit to Wellington. National museum staff, led by Best together with Maori ethnographers, collected sound recordings, artefacts, and written records. The team was regularly joined by Peter Buck (Te Rangi Hiroa), the Maori medical doctor and anthropologist who became director of the Bishop Museum in Hawaii (Henare, 2007: 99).

When World War I broke out, Buck with other Maori MPs recruited a volunteer Maori contingent. After fighting in Gallipoli, Buck was promoted to second-in-command of the Maori Battalion. While he was on hospital duty in Britain, Buck met Arthur Keith of the London Hunterian Museum and the eugenicist Karl Pearson who encouraged his interest in physical anthropology. After returning with his battalion in 1919, he participated in the Hui Araha, a gathering of love and mourning organised by Ngata in Gisbourne. Ngata supported the recording of the traditional activities by Best and associates (Henare, 2007: 99).

Building on the successful gathering of ethnographic data at Gisbourne, Best organised a second Dominion Museum expedition to the tourist centre of Rotorua in 1919, and Ngata again encouraged the trip. A third Dominion Museum expedition was organised in 1921 to the Whanganui River. Buck joined the expedition and applied in the field the anthropometric measurements he had learned in Britain, and purchased artefacts for display at the 1924 London Empire Exhibition. A fourth Dominion Museum expedition took place in 1923; Ngata invited Best and associates to his home at Waiomatatini on the East Coast. The team was joined by Ngata, Buck and Ngati Porou tribal elders (*kaumatua*). It was envisioned that ethnographic material collected on these expeditions was to be for anthropological knowledge as well as for ensuring that Maori culture was brought forward into the contemporary Maori world (Te Ao Maori) through the Young Maori Party (Henare, 2007: 100).

The Dominion Museum field-based anthropology pioneered by Best, Ngata, and Buck did not continue once anthropology gained a foothold in universities. The New Zealander Skinner, one of Haddon's students from Cambridge, was appointed in 1919 as the curator of the museum and lecturer in ethnology at Otago University; he did not continue the ethnological tradition established by Buck. Raymond Firth conducted his study of Maori economics in the 1920s under supervision from Malinowski. His teaching career developed at the LSE, and it was later that he influenced anthropology in New Zealand (Hanare, 2007: 102).

At the time, New Zealand was responsible for administering more than 144,000 Maoris and other Polynesians in mandates and dependencies in the Pacific. Maori social life was considered still worth studying, and Beaglehole called for an applied colonial anthropology school to teach government cadets in Wellington and for researchers to be available for providing scientific advice to departments "administering our native peoples" (Beaglehole, 1937: 161). A proposed school of anthropology, modelled on the London school for colonial service cadets or the Sydney department of anthropology for cadets, missionaries, and government anthropologists in the Territory of Papua, "might well act as a liaison officer between government and the native who, after all, is the one most affected by governmental regulation" (Beaglehole, 1937: 159). The study of anthropology was justified through its application to the difficult task of governing indigenous people, but colonial exploitation was challenged:

> "The cynic or the communist, of course, will say that this is prostitution of science in the interest of furthering capitalistic exploitation of powerless peoples. I know not the truth in this allegation, but I do know from personal experience that in some Pacific islands at least, where there is no exploitation, the inoculation of administrators and officials with the anthropological point of view would conduce immeasurably to a more efficient, tolerant, enlightened, and sympathetic government of the native peoples concerned."
>
> (Beaglehole, 1937: 166)

The sophistication of applied colonial anthropology for the educator, the missionary, the administrator, and the civil servant meant adopting an attitude of tolerance (Beaglehole, 1937: 166).

Conclusion

America

The commitment of Indigenous nations to collective ownership was a major obstacle to assimilation. Professor Boas published "Scientists as Spies" in *The Nation* in 1919 as an ethical critique of unnamed anthropologists who used the cover of anthropological research to work as World War I government agents.

Britain

Social anthropology theory and fieldwork methods were more suited to colonial administrative need. Professor Malinowski advocated a colonial strategy based on social anthropological knowledge to achieve desired evolutionary progress inexpensively and with minimal violence.

Canada

Anthropology shared a settler colonial discourse that the traditional lifeways of Indigenous people were irrelevant to life in the 20th century. Settler colonial intervention to transform and assimilate Indigenous people naturalised their oppression and marginalisation.

Australia

Australian anthropology was exclusively associated with the University of Sydney until after World War II. Applied anthropology aided government control, development and advancement of Aboriginal peoples and the Sydney department trained administrators and missionaries for Australia's overseas colonies.

New Zealand

Best, and the Maori anthropologists, Ngata and Buck, pioneered the Dominion Museum field-based anthropology. New Zealand was responsible for administering over 144,000 Maoris and other Polynesians in mandates and dependencies in the Pacific and Maori social life was considered still worth studying.

CHAPTER 4

Militarised Anthropological Intelligence in the Second World War

Introduction

America

Half of all American anthropologists applied their skills to World War II. Anthropologists were social engineers in the "M Project" initiated by President Roosevelt in 1942 and tasked with relocating millions of wartime refugees. The work of several institutions functioned as a kind of "brain trust," which included the Human Relations Area Files, the Smithsonian Institution and its Ethnographic Board, and the Institute of Social Anthropology. Anthropologists were also involved in more clandestine activities. A dozen anthropologists designed propaganda for Japanese audiences for the Office of War Information. The FBI's Special Intelligence Service embedded several anthropologists to coordinate cultural intelligence operations in Latin America. The spy agency Office of Strategic Services, established in 1942, was the precursor to the CIA.

Britain

British anthropologists in World War II directed their fieldwork skills at peoples within the colonial boundaries of the Empire. War interests conflated with the interests of colonialism as anthropologists administered or defended outposts of Empire. The key transnational figures of scholarly patronage and appointment were Haddon, Malinowski, and Radcliffe-Brown before the war, and Firth after the war. Professor Firth was posted to the Naval Intelligence Division of the British Admiralty to produce a series of geographical handbooks to inform naval operations and was later appointed as the first secretary of the Colonial Social Science Research Council.

Canada

There were no professional university academic anthropologists from Canada to participate in World War II.

Australia

Indigenous peoples in Australia were colonised without citizenship and political or civil rights, and were used in the pursuit of Australian war aims. The Northern Territory Special Reconnaissance Unit (NTSRU) under the command of Thomson was the only guerrilla fighting unit comprised of Indigenous people and designed as an insurgency against occupation of Japanese forces. The unit engaged in reconnaissance but had no opportunity for frontline fighting in northern Australia. The Directorate of Research and Civil Affairs (DORCA) was established, and directly recruited anthropologists to study the effects of the war on Indigenous peoples in New Guinea. The anthropologists Ian Hogbin, Camilla Wedgewood, K. Read, Ralph Piddington, Lucy Mair, and W.F.H Stanner were involved in DORCA's activities. With the battle for Australia fought in colonial New Guinea, there developed a sense of indebtedness to New Guineans for their sacrifice in the Australian war effort.

New Zealand

The use of anthropologists by colonial governments in the Pacific continued in the interwar years. The Empire before and during the war consisted of colonies and states interlocked through transnational intellectual, social, and cultural networks that bound the British world together beyond the mother country. New Zealanders Belshaw, Geddes, Freeman, Keesing, and Piddington were part of the transnational empire networks that were not diminished, but were actually strengthened, by war. It was accepted that enlightened colonial rule was beneficial for Indigenous peoples. The war resulted in a shift of power in the Pacific, with increasing dependency on America, the demise of British military power, and the onset of the Cold War.

America: Wartime Militarised Anthropology

In *Anthropological Intelligence*, Price (2008) critiques wartime anthropology, and documents that more than half of all American anthropologists applied their skills to World War II. Anthropologists were social engineers in the "M Project" initiated by President Roosevelt in 1942, which was tasked with relocating millions of wartime refugees. The work of several institutions functioned as a kind of "brain trust," which included the Human Relations Area Files, the Smithsonian Institution and its Ethnographic Board, and the Institute of Social Anthropology. These wartime institutions rapidly transitioned into Cold War area-study centres. Other anthropologists were involved in more clandestine activities. A dozen anthropologists designed propaganda for Japanese audiences for the Office of War Information. The FBI's Special Intelligence Service embedded several anthropologists to coordinate cultural intelligence operations in Latin America. The spy agency Office of Strategic Services (OSS), established in 1942, was the precursor to the CIA; conducted secretive missions that were, for example, carried out in South Asia by Gregory Bateson and in North Africa by Carleton Coon; the "war's needs shone so brightly that they seemed to blind anthropologists to the possibility that America's interests and those of the cultures they were studying might diverge" (Price, 2008: 89).

Three months after the attack on Pearl Harbor, the War Relocation Authority (WRA) was charged with the controversial internment of nearly 120,000 Japanese immigrants and Japanese-Americans (Price, 2008). Anthropologists involved in the WRA were captives of a government bureaucracy; the "WRA anthropologists reformulated the classic Boasian axiom: instead of confronting power with truth, anthropology was to supply information to power" (Starn, 1986: 705). Twenty-one anthropologists and sociologists were employed as 'community analysts' and among them, John Embree, John Province, Solon Kimball, Robert Redfield, Conrad Arensberg, Edward Spicer, and Morris Opler were previously researchers with the Indian New Deal programs (Wax, 2010). Anthropologists were deployed to provide the administration with knowledge of Japanese culture to enable smooth running of the camps. World War II extracted a high cost in terms of disciplinary autonomy. This is seen in the WRA community analyst program that valued anthropological information for the application of policy, not the creation of policy (Wax, 2010). The assumption that the contrived military-supervised internment camps were functioning communities limited and constrained anthropologists working in the camps. In WRA projects, for example, the language in which anthropologists could report their findings was regulated and euphemistic: "'registration' instead of loyalty oath, 'stop order' instead of permanent incarceration in the camp, 'community' instead of camp, 'internees' instead of evacuee or prisoner" (Wax, 2010: 161). Far from understanding resistance as a reasonable response to internment, the community analysts presented unwillingness to relocate as due to personal insecurity caused by maladjustment to camp life and to 'disloyals' and 'pro-Japans' (Wax, 2010). Moreover, "while many within the WRA rejected the racist premises inherent in the internment itself, the work of the community analyst allowed them to see the execution of the internment as essentially fair and democratic" and 'strikingly American' according to Robert Redfield (Wax, 2010: 161).

President Roosevelt implemented the M Project in 1942 as a post-war refugee-resettlement program. Henry Field, then Assistant Curator of Anthropology at the Field Museum, was given a commission as lieutenant in the navy, and assigned to administer the highly secretive M Project under the Librarian of Congress. For three years, Field and his staff reported confidential summaries of economic, geographic, cultural, and historical information to inform refugee-resettlement plans. The M Project mainly focussed on European refugees, and ignored the millions of people displaced in Africa and Asia. The reports hyped vast regions for occupation, implying that inhabitants "would welcome invaders moved from another continent at the behest of an American president" (Price, 2008: 128). The peoples identified for relocation were victims of the aggression of others (e.g., the Roma, Jews, etc.); "it was as if the reward of being victimised was being moved so that the aggressor could live in peace" (Price, 2008: 127). The provisional plans were never implemented; once declassified, the report summaries were published by Field (1962).

Several institutions functioned as a kind of "brain trust" (Price, 2008: 91). One was the Institute of Human Relations (IHR) interdisciplinary research centre established by Yale University in 1929. The historically significant Cross Cultural Survey was started by George Murdock in 1937; World War II transformed the Cross Cultural Survey from a theoretical to an applied orientation. Unclassified and restricted Civil Affairs Handbooks were prepared under the auspices of the Office of the Chief of Naval Operations, in accordance with the standardised organisational framework provided by the Cross Cultural Survey. The reductionist view of cultures provided in the handbooks facilitated co-option and management of the described culture, but their ethnographic usefulness proved to be minimal. In the post-war years, the IHR became the Human Relations Area Files (HRAF), and the cross-cultural database was used by academic anthropologists as well as the intelligence community (Price, 2008: 93–95).

The Ethnographic Board, established by the Smithsonian Institution in 1942, was another of the wartime brain trusts. The Ethnographic Board was open to all military and intelligence agencies, and served to connect knowledgeable individuals with specific requests. The Ethnographic Area Roster was considered the board's most significant contribution to the war; the roster identified more than 5,000 individuals with cultural and linguistic knowledge of more than 10,000 cultural groups (Price, 2008). The Ethnographic Board's most visible and widely distributed product was the waterproof book, *Survival on Land and Sea*, published by the Office of Naval Intelligence. By the end of 1944, close to a million copies of the survival guide had been distributed to soldiers and sailors in the Pacific theatre of war, but the book was not a neutral compendium of survival facts:

> "[…] it bore traces of anthropology's mid-century conception of "primitive" cultures, as well as universalist presumptions about the best way to deal with the "others" that soldiers encountered throughout the

world. The text's view of these "others" was consistent with a range of nascent anthropological frameworks, including the neo-evolutionary views of White, the cross-cultural computations of Murdock, and the cultural determinism of Boasians such as Mead and Benedict."

(Price, 2008: 106)

The Institute of Social Anthropology (ISA), created by the State Department in 1943, was a wartime brain trust for the collection of ethnographic information on Latin America. Julian Steward, the first ISA director, had already directed the production of the *Handbook of South American Indians*, and viewed his work on the compilation as contributing to the American war effort. Steward anticipated that work at the ISA would inform post-war modernisation in Latin America, and "thought it would be highly desirable to have social scientists, especially anthropologists and cultural geographers, trained to do research on a whole series of developmental problems" (Foster, 2000: 123).

American anthropologists were quick to join the wartime brain trusts, which were funded by large amounts of private and public money. Anthropological research projects analysed cultural information to help the Allies defeat the Axis. Anthropologists had long conducted ethnographic research that the agencies searched for; however, the contextual meaning of the data was transformed by the war in ways similar to colonial experiences. The wartime agencies rapidly transitioned to area-study centres in the Cold War, and area-study programs became financiers and directors of anthropological research. During the Cold War, funding from the Rockefeller, Carnegie, and Ford foundations focused cultural research on peasants, land reform, counterinsurgency, and the Green Revolution (Price, 2008).

The Office of War Information (OWI) was a more clandestine organisation established by Roosevelt in 1942. A dozen anthropologists designed propaganda for Japanese audiences, and John Embee was particularly important for his Japanese fieldwork and ethnography *Suye Mura: A Japanese Village* (1939). Embee worked for several military-intelligence agencies, including as 'principal community analyst' for the WRA and, as OWI supervisor of the Psychological Warfare Program. He also worked with Ruth Benedict and Clyde Kluckhohn. Embee was politically sophisticated and examined economic, demographic, and geopolitical factors, rather than analyses that reinforced commonly held prejudices. The roots of Japan's militarism were identified by Embee as the constraints of tariffs and resource limitations; not in internal psychological defects (Price, 2008).

Prior to her involvement in the OWI, Benedict had no research interest in Japanese culture, and she drew on her past culture and personality research to make wartime policy recommendations. Benedict's Japanese culture and personality study, started in June 1944, focused on the role of the emperor in Japanese culture. Her classified OWI report "Japanese Behavior Patterns" in 1945 provided a psychological profiling of Japanese culture:

> "Themes and passages in "Japanese Behavior Patterns" were later reproduced unaltered in Benedict's book The *Chrysanthemum and the Sword* (1946). With the postwar publication of *Chrysanthemum*, Benedict's work at OWI became the most famous American social-science contribution to the Second World War — although this fame contributed some misunderstanding of how her work (and that of others at OWI) was used and ignored by military and civilian agencies during the war."
>
> (Price, 2008: 177)

During World War II, FBI Director Hoover controlled most American intelligence in North and South America through the control of the Special Intelligence Service (SIS); this was created under the FBI by President Roosevelt in 1940. The SIS recruited American anthropologists to collect cultural intelligence in Central and South America; similar to the spying operations that had previously angered Boas in World War I. World War I archaeologist-spy Samuel Lothrop recreated the fieldworker role as pretence for espionage in World War II. Prior to joining the SIS, Lothrop was employed by the Carnegie Institute, which paid the salaries of those working temporarily in government service, and had a long history of supporting intelligence operations (Castaneda, 2005). Lothrop assumed the posture of the gentlemen spy, leisurely undertaking archaeological tours in Peru during the midst of the century's largest war. Although stationed long-term, Lathrop resented the lack of FBI support for his political and logistic problems, and he resigned in 1944. Lothrop returned to positions with the Harvard Peabody Museum and Carnegie Institution, and ended formal association with American intelligence agencies (Price, 2008).

While silences by former spies and spy agencies are understandable, the:

> "[...] careful silence maintained-and, at times, enforced-by members acting within professional associations such as the Society for American Archaeology are another matter...not to investigate in a scholarly way the extent of such past relations or to clearly and unambiguously prohibit all such relationships in the present creates serious dangers for fieldworkers operating around the world...all anthropologists will be placed at risk — a risk exacerbated by professional anthropological and archaeological associations' refusal to clarify that such covert relationships between anthropologists and intelligence agencies are inappropriate."
>
> (Price, 2008: 219)

From its inception in July 1942, the Office of Strategic Services (OSS) was a multidisciplinary military-intelligence agency. There were two dozen OSS anthropologists during the war, including Gregory Bateson and Carleton Coon, who ran secret missions in South Asia and North Africa. Bateson's OSS work mostly involved analysing shifting political conditions and producing scholarly reports for strategists. Bateson acknowledged the necessity of the war, but was concerned about the outcomes of anthropology's wartime contributions and alignment with colonial forces (Price, 2008: 242). Biographer David Lipset (1980: 174) clarifies that Bateson was disturbed with the OSS treatment of the natives.

Based on his anthropological authority on the Near East Theatre, Carleton Coon was recruited for subversive and demolition work, and he found that his limited Arabic was sufficient to instruct locals in techniques of sabotage and terrorism. Mule turd bombs were deployed in Morocco to stop the advance of German tanks. Coon led 50 Tunisian commandos who planted mule turd bombs, blew up railroad trestles, and kidnapped local boys as hostages, who "were imprisoned in the Cap Serat lighthouse until their fathers proved authenticated information about enemy positions" (Atkinson, 2003: 277). Coon apparently had no regrets about his time in

North Africa running covert operations, and he and the OSS viewed his anthropological skills as a bonus. The OSS was disbanded in 1945 and morphed into the CIA in 1947. After the war, Coon worked as a CIA scientific consultant between 1948 and 1950 (Price, 2008).

David Mandelbaum directed a unit that planned strategies for Detachment 101 of the OSS for coordinating Kachin armed resistance in Burma and the counterinsurgency work of Bateson and Coon. When counterinsurgency returned in such Cold War projects as Project Camelot and the Thai Affair, it did not value anthropology for specific knowledge or theoretical orientation, but for the methodological ability to "extract from informants information that may be useful in their own subjugation" (Wax, 2010: 162).

During the war, military officials had a tendency of "selectively ignoring and selectively commandeering social scientists' recommendations" (Price 2008: 198). Unfortunately, those who committed anthropology to war often found "themselves doing 'piecework' on large projects that had grand designs beyond their control or comprehension" (Price, 2008: 142), and "they were unaware that their actions were releasing a genie from a bottle, unleashing forces that they could not control in new, unimagined Cold War contexts" (Price, 2008: 280).

Britain: World War II Anthropology in Administering and Defending Colonial Outposts of Empire

After World War II, there was a new generation of academic anthropologists with the:

> "[…] succession of Raymond Firth to the chair at the London School of Economics (1944); Edward Evan Evans-Pritchard to the chair at Oxford (1946); Max Gluckman to a new department at Manchester (1949); and Meyer Fortes to the chair at Cambridge (1950), to be shortly joined by Edmund R. Leach, a new generation of scholars, all born after 1900, took over the leadership of the main academic centres of Britain with their new anthropology. Each had been shaped by Bronislaw Malinowski and A.R. Radcliffe Brown."
>
> (Barth, 2005: 32)

These British anthropologists in World War II directed their fieldwork skills at peoples within the colonial boundaries of the Empire. War interests conflated with the interests of colonialism as anthropologists administered or defended outposts of Empire (Price, 2008). The chairs of the major departments subsequently influenced their junior colleagues and students, and controlled field research through the Colonial Social Science Research Council (Barth, 2005).

The American Office of Strategic Services (OSS) sent anthropologist Jack Harris on a sham expedition to the Gold Coast in West Africa to liaise with British Intelligence services. Harris recalled that the:

> "British, with a long tradition of intelligence activities, had been in West Arica for some 80 years with a network of informants in place reporting to trained agents. In the Gold Coast, British intelligence utilized the services of at least one anthropologist, Meyer Fortes, a South African, who after the war taught at Cambridge."
>
> (Price, 2008: 245)

Meyers Fortes (1906–1983) "monitored economic and ideological developments in West Africa" (Price, 2008: 54) and found:

> "The ideological currents stirred up by the war in Europe, which reach West Africa very quickly now through the British propaganda machinery, have also stimulated [a] move to the Left. Ten years ago, for instance, many educated West Africans looked on Japan as a worthy model for imitation by a backward territory. Today, Japan is in dispute and the ideal is the U.S.S.R. The Atlantic Charter, the Philadelphia Charter, all our anti-Nazi Propaganda and our war-time slogans, as well as the solid social and economic achievements of Great Britain, from aircraft production to school meals have been publicized and widely discussed among the African elite."
>
> (Fortes 1945: 209)

Raymond Firth (1901–2002) was born in New Zealand. He graduated in economics from Auckland University College in 1921, took a MA in 1922, and a diploma in social science in 1923, and stared his doctoral research at the London School of Economics in 1924 (Huntsman, 2003).

Firth had planned on studying economics, but after an opportunistic meeting with Malinowski, decided to study economic and anthropological theory with Pacific ethnography (Huntsman, 2003). His doctoral thesis was subsequently published in 1929 as *Primitive Economics of the New Zealand Maori*. On completion of his PhD, Firth returned to Australasia for a position at the University of Sydney in 1927, when in 1928, a research opportunity took him to Tikpopia, which began an enduring research relationship. The first of 10 subsequent books, *We the Tikopia: A Sociological Study of Kinship in Primitive Polynesia*, was published in 1936 (Macdonald, 2002). With the departure of Radcliffe-Brown, Firth succeeded as acting Professor at the University of Sydney in 1933. Eighteen months later, Firth returned to take up a lectureship to the LSE, and became Reader in 1935. From 1939–1940, Raymond Firth engaged in new ethnographic fieldwork in Kelantan and Terengganu in Malaysia (Ortiz, 2004). Firth succeeded Malinowski as Professor of Anthropology at LSE in 1944, and he remained in the position for 24 years (Huntsman, 2003).

The British university system was dislocated during the war. The London School of Economics was moved to Cambridge; meanwhile, Professor Firth was posted to the Naval Intelligence Division of the British Admiralty to produce a series of geographical handbooks to inform naval operations. He wrote and edited four volumes concerned with the Pacific Islands for the Naval Intelligence Division Geographical Handbook Series during World War II (Clout and Voeks, 2003), which were sophisticated ethnographies similar to those produced for the Smithsonian's War Background Studies. Firth was later appointed as the first secretary of the Colonial Social Science Research Council (Price, 2008).

E.E. Evans-Pritchard (1902–1973) was an English academic who read history at Oxford and conducted a series of field studies in southern Sudan (Barth, 2005). During the war, Evans-Pritchard served in military intelligence in Ethiopia, Libya, Sudan, and Syria. He was commissioned into the Sudan Defence Force in 1940, and participated in British army counterinsurgency campaigns in Ethiopia and Sudan (Price, 2008). In Sudan, he raised irregular troops among the Anuak and fought with them in guerrilla warfare against the Italians in Ethiopia in 1940–1941 (Anderson and Killingray, 1991). Evans-Pritchard was ethnographically familiar with the Anuak, and had earlier published the *Political System of the Anuak of the Anglo-Egyptian Sudan* (1940).

Evans-Pritchard was next posted to the British Military Administration of Cyrenaica in North Africa in 1942, where he documented local resistance to Italian conquest. He saw no incompatibility between the roles of researcher and intelligence advisor, and was Tribal Affairs Officer in the British administration of Cyrenaica during the war (Feuchtwang, 1973). Evans-Pritchard combined ethnography among the Sanusi in Cyrenaica, Libya, with his war service, and subsequently published *The Sanusi of Cyrenaica* (1949).

Max Gluckman (1911–1975) was a South African social anthropologist whose Jewish origins and political views hindered his acceptance into British colonial society (Brown, 1979). Gluckman took up a Rhodes scholarship to Oxford (1934–1936, 1938–1939), where he was influenced by Evans-Pritchard and Radcliffe-Brown. He conducted a period of intensive fieldwork with the Zulu from 1938 to 1939. From 1939 to 1941, Gluckman was an assistant anthropologist with the Rhodes-Livingston Institute (RLI), which was the first research institute in British colonial Africa that provided anthropological knowledge to the colonial administration (Crehan, 1997). Within days of arriving at the RLI, World War II broke out and Gluckman received permission to be released from his post to return to Britain to enlist. However, his age and nationality made such enlistment impossible and he was reinstated (Brown, 1979). The research agenda of the RLI was set by colonialism and, during his time as assistant anthropologist, Gluckman conducted field research with the Lozi of Barotseland.

Gluckman directed the RLI from 1941–1947, and he was convinced of the importance of anthropology beyond the academy, and favoured closer cooperation between science and government; "Gluckman looked forward to a vastly expanded role for the sociologist: in place of the existing *ad hoc* consultation on specific problems he hoped for a system where sociological research would proceed in advance of administrative action" (Brown, 1979: 533).

Developments began undermining Gluckman's belief in applied anthropology. The relative harmony that prevailed due to the war gave way to conflict after peace with the growth in settler colonist and African political activity (Brown, 1979: 539). Through his involvement in the Native Land Tenure Committee, Gluckman came into more direct contact with the settler colonist side of the Northern Rhodesian political system. The settler colonists succeeded in ousting Gluckman from the committee. The Northern Rhodesian Government remained convinced of the value of the RLI, but settler colonists remained vehemently opposed, and called on the Legislative Council for it to be closed (Brown 1979). However, "Gluckman's activities helped to push the settler-oriented antiquarian of earlier anthropology onto the sidelines" (Brown, 1979: 540).

Chilver (1977: 239) observed, on behalf of the Colonial Social Science Council, that "by 1949 the impractical notion that anthropologists themselves should act as advisers to colonial governments was waning". Evans-Pritchard (1946) condemned applied anthropology and remained scientifically concerned chiefly with the 'primitive field'. Gluckman (1971a; 1971b) was a political activist theoretically engaged with the impact of colonialism on social conflict, racism, urbanisation, and labour migration, but he was not a revolutionary and was quite closely involved with the colonial state.

Edmund Leach (1910–1989) was a renowned British social anthropologist. Leach's *Political Systems of Highland Burma* (1954) ethnography of the Kachin became a classic, but he seldom wrote about his militarised role in conducting fieldwork in Burma during World War II (*see* Leach, 1977). The British colonised portions of coastal Burma in 1824–1826, southern Burma in 1852, and the remainder of the original kingdom in 1885. Armed resistance against British occupation continued through to 1940 and the frontier was under separate colonial administration (Leach, 1977). Although Leach assumed that anthropologists providing cultural understanding to colonial administrators was "better for the people who are being administered", and he maintained that "the principle task of academic anthropologists in the field is to pursue research which may lead to advances in sociological generalisation and that the anthropologist, as such, is not professionally concerned with whether administration is efficient or inefficient, just or unjust" (Leach, 1977: 192, 196).

In August 1939, Leach embarked on ethnographic fieldwork in the frontier Kachin highlands before the war brought the Japanese occupation to Burma (Leach, 1977). After Britain entered the war, Leach "signed up with the Burma Rifles and went into the field to Hpalang to conduct his research" (Tambiah, 2002: 40). Leach (1977) received military training from November 1939 to February 1940, and undertook military duty in Autumn of 1940. Leach utilised his ethnographic and linguistic skills to organise guerrilla forces known as the Northern Kachin Levies against the Japanese (Leach, 1977). According to Leach, "[a]s far as the British Army was concerned, I was odd man out, but I was potentially useful because I spoke the local language and the Kachin were, in effect, the Gurkas of the British Army" (Kuper, 1986: 377).

Leach (1977) fought with the Kachin from 1942 when British resistance to the Japanese was crumblin, until 1945, by which time Japanese resistance to the British was crumbling. Leach's *Political Systems of Highland Burma* is silent about the war's impact on the Kachin. In retrospect, he found "it very difficult to say just how relevant was my interest in anthropology to these activities, or how relevant were these activities to my subsequent development as an anthropologist. If I had not had my anthropological background, I would not have got seconded into the particular cloak-and-dagger activities" (Leach, 1977: 195). He assumed that "if I had been engaged in anthropology in Burma, in which neither colonial administrators nor army played their part, my anthropological assessment of Kachin society would hardly have been changed" (Leach, 1977: 196). Leach's biographer Tambiah, disagreed and assessed that:

> "Leach did not consider it relevant to discuss in detail how his extensive recruiting of 'frontier tribesman,' and his later involvement with the Kachin Levies which was 'a network of guerrillas and spies,' actually enabled him to collect information and to gain panoramic insights about the distribution and interrelations between the hill communities."
>
> (Tambiah, 2002: 417)

Canada: Academic Anthropologists Post-World War II

The hiring in 1925 of McIlwraith at the University of Toronto shifted the emphasis on professionalisation from government and museum to the university as the institutional framework for the emerging profession. Bailey received a PhD in history from the University of Toronto in 1934 and worked with McIlwraith. Bailey's ethnohistorical study of the emergence of Canada from settler contacts with Algonquian cultures in the 16th and 17th centuries identified the Canadian intersection of anthropology, history, and economics (Darnell, 1998). The university era of Canadian anthropology is marked by the first full-time lecturer in anthropology hired in 1925, the first department founded in 1936, and the first PhD awarded in 1956 (Hancock, 2006). The Depression, followed by World War II, derailed the university expansion of anthropology in Canada. Full-time positions for anthropologists did not occur at McGill and the University of British Columbia until 1947 (Darnell, 1998). There were no professional academic anthropologists from Canada to participate in World War II.

The global depression and World War II also impacted on the role of anthropology in Indigenous nation-state relations. The 'North American Indian Today' conference in 1939 brought together academics and government officials to address "the Indian problem", and signalled the intellectual connection of anthropology to public issues (Loram and McIlwraith, 1943). Anthropologists in the 1940s began to step outside simply recording and documenting Indigenous cultures before they vanished to tackling politicised issues of citizenship, racism, welfare, and democratic rights and responsibilities (Dyck, 2006). Lucien and Jane Hanks (1950) formulated a historically grounded extended case study of the Canadian state's administration of the Blackfoot people, and coined the term 'social syndrome of malsatisfaction' for the lack of Indigenous control over the management of their own affairs. Dunnings (1959) demonstrated that government contact with the Northern Ojibwa had not constituted a loss of Indigenous culture, and that the Ojibwa actively reshaped certain features of their socio-political context in response to the cash economy. By the 1960s, ethnographers were investigating Indigenous nation-state relations both intellectually and through more practical and political forms of participation (Dyck, 2006).

Australia: Militarised Anthropology and Managed Colonised Peoples in World War II

From early 1942, Elkin lost the Sydney monopoly on anthropological research and training with the creation of the Australian New Guinea Administrative Unit (ANGAU) and the army's Directorate of Research and Civil Affairs, which included the School of Civil Affairs. Government anthropologist F.E. Williams was in the team of ANGAU experts in native administration. Williams served in the Allied Geographical Section of Military Intelligence and, together with William Groves, the deputy director of the Directorate of Army Education, produced the booklet *You and the Native*, to guide soldiers in dealing with Papua New Guineans (Gray, 2005). Although the view of Indigenous peoples in the booklet was then considered enlightened, it encouraged European superiority (Gray, 2006).

In Australia's racially structured society, the loyalty of Indigenous peoples was considered a problem, especially by the army, the Commonwealth, and states' Native Affairs administrators. The military was particularly suspicious about Indigenous peoples in northern Australia and, in 1943, planned, but did not carry out, the removal of Indigenous peoples from northwest coastal areas to a distance inland of some 200 kilometres. For the most part, those considered Aboriginal and not of mixed descent were left to their own devices (Gray, 2006). The anthropologist Donald Thompson accused Native Affairs officials of retreating south and abandoning Indigenous peoples in need of protection and help (Long, 1992: 39). Thomson published a number of articles for Melbourne newspapers that were critical of the treatment of Aborigines in Northern Territory in 1946, and Elkin defended the government and accused Thomson of exaggeration (Gray, 1994).

A.P. Elkin, Professor of Anthropology at the University of Sydney, maintained a strong sense of public duty and moral rectitude, and was bent on shaping a new Department of Propaganda with himself as Head (Pomeroy, 2012). However, he had to content himself with public speaking, teaching, and welfare work. Elkin unsuccessfully advocated for the formation of an Aboriginal mixed-blood battalion, and pointed out there was growing support for extending citizenship rights for Aborigines (Pomeroy, 2012). Elkin's grasp of the dynamics of political power and influence was limited, and he was increasingly isolated from the development and implementation of public policy (Pomeroy, 2012). Elkin's biographer, T. Wise (1985: 147), summarised Elkin's contribution to the war effort as "a four-year campaign of patriotic speeches, surveys, questionnaires and pressing of unsolicited advice on the government and public."

Ethical concerns did not inform the effective use of anthropological knowledge during World War II. Indigenous peoples in Australia were colonised peoples without citizenship and political or civil rights, and were used in the pursuit of Australian war aims (Gray, 2006). The Northern Territory Special Reconnaissance Unit (NTSRU), under the command of Thomson, was the only guerrilla fighting unit comprised of Indigenous people, and designed as an insurgency against occupation of Japanese forces. The unit engaged in reconnaissance but had no opportunity for frontline fighting in northern Australia. Thomson, accompanied by a contingent of Torres Strait and Solomon Islanders, engaged in commando action in southwest Dutch New Guinea.

Thomson had previously conducted fieldwork for the government in 1935–1937 with the Murgin (Yolgnu) people in northeast Arnhem Land. Having served in the British Solomon Islands Protectorate, Thomson was promoted to Squadron Leader in 1941 to organise and lead the unique NTSRU. Thomson developed the guerrilla force from the Yolgnu men he knew for their hunting and fighting prowess, and whose language he spoke. Whereas killing Japanese had led to punitive government reprisals, the unit was now to fight the Japanese as a common enemy. The Yolgnu were not armed with guns because Thomson believed spears to be more effective and, if captured, they would not be considered an armed opposition (Gray, 2006).

Thomson's base was the ketch Aroetta, which he crewed with Solomon Islanders he knew, and included the Torres Strait Islander Kaipu Gagi. A total of 49 Yolgnu were recruited to the unit, and the guerrilla force patrolled the Arnhem Land coast during 1942. By 1943, the North Australia Observer Unit (NAOU) expanded and the NTSRU was abandoned (Gray, 2006). None of the 49 Yolgnu guerrillas were formerly enlisted and were thus denied the benefits from military service, including a cash wage or veteran's pension (Hall, 1992: 61).

In 1943, Thomson led two patrols for the First Australian Army and Merauke Force in the swamp-lands of the upper Obaa-Wildema Rivers to determine the extent of Japanese infiltration in southwest Dutch New Guinea. The Dutch regarded the country to be some of the worst in the world, and they had not subjugated the Indigenous people, for whom "headhunting was the spice of life" (Thomson, 1953: 4). Thomson carried out the patrols barefoot after years of barefoot travel with nomadic hunting groups of Yolgnu in Arnhem Land and leading NTSRU on reconnaissance, so as not to "leave a shod footprint to indicate to the enemy that a white man was leading the patrol" (Thomson, 1953: 4). When possible, Thomson travelled by canoe and lived off the land to conserve food and fuel. Part of the first patrol included savannah bushland landscape with flora and fauna that was reminiscent of the northern Australian bush of Arnhem Land and Cape York Peninsula, but most of the journey was remarked upon for its wretchedness.

Before the second patrol, Thomson retuned to General Headquarters in Brisbane, and collected Sergeants Dick, Richie, and Egan, the latter two had previously served on the NTSRU armed patrol vessel Aroetta on the coast of Arnhem Land. Kapiu Gagi, from the NTSRU, also accompanied Thomson along with four Torres Strait Islanders selected from Boigu and Saibai. There were numerous Indigenous people in the border country between Dutch control on the Digoel River in the south and the colonially untouched people of the interior who were relentless raiders and head-hunters. Subsistence was based on sago. Thomson recruited 75 villagers and 25 canoes for the second patrol from Mappi to the estuary of the Eilanden, which was obstructed by masses of floating weed. Once the patrol reached the headwaters of the Wildeman River, there was open water, but the Indigenous recruits were apprehensive about being in hostile country. Thomson kept two dugout canoes for the patrol, and sent the Indigenous recruits home with presents of fishhooks and knives (Thomson, 1953).

A raft was constructed across lashed together canoes and mounted with four Bren guns. By day, the raft was camouflaged against Japanese patrols on the bank of the river and floated silently downstream in the darkness, but no Japanese were encountered. The patrol did ominously encounter armed Indigenous men without women and children, who watched from their canoes far out in the open water. The estuary of the Eilanden River was reached without encountering Japanese occupation, and a camp was established some 45 kilometers from the nearest Japanese headquarters. The Indigenous men began to appear more treacherous with knives, axes, and machetes supplied by the Japanese. Sergeant Egan was left with the Torres Strait Islander troops and Thomson with Sergeant Richie and Kapiu made a reconnaissance of the estuary:

> "Early one morning as we were breaking camp on a narrow open strip fringing the jungle, the natives crowded us and attacked *en masse*, two hundred strong. We were overwhelmed, and three of us — Richie, Kapiu and myself — were severely wounded before we could get our Tommy guns into action… I myself was wounded three times. But the very smallness of our party and the overwhelming weight of the attackers were in our favour. After the first onslaught they could not see where to hit. We turned our machine guns on them and on the canoes moored along the foreshore. Then under the cover of Bren gun fire we carefully collected and embarked our equipment."
>
> (Thomson, 1953: 16)

With his left hand and shoulder out of action, Thomson made it back to the Egan base camp, and a relief party embarked the wounded 40 hours later. Thomson was no longer active in the war and, afterwards, returned to the University of Melbourne until his retirement in 1966 (Gray, 2006).

Alfred Conlon argued for a research section in 1942 to watch New Guinea because fighting the Japanese could leave behind a troublesome population. The Directorate of Research and Civil Affairs (DORCA) was established, and directly recruited anthropologists to study the effects of the war on Indigenous peoples in New Guinea. The anthropologists Ian Hogbin, Camilla Wedgewood, K. Read, Ralph Piddington, Lucy Mair, and W.F.H Stanner were involved in DORCA's activities. These anthropologists were not directly supporting the war but managed the impact of war on Indigenous peoples (Gray, 2005; 2006).

Unlike their British and American counterparts, Australian anthropologists were not deployed in frontline fighting or in advising frontline troops, with the exception of Donald Thomson and, to a lesser extent, W.F.H. Stanner. NAOU was created as a mobile commando unit in 1942 and commanded by Stanner (Gray, 2012). The NAOU unit guarded 3,000 kilometers of northern Australian coastline against Japanese invasion. Stanner was reluctant to involve Aboriginal people in the war, and each company hired only a few Aboriginal trackers, guides, and horse handlers, the unit employed 59 Aborigines and 465 white members. Aborigines were treated poorly and paid in kind with tobacco and clothing.

Stanner (1905–1981) transferred from commander of the NAOU to the Directorate of Research in 1943 (from 1945, it was the Directorate of Research and Civil Affairs or DORCA), and was made Assistant Director of Research (Gray, 2012). Stanner prepared papers on British colonial policy and its application to the South-West Pacific. Stanner was on the side of reforming colonial government, rather than calling for decolonisation. Despite the beginnings of debate over the future of decolonisation, self-government, and independence for the British colonies, Stanner remained convinced of the colonial mission. Stanner's support for a reformed colonial system for post-war Papau New Guinea was unacceptable to his directorate colleagues Hogbin and Wedgwood (Gray, 2012).

At the request of the American Institute of Pacific Relations, Stanner surveyed post-war rehabilitation and reconstruction in the Southwest Pacific in 1947, which was published in 1953. As an advisor to the Department of External Affairs, Stanner helped establish the South Seas Regional Commission. The South Pacific Commission was created in 1946 to promote development in the Pacific Island territories under the control of administering powers, but Stanner was not offered a position. Stanner returned to London to work for the Colonial Office and in Uganda. He declined the offer of a Chair of Anthropology from Auckland University College and, instead, accepted an appointment as Reader in Comparative Social Institutions at ANU in 1948 (Gray, 2012). Stanner's academic reputation was in steady decline; when Elkin retired in 1955, Stanner applied for the Sydney Chair but Barnes was the appointee. Barnes later resigned from the Sydney Chair in 1958 to take the ANU Chair, and Stanner's Sydney application was again unsuccessful (Gray, 2012). He was appointed to a personal chair in 1966 and later to the Council for Aboriginal Affairs, headed by H.C. Coombs, and resigned due to ill health in 1976 (Gray, 2012).

After a period in the British Army as a psychologist, Piddington enlisted in the Australian Army and was appointed deputy principal of the School of Civil Affairs in 1944, which was created to train officers for service in Papua New Guinea. In 1945, Piddington proposed studies of the effect of war on New Guineans but there were no resources available from the administration. Funding was denied by Elkin as chair of the ANRC's Committee for Anthropological Research. In 1949, Piddington was appointed the foundation Professor of Anthropoogy at the University of New Zealand in Auckland (Gray, 2005; 2006).

Lucy Mair, British anthropologist and colonial administration expert, assisted DORCA formulate a colonial policy and lectured on colonial administration in Papua New Guinea. Mair's book *Australia in New Guinea* was published in 1948, but her views were rejected by the change of government and the new administrator for Papua New Guinea (Gray, 2012). In Stanner's (1949: 394) opinion, Mair's "appraisal of the new policy is not merely a loss of objectivity but a flight from it, which mar an otherwise excellent book."

Ian Hogbin immigrated to Australia from England in 1914. In 1929, he enrolled at the London School of Economics under Malinowski; his dissertation was published as *Law and Order in Polynesia* (1934). He returned to the Sydney anthropology department in 1931, conducted extensive fieldwork in the Solomon Islands and New Guinea, and was appointed permanent Lecturer in Melanesian ethnography in 1936 (Gray, 2012).

Hogbin enlisted in April 1942 and spent most of his time in the war in Papua New Guinea. An early task was to research the Army's use of labour from native men removed from their villages. Hogbin's report was critical of the recruitment practices of the Australian New Guinea Administrative Unit (ANGAU), another field organisation involved in the 'native affairs' of Papua and New Guinea (Wetherell, 2012). He found that Australian and American armies deployed New Guinea labour beyond operational requirements. He considered that removing 25% to 30% of adult males from their villages undermined social structure, and should be reduced to around 5% (Gray, 2012). Hogbin's work for the Army enabled him to pursue his applied anthropological interests in culture contact, changing society, and ethnographically informed colonial administration (Gray, 2012). His book *Transformation Scene* (1951) was one of the few ethnographic analyses of the war's effect on Papua New Guinea.

The Commonwealth set up the Native War Damage Compensation Committee in 1944, and most of the work fell to Ian Hogbin. The scheme was generous and was a rare policy among other Allied victors. Hogbin continued to advise the Papua New Guinea administration after he left DORCA and the School of Civil Affairs (later ASOPA). After the war in 1946, he returned as Reader to the University of Sydney, and he also lectured in anthropology at the ASOPA and continued until retirement in 1970 (Gray, 2012).

Read taught at the School of Civil Affairs while taking an MA under Elkin's supervision at Sydney. Read wrote *Effects of the War in the Markham Valley, New Guinea* (1947), an ethnography on the effect of the war on the Markham Valley. He moved to London and received his PhD in 1948 from the London School of Economics. Read returned and taught for 18 months at ASOPA, the successor to DORCA's School of Civil Affairs. He received the first Australian National University (ANU) Research Fellowship and returned to New Guinea in 1951–1954. In 1956, he moved to a Professorship at the University of Washington in Seattle.

Camilla Wedgwood qualified in anthropology for a Cambridge MA in 1927, but the university did not award degrees to women until 1948. She held teaching and research positions under Radcliffe-Brown at the University of Sydney from 1928–1930. In 1933–1934, she attended Malinowski's seminar at the London School of Economics and conducted research on Manam Island in New Guinea. She was in her sixth year as Principal at Women's College at the University of Sydney when the war in the Pacific began (Wetherell, 2012).

Wedgwood converted from pacifism to acceptance of the doctrine of a 'just war'. In 1944, she was commissioned in the Australian Army Medical Women's Service. She was appointed to DORCA and, from 1944–1946, conducted research on native education. For Wedgwood, the first essential was to link educational curricula to local culture; the diffusion of Westernisation was considered inappropriate. The aim was to devise an education program suited to New Guinea's rural culture (Wetherell, 2012).

Wedgwood was widely regarded as a feminist; she was the only woman lecturer in anthropology at Sydney University and the only wartime woman lieutenant colonel in Papua and New Guinea. However, she rejected being labelled a feminist, and recognised gender stratification and marriage as the natural order of society (Wetherell, 2012). She did not envision the opposition that emerged to her education policy. After the war, rural education was no longer considered adequate; Indigenous people in Papua

New Guinea were not satisfied with a program of education that confined them to village life. In 1945, she taught at the School of Civil Affairs and continued lecturing on native education at ASOPA until she died in 1955.

No indigenous guerrilla units like the NTSRU were created in New Guinea. Despite anthropological recommendations, the military tended to pursue their own interests through ANGAU in New Guinea, and used New Guineans as carriers and labour during the war. Without undertaking fieldwork, Stanner wrote a positive report on ANGAU on the conditions and treatment of New Guinean labour, but Hogbin, who undertook research, was critical of the systematic brutality of ANGAU overseers (Gray, 2006). Since the battle for Australia was fought in colonial New Guinea, there developed a sense of indebtedness to New Guineans for their sacrifice in the Australian war effort (Elkin, 1943; Hogbin and Wedgwood, 1943; Cranswick and Shevill, 1949). Powell (2003) developed this theme in his book on ANGAU, and contended that there would not have been the victory in New Guinea without the considerable sacrifice of New Guineans.

ANU was established in 1946 and the first Chair of Anthropology went to Fred Nadel in 1950, where he was Professor of Anthropology and Dean of the Research School of Pacific Studies, until his sudden death in 1956. In 1937, he lectured to the Summer School on Colonial Administration at Oxford University. In 1938, he was appointed as Government Anthropologist to the Government of the Anglo-Egyptian Sudan, and conducted fieldwork with the Nuba, a decade after military action against them had ceased. Nadel's task was to report on pressing problems created by increasing contact, and he produced a "comparative survey which blended scientific accuracy with practical suggestion in a way which gave great satisfaction to the administration" (Firth, 1957: 119). Nadel considered the Nuba to be:

> "Powerfully affected by the authority of the Government, the forces of economics and the influence of science…Their lives were still largely conditioned by superstitions and customs imperfectly known to the administration…Keen officials, especially technical officials, were apt to override native customs rather than make use of them."
>
> (Nadel in Gonzalez, 2009: 113)

For Nadel, making use of Nuba customs included establishing native courts and government sponsored chieftainships or securing indirect rule. Nadel was incapable of seeing beyond colonialism and the role of the anthropologists as other than of practical value to the administrators seeking to control Indigenous peoples. This was anthropological complicity with the colonial enterprise that did not challenge the colonizers right and obligation to decide what was best for Indigenous peoples (Gonzales, 2009: 114).

Nadel enlisted in the Sudan Defence Force in 1941 and transferred to the British Army, East African Command. For a year, he was in charge of an Eritrean-Ethiopian frontier post, and became Secretary of Native Affairs in the British Military Administration. In 1945, he moved as a Major to the Home Establishment and then transferred as Lieutenant-Colonel to Tripolitania, where he was Secretary of Native Affairs and Deputy Chief Secretary in the British Military Administration (Firth, 1957: 119).

The war more widely impacted on anthropology in Australia. ASOPA took over the training of colonial field officers from the Sydney Anthropology Department. ANU promoted research in the Highlands of Papua New Guinea, leaving the investigation of Aboriginal Australia to the Sydney department. The nature and direction of anthropological research shifted direction from Sydney to Canberra and from domestic issues of Aboriginal welfare to strategic issues of administering the South West Pacific and Papua New Guinea (Gray, 2006). Anthropological colonial expertise deployed in World War II also set the stage for more troubling chapters in the history of the discipline, including the 'Thailand controversy' that fractured the anthropological communities of Australia and America in the early 1970s.

New Zealand: Anthropology and Shared Wartime Colonial Intelligence in the Empire

Historical geographer Farish (2005: 673) contends that anthropology's field method of assuming an informant's view of culture represented a particularly relevant approach for those soldiers in World War II who would be engaging in 'social control at the local level'. The use of anthropological knowledge during the Pacific War corresponded to a continuation of the use of anthropologists by colonial governments in the Pacific in the interwar years (Farish, 2010: 101–146). The pre-war and war developments in anthropology between Britain and Australia contrasted with conditions in New Zealand:

> "The British Colonial service has in the past been able to make use of anthropologists in the service of colonial administration, notably in Africa. Administrators have also often profited by training in anthropology at one of the English universities. Australia again, has had its government anthropologist in Papua and in New Guinea. It has been able to make use of additional skilled anthropological surveys in various sections of both mandate and territory. The New Zealand government and its island administrations have remained consistently and continuously unaware of the benefits that would accrue to Pacific administration by the use of government anthropological service."
>
> (Beaglehole, 1944: 69–70).

The New Zealand government did not demonstrate interest in utilising anthropologists during World War II, nor was there an equivalent of the Australian Army's Directorate of Research.

The Empire before and during the war consisted of colonies and states interlocked through transnational intellectual, social, and cultural networks that bound the British world together beyond the mother country. Transnational empire networks were not diminished by war but were actually strengthened by war. The key transnational figures of scholarly patronage and appointment were Haddon, Malinowski and Radcliffe-Brown before the war and Firth after the war (Gray, Munro and Winter, 2012).

New Zealander (now Canadian) anthropologist Cyril Belshaw received an MA from Victoria College. He volunteered for the British Solomon Islands Defence Force, and later took up an offer with the New York-based Institute of Pacific Relations to survey colonial government and reconstruction in New Caledonia and the British Solomon Islands, from which he published *Island Administration in the South West Pacific* in 1950. Subsequently, the London School of Economics accepted Belshaw's wartime service as a substitute for fieldwork, and he submitted a library thesis published as *The Great Village: The Economic and Social Welfare of Hanubada, An Urban Community in Papua* in 1957. Before taking a position with the University of British Columbia in 1953, he was a research fellow at the Australian National University. Belshaw was appointed Head of the UBC Anthropology, Criminology and Sociology Department from 1968–1974, and thereafter remained on staff as a professor (Gray, Munro and Winter, 2012).

After taking the one-year anthropology course offered by Skinner at Otago University, William Geddes (1916–1989) served in the 2nd New Zealand Expeditionary Force from 1941–1945. Most of his time was spent in Fiji as a staff sergeant, which provided the opportunity to publish the Polynesian Society memoir, *Deuba: A Study of a Fijian Village* (1945). After the war, Geddes attended the London School of Economics and submitted his PhD thesis, *An Analysis of Cultural Change in Fiji*, in 1948. He lectured in psychology at the University of London Birkbeck College and, in 1951, took a lectureship in anthropology at Auckland University College. Later in 1958, Geddes became Professor of Anthropology at the University of Sydney (Gray, Munro and Winter, 2012).

Derek Freeman was born in Wellington on 16 August 1916, and in 1934, enrolled at Victoria University in psychology, philosophy, and education. Ernest Beaglehole, a psychologist and anthropologist, encouraged Freeman to consider fieldwork in Polynesia. Beaglehole interested Freeman in Mead during a graduate seminar in 1938, and promoted Samoa to Freeman at the time the government was advertising for teachers. Freeman accepted a teaching position at the Leifiifi School in Apia and, without finishing his degree; Freeman was appointed the Assistant Master. Freeman found a stone adze that led him to the village of Sa'anapu, which became the fieldwork village for investigating Samoan culture. He spent 19 months in close scrutiny, which included five months of ethnographic research in Sa'anapu during 1942–1943 (Hempenstall, 2012).

Freeman's opposition to World War II for the breakdown of international order and his fraternisation with Samoans in their villages saw him ostracised by the Samoan expatriate community. After the Pearl Harbor attack, Freeman joined the local defence force and patrolled the islands. He returned to New Zealand in 1943, and joined the Navy under 'Scheme B' for officer training in Britain. Once in England in 1944, Freeman received training in signals, weapons, officer leadership, navigation, and sailing. Upon graduation as an officer, Freeman applied to Naval Intelligence and studied Japanese. He was assigned as watch officer on-board a landing ship tank and after the atomic bomb was dropped on Hiroshima was dispatched to Borneo to take the Japanese surrender. Travelling up and down the coast enabled Freeman to have his first encounter with the Iban. Though Freeman "served in the royal Navy, he did so as a Kiwi, and he remained a Kiwi till his dying days" Hempenstall (2012: 185).

While in England, Freeman contacted Firth about his ethnographic study in Samoa and Firth encouraged him to register for a PhD. However, Freeman was unable to enrol because he had not completed his bachelor's degree, but was compensated with a New Zealand Rehabilitation Board support to study in London for a Postgraduate Academic Diploma. In 1947, Freeman was back in London on his rehabilitation bursary and enrolled with Firth to study anthropology. In 1948, he submitted his diploma thesis, *The Social Structure of a Samoan Village Community*. Fieldwork followed among the Iban between 1949 and 1951 under Leach's sponsorship with the Colonial Social Science Research Council. Freeman joined Fortes at Cambridge and was awarded his PhD in 1953 (Hempenstall, 2012). With opportunities for anthropologists limited in New Zealand, Freeman moved to ANU and was there for the remainder of his academic life (Munro, 2012).

New Zealander Felix M. Keesing was based in America, with the Institute of Pacific Relations in 1941, when he published *The South Seas in the Modern World*, which examined contemporary experiences and problems of Indigenous peoples in the Pacific (Gray, Munro and Winter, 2012). During the war, Keesing served in the Research and Analysis Branch Pacific Island section, which was designated as the South-West Pacific. He "directed the compilation of information...on all phases of psychological warfare, morale, politics, diplomacy, public administration, law personnel and social affairs in the area" (Price, 2008: 222–223).

Piddington, an Australian, started his PhD in 1932 at the London School of Economics and completed it in 1938. He never returned to

Australia as an academic. During World War II, Piddington initially served in the British Army as a psychologist (1941–1944). In 1944, he worked in the Australian Army's Directorate of Research and Civil Affairs, and in 1945, moved to the School of Civil Affairs, which later became the Australian School of Pacific Administration. He was appointed Deputy Principal of the School of Civil Affairs in 1944, which was created to train officers for service in Papua New Guinea. In 1945, Piddington proposed studies of the effect of war on New Guineans but was blocked by Elkin. In 1949, Piddington was appointed the Foundation Professor of Anthropology at the University of New Zealand in Auckland (Gray, 2005; 2006).

The Pacific was the last to be colonised and the last to be decolonised. Australia and New Zealand had gained New Guinea and Samoa. There was a crisis of colonialism with the colonised having seen the weakness of colonial governance. Anthropology expanded as the dominant social science of colonised peoples and colonial rule. Australian and New Zealand anthropology rarely examined colonial legitimacy, and accepted that enlightened colonial rule was beneficial for Indigenous peoples. There developed a tension between re-establishing colonial rule and the international push for decolonisation. The war resulted in a shift of power in the Pacific with increasing dependency on America and the demise of British military power and the onset of the Cold War (Gray, Munro and Winter, 2012).

Anthropology represented itself to colonial administrations and the governments of America, Britain, Canada, Australia, and New Zealand as an academic discipline with practical credentials for assisting in the control, management, and advancement of the colonised peoples in British African colonies and of the Indigenous peoples in the settler colonial states of America, Australia, Canada, and New Zealand. The World War II professionalised anthropology in Australia and New Zealand (Gray, Munro and Winter, 2012). Publications from Australian and New Zealand anthropologists in the post-war and mid-1950s period began to call for a new deal for Pacific Islanders, and some asserted that the colonial powers were indebted to the Indigenous peoples who had assisted the Allied war effort.

Conclusion

America

Anthropologists were involved in clandestine activities in World War II. The FBI's Special Intelligence Service operations in Latin America and the spy agency Office of Strategic Services established in 1942, was the precursor to the CIA, and had embedded several anthropologists to coordinate cultural intelligence. The work of several institutions functioned as a kind of "brain trust," which included the Human Relations Area Files, the Smithsonian Institution and its Ethnographic Board, and the Institute of Social Anthropology. Half of all American anthropologists applied their skills to World War II.

Britain

World War II interests conflated with the interests of colonialism as anthropologists administered or defended outposts of Empire. The key transnational figure Professor Firth was posted to the Naval Intelligence Division of the British Admiralty to produce a series of geographical handbooks to inform naval operations and was later appointed as the first secretary of the Colonial Social Science Research Council.

Canada

There were no professional university academic anthropologists from Canada to participate in World War II.

Australia

Indigenous peoples in Australia were colonised without citizenship and political or civil rights and were used in the pursuit of Australian war aims in the Northern Territory Special Reconnaissance Unit. The battle for Australia was fought in colonial New Guinea and the Directorate of Research and Civil Affairs (DORCA) was established and directly recruited anthropologists to study the effects of the war on Indigenous peoples in New Guinea.

New Zealand

Britain consisted of colonies and states interlocked through transnational Empire networks that were actually strengthened by war. Anthropologists were used by colonial governments in the Pacific and enlightened colonial rule was considered beneficial for Indigenous peoples. The war resulted in a shift of power in the Pacific with increasing dependency on America and the demise of British military power and the onset of the Cold War.

CHAPTER 5

The Cold War and the Demise of Colonial Empire

Introduction

America

The anthropological account of occupied Seoul, *The Reds Take a City* (1951), was disseminated by the State Department as a standard anti-communist text. In the Vietnam War in 1968, the CORDS program linked counterinsurgency and rural development projects with the Phoenix program which eliminated the Viet-cong command structure and more than 35,000 Vietnamese civilians were killed. Militant opposition to Vietnam War counterinsurgency galvanised dissent in the universities and brought ethics to anthropology; AAA's first Code of Ethics declared that anthropologists should not conduct covert research, not issue secret reports, use pseudonyms, and show primary loyalty to those they studied.

Britain

Significant political critique was mounted against structural functional anthropology in the 1930s to 1960s for accommodating to and enhancing the powers of the Empire and becoming complicit in it. Asad's *Anthropology and the Colonial Encounter* (1973) had a counterpart in America, with the appearance of *Reinventing Anthropology*, edited by Hymes (1969), that was similarly critical of anthropology's history and future. If British anthropology was concerned with the role of colonialism in former and current colonies; the counterpart for Americans was the settler colonial relationship to Indigenous nations.

Canada

Canadian anthropology grew up during the Cold War. More than 125,000 American draft dodgers and deserters came to Canada between 1964 and 1977; it was the largest political exodus in American history and more than half stayed in Canada. Politically activist anthropologists engaged theory with practice and worked effectively with First Nations. Engagement became more challenging as First Nations gained ever greater control over their resources and acquired increased political autonomy.

Australia

In the Cold War, Aboriginal ethnography gave way to a broader Asia-Pacific research focus. Australia contributed small contingents of troops to Korea and Vietnam as a way of cementing support for the American alliance. Vulnerability to the communist menace and the growing opposition to military counterinsurgency in the Vietnam War created similar political climates on Australian and American universities. A rancorous conflict centred on counterinsurgency intelligence research conducted in Thailand by members of the anthropology department at the University of Sydney.

New Zealand

Maori participation in anthropology began to flourish again in the 1960s to 1970s. Sir Ian "Hugh" Kawharu was a distinguished academic and paramount chief of the Ngati Whatua Maori. He gained a MA in anthropology from Cambridge and a DPhil form Oxford. In 1970, Kawharu became the Foundation Professor of anthropology and Maori Studies at Massey University, and from 1985–1993, he was Professor of Maori Studies and Head of the Department of Anthropology at the University of Auckland. Maori anthropologists were politically active and reasserted old claims to redress injustices during settler colonialism.

America: Korean War, Counterinsurgency in Vietnam and the Ethical Rejection of Militarised Anthropology

The direct involvement of American anthropologists in the Korean War from 1950–1953 goes largely unrecognised. Three university-employed social scientists together, with a CIA psychological warfare specialist, were dispatched in 1950 to study the North Korean occupation of the South. They departed after a month and subsequently produced reports on "Sovietisation" and the "impact of Communism" for the government, as well as a popular book on occupied Seoul, *The Reds Take a City* (Riley and Schramm, 1951), that was disseminated by the State Department as a standard anti-communist text (Oppenheim, 2008).

In the post-war period, Wilbur Schramm helped develop the academic discipline of communications. Other members of the multidisciplinary team included John Riley, a follower of communications from the Rutgers sociology department, and John Pelzel, a Harvard anthropologist. Pelzel's study of two occupied villages south of the 38th parallel in Korea set the model of similar wartime research by other United Nations and American researchers (Oppenheim, 2008). Simpson (1994) critiqued the field of communications because of anti-democratic propaganda and psychological warfare opinion management and identified Sovietisation studies with the co-optation of American academics through military and intelligence-related funding.

The direct sponsor of the Korean War Sovietisation study was the Human Resources Research Institute (HRRI), an Air Force research body linked to the Air Force-affiliated RAND Corporation. The study illustrated connections between anthropology and post-war military–social scientific relations. John Bennett, Director of the Public Opinion and Sociological Research (PO&SR) Division of the Supreme Command for Allied Powers (SCAP), approached Kluckhohn through Harvard's interdisciplinary research centre to collaborate in the HRRI project on Sovietisation in Korea, resulting in the selection of Pelzel from Harvard to be part of the team. Pelzel, the area expert, preceded Bennett as the first Head of the PO&SR Division in Japan. Frederick William, the fourth member of the research team, was assigned from the CIA as Assistant Director of HRRI (Oppenheim, 2008).

PO&SR functioned as an in-house contract interdisciplinary anthropology research agency for the SCAP occupation of Japan. PO&SR anthropological research emphasised understanding and effecting socio-political change, and defined itself against culture and personality research. The ethnographic village studies that Pelzel presented as part of the HRRI "Preliminary Study" provided the fine-grained, individuated analysis of local institutional politics that was PO&SR's stock in trade. Air Force concerns motivated the HRRI study, which used social scientific methods of sampling, survey, and participant observation, as well as dialogues with English-speaking educated Koreans and government elites (Oppenheim, 2008).

Anthropology played a significant but little acknowledged social scientific role in the Korean War. Military interests were certainly relevant to this episode and Cold War anthropology in general. Understanding Pelzer's anthropological networks and practical–theoretical orientation, and such ideological products as *The Reds Take a City* requires the consideration of the demands and needs of SCAP administrators in Japan. Pelzel, Riley, Schramm, and Bennett shared a liberal anti-communism that conflicted with William's militarism political ideology. Colonialism and occupation were discussed in HRRI: "Bennett put himself on the line for PO&SR Japanese employees accused of being communists," "Schramm took a visible role in opposition to the imposition of loyalty oaths at the University of California," and "Riley wrote home unsparingly about the violence of ROC policemen who were alienating their own populace" (Oppenheim, 2008: 250).

The Vietnam War and political upheavals of the 1960s profoundly affected anthropology much more than World War II or the Korean War. The 1960s were a period of political turmoil in America:

> "The early years of the decade had seen the civil rights movement, and by 1965 both the Vietnam War and the antiwar protests moved into high

gear. Then 1968, the year so critical for academics worldwide, brought the United States the Martin Luther King Jr. assassination; Lyndon Johnson's concession of defeat by the antiwar demonstrators; student revolts and occupations of campus buildings; the Democratic Party convention in Chicago, where violent clashes with the local police erupted; the flourishing of the new youth culture; and more. For anthropologists the Camelot affair was a recent memory and the spectre of clandestine research would soon arise again in the context of Southeast Asia."

(Silverman 2005: 310)

Anthropological scholars in peasant studies were inevitably drawn into peasant involvement in armed political movements, and Wolf's book *Peasants* (1966) systematised the anthropology of peasantry. Anthropologists were at the forefront of the protest against the war in Vietnam (Silverman, 2005). The anthropologist Marshall Sahlins invented the concept of the teach-ins in March 1965 and Wolf was a founder of the movement (Jorgensen and Wolf, 1970). Wolf wrote a briefing paper on Vietnam for the teach-in at the University of Michigan and developed it into a full-scale comparison of six peasant revolutions in Mexico, Russia, China, Algeria, Cuba, and Vietnam that was published as *Peasant Wars of the Twentieth Century* (1969).

Anthropologists conspicuously intensified anti-war activism. American anthropologists were drawn into the political ferments on their campuses, but it was the Vietnam War and the American government's involvement in counterinsurgency that galvanised dissention in the universities. The first crisis erupted over anthropologists being recruited for counterinsurgency work with the 1964 Project Camelot, an Army mission to "assist friendly governments in dealing with active insurgency problems" (Silverman, 2005: 290). Project Camelot planned to use anthropologists to develop counterinsurgency tactics for application in Latin America. The effort to recruit Norwegian sociologist Johan Galtung for Camelot's Chilean counterinsurgency program proved futile and Galtung publically exposed the project, which caused a public uproar. The American Anthropological Association (AAA) established a committee to scrutinise the use of anthropology to inform counterinsurgency, and the resulting report foreshadowed ethical principles to appear four years later in the first AAA ethics code (Price, 2011).

Although Project Camelot galvanised academic anger in the mid-1960s, it was but one of many counterinsurgency programs drawing on anthropologists. Anthropologists working for RAND in Vietnam supported a number of rural agricultural counterinsurgency programs. Anthropologists worked on Strategic Hamlet Programs in Vietnam, and began working on a number of so-called "Modernization Programs" managed by the US Agency for International Development:

> "In the 1960s, military strategists and intelligence analysts suddenly rediscovered the value of anthropology, and began dreaming that culture may hold answers to their military problems. The Special Operations Research Office (SORO) and its cousin-organization CINFAC (Counterinsurgency Information Analysis) published a whole series of crazy sounding (and reading) papers on counterinsurgency related topics like the 1964 classic, "Witchcraft, Sorcery, Magic and Other Psychological Phenomena and Their Implications on Military and Paramilitary Operations in the Congo," or CINFAC's "An Ethnographic Summary of the Ethiopian Provinces of Harar and Sidamo," and a series of counterinsurgency related documents. The military and the CIA were in over their heads with a mix of overt and covert operations around the world, and they held out hopes that "culture" was the panacea for the forms of social control they envisioned."
>
> (Price, 2011: 24)

In Vietnam, the CORDS (Civil Operations and Revolutionary Development Support) program was made operational in 1968. John Vann, a key author of CORDS, resigned his commission in 1963 due to disillusionment with the ineptness and corruption of the Diem regime. Vann returned to Vietnam in 1965 as a US Agency for International Development (USAID) official. From his position, Vann argued for a uniform chain of command for development, psychological operations, and intelligence. CORDS linked counterinsurgency and rural development projects, and centralised the USAID, the CIA, and the United States Information Service under one civilian director reporting directly to the US military command (Hevia, 2010). CORDS became one component of the counterinsurgency strategy, with the Phoenix program as the other component, which was designed to eliminate the Viet-cong command structure through assassination and incarceration

(Sheehan, 1988: 730–732). Phoenix was not remotely calculated to win hearts and minds, and sought to attain the crossover point when the dead and wounded exceeded the National Liberation Front's ability to replenish itself. The State Department acknowledged that, during President Nixon's first two and a half years in office, the Phoenix program murdered or abducted 35,000 Vietnamese civilians (Jacobsen, 2010).

It was anthropology deployed for counterinsurgency that posed the most fundamental ethical and political questions, because "using anthropology to alter and undermine Indigenous cultural movements cut against the grain of widely shared anthropological assumptions about the rights of cultures and peoples to determine their own destiny" (Price, 2011: 25).

Rejecting the use of anthropology for counterinsurgency continued to drive debate and, in 1968, more than 800 anthropologists petitioned against a Vietnam War psy-op counterinsurgency position that appeared in the *American Anthropologist*. The petitioners successfully introduced a new policy that directed the AAA to refrain from accepting advertisements for employment that produced secretive reports. In 1967, a self-identified Radical Caucus of anthropologists seized political power at the AAA's annual meeting and effectively pushed the AAA board to draft a set of ethics known as the Principles of Professional Responsibility. The draft ethics code "mandated members to do no harm, disclose funding sources and uses of research and forbid covert research and the production of secret reports" (Price, 2011: 25).

Anthropological protest to involvement in counterinsurgency escalated in 1970 when Eric Wolf, as Chair of the AAA Ethics Committee, received stolen documents from the Student Mobilization Committee (SMC) that established the involvement of anthropologists in counterinsurgency operations in Thailand (Jorgensen and Wolf, 1970). Excerpts from the documents appeared in the radical newspaper *The Student Mobilizer* and were distributed at the Association of Asian Studies annual meeting. Professor Gerald Berreman issued a statement distributed by the SMC in San Francisco on April 3, 1970:

> "The evidence clearly demonstrates the direct complicity of scholars in the antischolarly tasks of implementing counter insurgency programs in

Thailand. This comprises untenable corruption of social science and scholarship which promises to discredit not only those who have participated, but to cast suspicion on all of those who study and work in Asia and, in fact, anywhere else. It also betrays social scientists and area specialists in their role as scholars within American society, for it identifies them as hirelings to agencies whose purposes are, as this document confirms, to intervene politically in the internal affairs of sovereign nations. This is an intolerable affront to the academic community and the public which supports it. It is an insult to the people we area specialists know, study, work with and trust in Asia and elsewhere."

(Wakin, 1992: 159)

Unaware of the steps planned by SMC, Wolf privately wrote the named anthropologists for clarification enclosing the statement:

"Since these documents contradict in spirit and in letter the resolutions of the American Anthropological Association concerning clandestine and secret research, we feel that they raise the most serious issues for the scientific integrity of our profession. We shall, therefore, call the attention of the American Anthropological Association to these most serious matters."

(Jorgensen and Wolf, 1970)

With the charges made public, the AAA exploded in controversy and highly charged debates between anthropologists across the country. The AAA Executive Board criticized Wolf, who resigned as Chair of the Ethics Committee, and appointed an independent committee chaired by Margaret Mead, then the most prominent member of the discipline, to investigate the charges as well as counter charges that the ethics committee had acted improperly by questioning colleagues (Wakin, 1992).

The Mead committee reported in late 1971, and chastised the ethics committee and vindicated those originally charged, but the report was rejected by the AAA membership and proved to be a disaster and humiliating repudiation of Mead (Silverman 2005). The Radical Caucus occupied the 1971 AAA Council Meeting, marshalled the numbers to take control of the agenda, and succeeded in motioning, seconding, and adopting the rejection of the Mead report. More significantly, the protest over using anthropologists in counterinsurgency in the unsuccessful Camelot Project and in Southeast Asia galvanised the AAA membership's vote to adopt the Principles of Professional Responsibility. The AAA's first Code of Ethics declared that anthropologists should not conduct covert research, not issue secret reports, use pseudonyms, and show primary loyalty to those they studied (Price, 2011: 26).

The Vietnam War brought ethics to anthropology. The political and cultural upheavals of the 1960s created long-lasting divisions within anthropology that reflected theoretical differences. On the one hand, the 1960s ushered in a level of political engagement that prompted efforts to reinvent anthropology; on the other hand, there was reluctance to take on work with political implications that sparked a retreat into trivia (Silverman, 2005). By the 1980s, political economy shifts in anthropology loosened the AAA's Code of Ethics to allow for more secrecy in the production of proprietary reports for industry. As more anthropologists worked in corporate or government settings, the AAA Code of Ethics was relaxed in 1990 to allow for proprietary, secretive reports. Many academic anthropologists were uncomfortable with inverting the appropriate relationship between professional ethics and the desire to produce or control knowledge (Price, 2011: 27).

Britain: Structural Functional Juggernaut and the Colonial Encounter

Anthropological research in Britain from the 1940s to 1970s was defined by the attempt to generalise and expand the application of Radcliffe-Brown's structural functionalism. The senior British anthropologists of the 1940s to 1970s held considerable discretionary power over junior academics and autocratically controlled research grants and appointments. There was substantial unity of the structural functional orthodoxy because the ideas offered were exciting and internal criticism was stifled. Although there was shared theoretical achievement, there was also delayed critical work and reduced individual creativity; the "power of lineage theory to extract its object from the complexity of social life and to deliver a generalizable set of characterisation of groups seemed increasingly questionable" (Barth, 2005: 37).

Although, in "mainstream British anthropology, the structural-functional juggernaut moved on for a considerable time" (Barth, 2005: 37), there were several factors that brought the orthodoxy to a halt. The senior anthropologists mostly retired as a cohort; Evans-Pritchard retired from Oxford in 1970, Fortes retired from Cambridge in 1973, Firth retired from the London School of Economics in 1968, and Gluckman retired from Manchester in 1971. Leach did not receive his personal chair at Cambridge until 1972, and retired as Provost of Kings College in 1979. The global student uprising of 1968 shattered institutional constraints and changed relations of power in British academia, and the arbitrary power of the senior anthropologists was replaced by committees, and students and junior academics could no longer be so effectively disciplined (Barth, 2005: 45). Finally, significant political critique was mounted against the British structural functional juggernaut, most effectively from Talal Asad's edited volume, *Anthropology and the Colonial Encounter* (1973).

Anthropologists have variously conceptualised colonialism as a combination of the universal evolutionary progress of modernisation, a strategy of domination and exploitation and as unfinished struggle (Pels, 1997). Past colonialism cannot be demarcated from struggles in the present; therefore, anthropology of colonialism is concerned with contemporary anthropology as well as the colonial circumstances from which it emerged (Thomas, 1994). Critical approaches have questioned the nature of anthropological knowledge required for colonial rule, and raised doubts about the claim to scientific independence from colonial circumstances (Asad, 1973).

Asad addressed ways British anthropology, especially the period from the 1930s–1960s, accommodated to the empire and became complicit in it. Structural functional analysis was viewed as particularly well suited to enhancing the powers of the empire (Loizos, 1977). Power relations between anthropologists and other colonials and the colonial masses served to distort the practice of fieldwork and anthropological representation (Barth, 2005). Further complicity was:

"[…] rooted in an unequal power encounter between the West and Third World…that gives the West access to cultural and historical information about the societies it has progressively dominated, and thus not only generates a certain kind of universal understanding, but also reinforces the inequalities in capacity between the European and the non-European worlds."

(Asad, 1973: 16)

Asad's *Anthropology and the Colonial Encounter* (1973) had a counterpart in America, with the appearance of *Reinventing Anthropology*, edited by Hymes (1969) that was similarly critical of anthropology's history and future (Silverman, 2005). If British anthropology was concerned with the role of colonialism in former and current colonies; the counterpart for Americans was the settler colonial relationship to Indigenous nations. The Sioux scholar Vine Deloria's book *Custer Died for Your Sins* (1969) challenged on behalf of all colonised Indigenous nations that anthropology exoticised and primitivised the Indians. The voice of the colonised 'native' that critiqued anthropology and sought entry into academy raised the ire of some anthropologists but drew attention to others of the legitimate concerns and the need to incorporate colonial perspectives.

Settler, indirect, direct, and hybrid were the four types of British colonialism (Lange, Mahoney and Hau, 2006). Settler colonialism was the most extensive form, with settlers transplanting British institutions while destroying pre-colonial ones. In contrast, indirect colonialism involved a low level of institutional transfer from Britain and implanted a combination of central bureaucratisation and peripheral patrimonialism. Direct colonialism established a colonial state without large-scale British settlers, due primarily to the disease climate. Hybrid colonies combined indirect with settler or direct colonialism as in South Africa.

The mission of the RLI was to utilise social anthropology to generate scientific knowledge about the subjects of British colonial rule, as well as to provide the colonial authorities with information to facilitate the smooth and humane operation of colonial rule (Crehan, 1997). The relationship between the RLI and the colonial state was a complicated one. A significant feature of the colonial state in British Africa was the commitment to the principle of indirect rule that combined the inexpensive use of locals to police its lower tiers, together with the illusion of local autonomy. It was believed that in some essential sense, African society retained pre-colonial social organisation, when in fact the imposition of colonial society represented a fundamental rupture. Behind the enthusiasm for indirect rule was the silent denial that the establishment of *pax Britannica* necessarily eroded the power base on which pre-colonial political authority rested. It was within this project of understanding and controlling the colonised society that the work of the RLI anthropologists was located (Crehan, 1997).

Social anthropology was useful to colonial administration for its small-scale, intensive, and timeless ethnographies: "as far as Africa is concerned, it is mainly in colonies governed under the system of Indirect Rule, where economic policy is to encourage independent native production, that the study of social anthropology receives official encouragement" (Lucy Mair, 1938: 1). There was supposedly no scientific incompatibility with accepting imperial policy; Evans-Pritchard (1946: 98), for example, was scientifically concerned with the 'primitive field'. Primitive societies were accepted as administrative and cultural facts, unquestioned until their decolonisation and conversion to new nations was imminent (Feuchtwang, 1973: 95).

Social anthropology did not analyse colonialism; rather, it reproduced the colonial divide in an inverted form as a colonial 'us' interpreting a colonial 'them'. Indirect rule in Africa was shaped by British structural-functional anthropology, and indirect rule gave to anthropology small-scale social formations as units of study to be treated as complete social systems. The units were studied in relation to universal humanity and for recommendations on short-term effects of colonial policy (Feucthwang 1973: 99); for structural functionalism:

> "Real participant observation, the comparison of socio-economic types, an historical science of social formation and of the transition between types, and the study of imperialism as a system, these are the parts of a social science that could logically have been anthropology, but have not been."
>
> (Feucthwang, 1973: 100)

When the Colonial Development and Welfare Act of 1940 constituted the Colonial Social Science Research Council (CSSRC) in 1946, Firth became the first secretary. As Colonial Research Fellows in the late 1940s, Firth had worked in West Africa and Malaya, Leach in Sarawak, and Richards in East Africa. Although administered by Firth and other academics, the grants were guided by colonial policy priority lists (Feuchtwang, 1973: 94). Half of the Colonial Research Studies series written by its Colonial Research Fellows and members between 1944 and 1962 were by anthropologists, and half the CSSRC's total allocation of funds established institutes in the colonial territories (Feuchtwang, 1973: 86).

Discourses of 'culture' and 'ethnography' developed under and for colonial rule are still operative in contemporary anthropology (Fabian, 1983). Anthropological concepts of ethnography, fieldwork, participant observation, and culture need to be placed in historical context (Pels, 1997). In the history of colonial sciences, ethnography, geography, and botany set up the exotic as a field to be observed (Grove, 1995). There are continuities between past colonial and today's professional ethnography (Pels and Salemink, 1994).

Evolutionism surreptitiously continued in British structural functionalism in the dualist vocabulary used to identify anthropology's subject matter of primitive/modern and simple/complex, and noted that the anthropologist studies the peasant, the farmer, the labourer; never the imperial, government-advising or funding agency (Worsley, 1970). Moreover, anthropologists went unchallenged by its subjects, who were unable to read the finished work. The Indigenous voice of Vine Deloria (2004: 3–4) addressed the evolutionary role Indigenous nations played in the stage of human development:

> "Tribal peoples have traditionally been understood by Westerners as the last remnants of a hypothetical earlier stage of cultural evolution, and this so-called "primitive" stage of human development is a necessary preamble to any discussion of human beings and the meaning of their lives. Indeed, the stereotype of primitive peoples anchors the whole edifice of Western social thought. We need the primitive so that we can distinguish Western civilisation from it and congratulate ourselves on the progress we have made. John Locke and Thomas Hobbes may have articulated the idea formally by beginning their theories of the social contract with the hypothetical stage wherein primitive people established a society, but subsequent generations of Western people have

wholeheartedly accepted the image without any critical examination of its validity. Thus the attitude of many philosophers is that American Indians must represent the stage of human development in which superstition and ignorance reigned supreme."

Anthropology has only recently examined colonialism as a struggle and researched the violent beginnings of colonial occupation. Conquests and colonial wars and their routines of reconnaissance structured colonial rule (Pels, 1997). A significant difference between the Europeans and the colonised was the colonisers' extreme capacity for violence, both technologically (Reid, 1994) and culturally (De Silva, 1994).

Evans-Pritchard's (1949) book on the Sanusiya Islamic brotherhood of Sufi mysticism addressed the historic association between the pragmatic Bedouin and their spiritual leaders, which:

> "[…] lies in the lineage structure of Bedouin internal rivalries. The Bedouin welcomed independent arbitration, and the immigrant tribes and their saintly lineages were glad to provide it (an anthropological approach). The rest of the answer lies in the pressures of Italian colonialism and war (a historical approach). The personalities of the Sanusi leaders fused with the fiery independence and physical endurance of Bedouin herdsmen."
>
> (Douglas, 1980: 47)

Evans-Pritchard promoted his book as an exemplary historical analysis, but it was deeply flawed in its historical approach because he ignored his role in counterinsurgency against Italian colonial occupation, and it was also flawed in its anthropological approach because he relied on the orthodox lineage paradigm. Peters' (1990) posthumous assessment of Evans-Pritchard's orthodox anthropological lineage paradigm was highly critical of the Sanusi monograph as "static in its assumptions and arguable deeply flawed in its account…could hardly be exaggerated" (Barth, 2005: 45).

Although military struggles have been taken for granted, anthropology has provided little informed study of tactical engagements between colonial soldiers and the Indigenous resistance to colonisation (Byrnes, 1994).

Leach's Kachin forces deployed brutal counterinsurgency tactics against the Japanese. Fire-hardened bamboo panji-sticks covered in human excrement were hidden to impale Japanese soldiers and inflict lethal infections (Price, 2008). In addition to panji-sticks, other Kachin guerrilla tactics included "making booby traps of trip wires attached to hollowed-out bamboo cups, beneath which they placed instantaneously fused hand grenades...when [tripped] the grenade's spring-loaded firing lever would pop upward, setting off the explosive and taking more casualties" (Webster, 2003: 53). US Army General Stilwell questioned a Kachin soldier on how he could be so confident they had killed thousands of Japanese soldiers:

> "[…] the Kachin unhooked a bamboo tube that had been hanging on his belt. Then he pulled a stopper from the tubes top and — turning the tube upside down — he dumped a pile of small blackish lumps onto the tabletop between himself and the general. The blackened lumps resembled bits of dried fruit: apricots or perhaps peaches. Divide all these by two and you know exactly how many Japs I've killed."
>
> (Webster, 2003: 55)

When the general learned they were Japanese ears, he ordered an end of the practice (Price, 2008).

Leach's understanding of Kachin culture and language helped provide the British Kachin-based counterinsurgency program with the lethal upper hand against the Japanese, but the sanctioning of violence against the Japanese created problems in the post-war period (Price, 2008). The attempt to distinguish between utilising anthropological techniques and knowledge for defensive/liberator as opposed to offensive/occupier purposes was difficult because "liberation arguments can be complicated to maintain, as liberators can easily become occupiers, and occupiers can make impressive historical arguments that frame occupations as acts of overdue liberation" (Price, 2008: 72). The Kachin maintained armed resistance against British colonial occupation as well as Japanese wartime occupation, and have continued armed resistance against attempted occupation from the Burmese state. The culture of resistance and military prowess, and the relative lack of success *vis-à-vis* colonial armies tended to leave a legacy of ethnic distinctiveness under subsequent phases of colonial rule (Forster, 1994; West, 1994). Anthropology's role in the conduct of colonial violence is important for rethinking the contemporary application of anthropology to understand culture and violence in postcolonial conflicts between nations and states.

Canada: American Anti-war Political Exodus and Anthropology Engagement with Indigenous Activism

Canadian anthropology grew up during the Cold War. Anthropology was a very small discipline in Canada until the 1960s; only the University of Toronto granted the PhD. The National Museum of Canada was the only anthropological institution of international prominence until the 1960s. Founded in 1880 and becoming an independent institution in 1910, the Museum operated as a branch of the Geological survey of Canada. Sapir was the chief anthropologist of the anthropology research program from 1910–1925. Anthropology university staff grew from a few to more than 120, and departments offering a doctorate grew from one to 10 in the period from 1950–1960 (Graburn, 2006).

The effect of large numbers of students taking sanctuary in Canada during the Vietnam War probably had a greater impact on social sciences in Canada then the Cold War (Graburn, 2006). It is estimated that 125,000 American draft dodgers and deserters came to Canada between 1964 and 1977. For the most part, they had left-leaning tendencies and their movement across the border represented the largest political exodus in American history. According to the 1986 census, more than half the wave of Vietnam War draft dodgers and deserters stayed in Canada. They blended into Canadian life, with many becoming part of Canada's intelligentsia and, during the 1960s, they swelled the ranks of students and faculty. Beginning in the 1970s, preferential hiring of Canadians was introduced to discourage American academics (Graburn, 2006).

In the 1960s, there was a growth in 'area studies' in North American social sciences informed by the need to better understand previously neglected culture areas. This translated in Canada to dealing with Indigenous peoples inconveniently living in the potential Cold War frontline between America and the Soviet Union. A number of 'joint' Arctic weather stations were built by America and, in the 1950s, the

American military was permitted to build the Mid-Canada Line along the 55th parallel to detect Soviet bombers. Airstrips and modern technology penetrated the subarctic inhabited by the Algonquian, Dene First Nations, and the Metis. Later, the DEW Line military sites for detecting intercontinental ballistic missiles were constructed further north in the homeland of the Inuit. The Canadian federal government abandoned their policy of benign neglect of Indigenous peoples and initiated assimilation policies based around education and permanent settlements (Graburn, 2006).

In the early 1960s, social scientists were employed by the Northern Research Coordination Centre (NRCC) to carry out community and social impact research with First Nation, Metis, and Inuit in the North. Over a four-year period, more anthropologists conducted fieldwork under the auspices of the NRCC than any other research organisation in North America. Research became more applied and concerned with wider social issues such as Inuit relocation and employment. Inuit men from communities associated with military bases were nominally employed as scouts or spotters and were 'paid' in rifles and ammunition (Graburn, 2006).

Although Canada became a member of NATO and sent 25,000 troops to the Korean War; it did not send troops to the Vietnam War. Canada worried about their position *vis-à-vis* the US, and was often seen to take a stance different from and to the 'left' of the US. The motivation for Canada's political positioning was less ideological and more of an attempt to fashion a national identity. Canada takes a more internationalist and Eurocentric posture and, in the Cold War, established an 'honest broker' stance between American McCarthyism and other smaller states (Graburn, 2006).

The Canadian anthropological identity to emerge out of the Cold War was shaped by:

> "[…] a significant presence of left-wing antiwar personnel, a style somewhat influenced by the francophone intellectually engaged tradition, and an involvement in the North and/or direct concern with Native activism. These influences have led a greater proportion of academic anthropologists into applied work, in their own (adopted) country, and often directly into the fray of social conflict."
>
> (Graburn, 2006: 251)

Cold War politically active anthropologists engaged theory with practice and worked effectively with First Nations.

Not until the 1960s and 1970s did Canadian anthropologists cease endorsing assimilation and grounding their ethnographic research in the practical desires of Indigenous peoples themselves. The continued assertion of Indigenous peoples of their rights gained national prominence as the public concern increased for issues of human rights and social justice. Debates around the 1969 White Paper, the James Bay hydroelectric project, the Mackenzie Valley pipeline, the identification of First Nation rights in the Constitution, as well as continuing land claims, provoked anthropologists to confront the oppressiveness of Canadian Indigenous policy and administration. Since the 1970s, anthropology assumed a more politically committed stance and developed a more collaborative anthropological practice that intervened between Indigenous peoples and Canadian society. Engagement became more challenging as First Nations gained ever greater control over their resources and acquired increased political autonomy (Buchanan, 2006).

By the 1970s, there was unprecedented participation of Indigenous peoples in the politics of Indigenous nation-state relations, and provocative ethnographies of Indigenous people's dealings with government appeared. In the 1980s, many anthropologists sought comparisons with Australia and New Zealand, where Indigenous nations were also encapsulated in settler states (Darnell, 2010). Dyck (1985) drew on Fourth World theory to compare the trajectories of Indigenous nation-state relations in Canada, Australia, and Norway.

Australia: Thailand Counterinsurgency Controversy and the Ethical Impact on Anthropology

The 1960s and 1970s were a critical period in the development of Australian anthropology. There was a rapid expansion of universities and postgraduate education in the post war Menzies Government. As a consequence of Australia's new strategic interests, Aboriginal ethnography gave way to a broader Asia-Pacific research focus. Hobsbawm referred to the period from the end of World War II to the early 1970s as the 'golden age' of capitalism. The demise of the old colonial empires was followed by the Cold War, with the superpowers competing for influence over the newly independent underdeveloped states. The discourse of development emerged for the management of the poor. The superpower competition resulted in armed conflicts in Korea and Vietnam, which contributed to Australia's settler colonists feeling threatened by the communist menace and vulnerable to the 'yellow peril' moving down from their near north. Australia contributed small contingents of troops to Korea and Vietnam as a way of cementing support for the American alliance to ensure regional security (Robinson, 2004).

The foreign policy sense of vulnerability to the communist menace and the growing opposition to military engagement in Vietnam created similar political climates on Australian and American universities. Mass-based opposition to the American involvement in Vietnam led to the New Left critique of American society and politics and the reawakened radical tradition of scholarship (Robinson, 2004).

In Australia, a dispute centred on the research conducted in Thailand by members of the anthropology department at the University of Sydney. The debate focused on the public uses of anthropological knowledge and the responsibilities of anthropologists in understanding the power contexts in which their knowledge would be deployed. The University of Sydney anthropology department in the late 1960s intellectually reflected structural functionalism of Radcliffe-Brown, the founding professor. Structural-functionalism had involved British anthropologists in colonial administration, particularly in Africa (Asad, 1973). Elkin followed Radcliffe-Browns departure in 1931; he continued functionalism, while advancing the practical application of anthropology and providing expert advice to government. When Elkin retired in 1956, he was replaced by the British anthropologist Barnes, who moved after a short while to take the Chair in anthropology at ANU following the death of Nadel. Later in 1958, the New Zealander Geddes, who received his PhD from LSE, became the professor of anthropology at the University of Sydney (Robinson, 2004).

The intellectual climate at the University of Sydney in the late 1960s was challenged by political activism under the banner of the New Left. As with the response to the Vietnam War on American universities, the student body was increasingly politicised and involved in massive mobilisations against Australian involvement in the Vietnam War and against drafting conscripts to the war, many of them students. The rancorous conflict that enveloped the anthropology department at the University of Sydney in the early 1970s flowed from the New Left politicisation that grew out of the anti-war movement. The naïve optimism of the research ethics associated with structural functionalism that the researcher can stand as a neutral observer was challenged (Robinson, 2004). More recently, this debate about ethics and anthropological engagement has refocused on the tension between moral/activist (Scheper-Hughes, 1995) and scientific/objective (D'Andrade, 1995) approaches in anthropology.

In response to New Left politics of the Cold War, the American Anthropological Association (AAA) developed a code of ethical practice in 1967 in response to the revelation that anthropologists had conducted research in the service of American counterinsurgency operations. In 1967, the AAA also set up an ethics committee:

> "[…] framed against the background of the war in Vietnam…but more generally it sought to guard the integrity of anthropologists whose specific knowledge and experience, based on fieldwork in the third world, obviously commended them to the executors of government policy on counter-insurgency and related forms of clandestine research."
>
> (Jorgensen and Wolf, 1970: 26)

Wolf (Chairman) and Jorgensen, as members of the newly formed AAA ethics committee, received copies of documents from the Student Mobilization Committee against the War (SMC) that named anthropologists that had been involved in counterinsurgency. Wolf and Jorgensen wrote to the named individuals requesting clarification. Jorgensen and Wolf (1970) resigned the ethics committee and published "Anthropology on the Warpath in Thailand" in the *New York Review of Books*. The article added new information concerning the Tribal Research Centre (TRC) in Chiang Mai, Thailand, that documented a 1970 consultants meeting involving anthropologists, Thai government officials, and representatives from US agencies and SEATO, which had funded establishment of the centre. Jorgensen and Wolf (1970) focused on the 'Proposal for Village Data Card' distributed to participants at the meeting, which requested information not normally gathered by anthropologists and would mainly be used to support such counterinsurgency measures as revealing precise locations of villages. Precise locational data had been used for aerial surveillance in the Malayan Emergency (Robinson, 2004).

In Hinton's view (2002: 171), the term counterinsurgency:

"[…] was taken up with enthusiasm by those trying to open up the Thailand controversy. It was used indiscriminately to label any social scientist who was researching for an 'enemy' government. So it did not matter if one was helping the military plan strategic hamlets in Vietnam, or studying the curative rites of one of the hill peoples of Thailand for a Tribal Research Centre which had nothing to do with the military. One was still perceived to be a collaborator with a social order which stood in the way of the progressive forces of the region."

The TRC had been set up with funding from SEATO, then the main arm of the Australian and American defence agreement. The allegation from Jorgensen and Wolf (1970) that the TRC was part of a counterinsurgency system set up by the American Defense Department created a furore in Australia. According to Miles (2008: 256–257):

"In the context of the 'Thailand controversy', Bill's [Geddes] judgement was tragically flawed. I emphasise the fact that both Hinton and Geddes were in Thailand funded by Australia's Department of External Affairs and as advisors of the SEATO, of which Thailand was a member and whose headquarters were in Bangkok. During their heyday, Geddes and Hinton were arguably the most academically qualified, the best scholars on the kingdom's north. They had the confidential ear of the generals, ambassadors and foreign ministers. Yet, what mobilised opposition to the two scholars in the 'Thailand Controversy' was that each declined to confirm to an inquisitive academic community that the Royal Thai Army and other armed forces at its command were actually at war and in full combat against significant sectors of the northern population."

Conflict in the remote Thai highlands remained largely unnoticed by the outside world. For Miles (2008), the 'Thailand Controversy' was not ignited by Jorgensen and Wolf (1970), but began two years earlier in 1968, when the village field site where he and his family resided was bombarded by the Royal Thai Air Force: "Geddes, who dedicated himself to the establishment of a TRC with funds and equipment largely from the

Australian Government, would have had good reason to worry once enquires began into whether the army of the Thai government was actually at war against people whose welfare Australian assistance was supposedly to benefit" (Miles, 2008: 257).

The ethical impact of the Thailand Controversy endured well beyond the unsuccessful closure of further debate in 1972 by the AAA and the Australian Association of Social Anthropologists. Anthropologists continued to work in areas with high levels of conflict, where global economic and cultural processes raised questions of neo-colonial power relations in new and complex forms. Changes in Indigenous nation-state relations in Australia altered the context that anthropologists considered issues of ethical research practice. With the passage of the Northern Territory Land Rights Legislation in 1976, many anthropologists found themselves in the centre of contests between Indigenous peoples, governments, and white landowners over claims to land rights. Issues of power and inequality are at the core of anthropology, and anthropologists are courted for their inside knowledge of the powerless. Universities received increasing volumes of funding for teaching and research from outside agencies with an interest in the product, from designated corporation named chairs and from tied scholarships to industry research or governmental foreign policy interests, while anthropologists became increasingly vilified for representing the powerless in their challenges to the institutions of the state and dominant elites. Ethnography involves the production of meaning, much of which is over-determined by rapidly shifting economic, political, and cultural networks of the modern world (Robinson, 2004).

New Zealand: Post-War Professionalising of Anthropology and Maori Studies

Piddington, an Australian student of Malinowski and Radcliffe-Brown, was appointed as Foundation Chair at Auckland University College in 1949. His appointment illustrated the networks of the small circle of anthropologists in Australia and New Zealand to the 'mother' country. Advice on the appointment was sought from the Association of the Universities of the Commonwealth, and the committee consisted of Firth as chair, with Evans-Pritchard and Forde (Gray, Munro and Winter, 2012). Piddington was undeterred by conservative opposition in establishing a new anthropology department and, in the 1950s, launched teaching and research in social anthropology, Maori studies, physical anthropology, prehistory, and linguistics. Bruce Biggs, who was sent to Fiji in the war, became the inaugural lecturer in Maori language. In the 1950s and 1960s, a new generation was trained under Piddington. Archaeology emerged after World War II as the main source of data on Polynesian culture history because of the heightened scientific interest in the Pacific Islands generated during World War II, when a number of influential American anthropologists had worked closely with military intelligence in the Pacific. There was a resurgence of field archaeology by the mid-1950s throughout Polynesia that inspired a radical rethinking of culture history. Polynesian origins were traced back to a southeast homeland with dispersals through the Melanesian archipelagos and not Micronesia, as Buck had advanced (Kiste and Marshall, 1999).

Maori participation in anthropology began to flourish again. Piddington created an environment that welcomed and nurtured Maori scholars, several of whom completed Oxbridge doctorates. Sir Ian "Hugh" Kawharu was a distinguished academic and paramount chief of the Ngati Whatua Maori. He gained a MA in anthropology from Cambridge and a DPhil from Oxford. In 1970, Kawharu became the Foundation Professor of Anthropology and Maori Atudies at Massey University, and from 1985–1993, he was Professor of Maori Studies and Head of the Department of Anthropology at the University of Auckland. Maori anthropologists were politically active and reasserted old claims to redress injustices during settler colonialism (Henare, 2007: 102). Piddington was a proponent of action anthropology aimed at empowering Indigenous peoples, and advanced processes of emergent development and cultural symbiosis that were ignored by government officials working to assimilate Maori (Metge, nd).

Conclusion

America

The CORDS program in the Vietnam War linked counterinsurgency and rural development projects with the Phoenix program, which targeted and eliminated the Viet-cong command structure and killed more than 35,000 civilians. Militant dissention in the universities was galvanised in opposition to counterinsurgency. Disagreement with the Vietnam War brought ethics to anthropology. The first Code of Ethics established that that anthropologists should not conduct covert research, not issue secret reports, use pseudonyms, and show primary loyalty to those they studied.

Britain

Structural functional anthropology was critiqued in the 1930s–1960s for accommodating to and enhancing the powers of the Empire and becoming complicit in it. Asad's *Anthropology and the Colonial Encounter* (1973) was concerned with the role of colonialism in former and current colonies. The American counterpart *Reinventing Anthropology* (Hymes, 1969) was concerned with the settler colonial relationship to Indigenous nations.

Canada

More than 125,000 American draft dodgers and deserters came to Canada between 1964 and 1977; it was the largest political exodus in American history and more than half stayed in Canada. The Cold War marked the establishment of anthropology in Canada. Many anthropologists effectively engaged with First Nations. First Nations pursued greater control over their resources and more effective political autonomy, which was a challenge to the engagement of anthropology.

Australia

In the Cold War, Aboriginal ethnography gave way to a broader Asia-Pacific research focus. Australia contributed small contingents of troops to Korea and Vietnam as a way of cementing support for the American alliance. Vulnerability to the communist menace and the growing opposition to military counterinsurgency in the Vietnam War created similar political climates on Australian and American universities. A rancorous conflict centred on counterinsurgency research conducted in Thailand by members of the anthropology department at the University of Sydney.

New Zealand

Maori professionalised as anthropologists in the 1960s and 1970s. Sir Ian "Hugh Kawharu" earned a DPhil from Oxford and became the Foundation Professor of Anthropology at Massey University in 1970. Maori anthropologists were politically active and reasserted old claims to redress injustices of settler colonialism.

CHAPTER 6

Socio-political Status of Anthropology and Indigenous Resistance

Introduction

The parasitic anthropological dependence on the study of Native Americans lasted into the 20th century, when anthropology was dismissed by the Red Power Movement. In Canada, few anthropologists ethnographically engaged with studies of nation-state settler colonial relations. Aboriginal and Torres Strait Islander academics now teach and research in their own university-based units. Accusations of invented and therefore inauthentic culture resulted in university Maori studies separating from anthropology. In Britain, programs developed in minority and postcolonial studies attracted some anthropologists. Paradoxically by the 21st century analysis of global internationalised nation-state relations shifted from anthropology into the hands of Indigenous scholars.

America

Professor Steward worked on the side of the colonial authorities to undermine the land rights of Indian nations, thus contributing to the settler logic of elimination. In the 1970s the gap widened between materialism,

Marxism and political economy, on the one hand, and those of idealism, symbolism and interpretivism, on the other. The Red Power Movement promoted Indian pride, activism and resistance to white settler domination. There was an estrangement between anthropology and Native Americans and few anthropologists involved themselves in university interdisciplinary Indigenous studies programs.

Britain

British Anthropology embraced Marxism around 1970. Ethnic and race politics on campus translated into academic programs focused around minority and postcolonial studies and some anthropologists took part in these university programs. The subsequent turn towards multiculturalism and migration, which largely excluded ethnic and race studies, established a new home in cultural studies and developed independently of anthropologists.

Canada

The 50 Indigenous nations of the Assembly of First Nations are represented by 630 First Nation chiefs. Settler colonial interests of Canadian society were motivated by the importance of land, while simultaneously First Nations pursued local and place-based resistance. There were anthropologists that placed emphasis on the local relationship with settler colonialism and First Nations, such as Dyck's (1985) treatment of nation versus state Fourth World politics. By the end of the 20th century, analysis of global internationalised nation-state relations shifted into the hands of Indigenous scholars. Fewer anthropologists were any longer ethnographically engaged with studies of nation-state settler colonial relations and a regime of compulsory research ethics based on biomedical models discouraged ethnographic research into nation-state relations.

Australia

Dispossession of Indigenous land has been the hallmark of settler colonialism and reclaiming the land has been the focus of the Indigenous sovereignty movement. Native title and land rights both recognised

Indigenous people's right to land but differed socio-politically and legally. Indigenous academics now teach and research in university-based Aboriginal and Torres Strait Islander units in law, education, political science, and health manage and run significant national bodies.

New Zealand

From the early 1900s, the Maori political movement has been characterised by the recovery of lost sovereignty. In the Maori language, *Waitangi* Treaty '*tino rangatiratanga*' (sovereignty) was retained by Maori, and '*kawanatanga*' (a more limited power of governorship) was granted to the British. The Maori were angered by the contention of some mentalist Anthropologist's that Maori culture was invented and therefore inauthentic and as a consequence Anthropology and Maori studies separated across the universities of New Zealand.

America: Anthropology and the End of Parasitical Dependence on the Study of Indigenous Nations

The Boasian historical particularist paradigm was challenged by neo-evolutionism in the post-WWII period. Julian Steward coined the term 'cultural ecology' to describe the nexus of resources, technology and labour (Silverman, 2005). Steward's cultural ecology project, most fully presented in *Theory of Culture Change: The Methodology of Multilinear Evolution* (1959), promised an anthropology that sought explanation by purporting to offer a scientific method to the study of society in relation to environment (Haenn and Wilk, 2006) and prompted Harris (1968: 666) to observe that "Steward's 'The Economic and Social Basis of Primitive Bands' must be reckoned among the important achievements of modern anthropology." Typically, Steward's method is understood to offer an objective ethnographic portrayal of the American Great Basin and "the representations of Indigenous societies that flow from it are the result of objective, scientific analysis and, therefore, represent a value-free foundation for the study of society in general and of Indigenous societies in particular" (Pinkoski, 2008: 181).

The American Congress passed the Indian Claims Commission (ICC) and the Act (1946) was organised as a "tribunal for hearing and determination of claims against the United States...by any Indian tribe, band, or other identifiable group of Indians living in the United States." Anthropology's relationship with settler colonialism continued with the connection between law regarding rights and title and the representation of Indigenous peoples as primitives. The relationship between Steward's application of his theory and method — what he called 'levels of sociocultural integration' and his testimony to deny Indigenous claims to land for the US government before the ICC was first presented by Ronaasen et al. (1999). Chapter 6 of Steward's *Theory of Culture Change*, The Great Basin Shoshonean Indians: An Example of a family Level of Sociocultural Integration," became the Department of Justice's statement of defence *in verbatim* (Ronaasen et al., 1999).

The ICC mandate assumed that the 'Indian problem' could be addressed through compensation for lands taken. However, the defined list was consistent with the settler colonial logic of elimination because it:

> "[...] opened the door for an argument that there could be a group of Native Americans that was not an "identifiable" group, as it could be argued that the particular claimant was not a band, tribe of group, based entirely on social evolutionary conjecture, and thus, as a consequence, had no legal standing before the Commission because of some sort of 'ethnological difference'."
>
> (Pinkoski, 2008: 182)

The American Department of Justice frequently and continually questioned the level of social organisation of Indigenous peoples before the ICC (Wallace, 2002) and both claimants and the federal government solicited expert testimony, which enabled anthropologists to determine Indigenous interests in land (Barney, 1955). The acceptance of neo-evolutionism and scientific expertise meant that the "very nature of the ICC placed anthropologists in a position to legitimize the denial of Indigenous rights to collectively held land" (Ronassen et al., 1999).

In 1949, the Department of Justice contacted Steward to assist the government in determining cases of Indigenous occupancy. Steward accepted and quickly outgrew his expert role and became an advisor and strategist for the government for the next seven years. Steward identified characteristics of recognisable social organisation in law (Pinkoski, 2008). For Steward the Ute, Bannock, Shoshoni and Paiute were not aboriginal names and none were aware of common culture or political unity. The new mode of subsistence enabled by acquiring the horse was not aboriginal and did not include farming, consequently with limited territorial rights land could be sold to the state for white settlement and development (Pinkoski, 2008).

For the ICC Paiute cases, the federal government legal defence denied Indian Title based on Steward's (1955) theorised "levels of sociocultural integration", which represented the Paiute as without cohesion, leadership or common identity. Steward (1955) believed in evolutionary typologies and assumed that when small Indigenous peoples were naturally assimilated by more complex forms, the newly emerged form was not an aboriginal one. Subsistence technologies adapted to the environment provided the most important cultural features; social organisation and superstructure arose as epiphenomena of the culture core (Steward, 1955: 37). Steward alleged the family level occupied the bottom scale of sociocultural integration and naturally yielded to the folk level, which in turn yielded to the national level.

For the ICC Paiute cases, the federal government assumed no liability for claims based entirely on Steward's assertion that the Paiute did not hold original Indian Title because they were not a recognised group based on his neo-evolutionist theory of the levels of sociocultural integration (Ronaasen *et al.*, 1999). Steward claimed the Paiute were a Shoshonean people at the lowest family level of sociocultural integration and described them as motivated solely by their want of food (Pinkoski, 2008: 193). Testimony to the ICC was untenable when contrasted with Steward's original position in: "The Economic and Social Basis of Primitive Bands" (Steward, 1936), where all bands are 'politically autonomous,' 'community landowning,' have 'rules for land inheritance,' and 'all people live in this state of social organisation, at a minimum.'

By comparison, Omer Stewart, the expert for the Paiute, effectively established through the use of place names that the Paiute had territory. Stewart (1985) noted that the ICC rejected Steward's testimony and that Steward lost every case where he was an expert witness. Despite futility before the courts, Steward contended his testimony should be understood as scientific, not as political. Steward's focus on traditional culture supported settler colonialism that oppressed Indigenous peoples (Sponsel, 2006). Steward worked on the side of the colonial authorities to undermine the land rights of Indian nations, thus contributing to the settler logic of elimination:

> "Steward took a leading advocacy role on behalf of the colonial project by locating himself as an advisor to and expert witness for the U.S. Government's Department of Justice, that he helped to develop an ethnographic image and legal opinion that the Indians of the Great basin were the lowest order of social evolution, and that his academic, proclaimed, and celebrated "objective" work, is in places his verbatim testimony before the ICC that had the explicit goal of creating a jurisdictional vacuum in the Great Basin; specifically creating a social evolutionary ladder, in the concept of "the levels of sociocultural evolution," that had exact applicability for undermining the rights to land of the people he was testifying against in court."

(Pinkoski 2008: 196)

Steward's neo-evolutionism and his promise of an anthropology that sought explanation appealed to a new cohort of graduate students with materialist and leftist political leanings. At Columbia Sidney Mintz and Eric Wolf were founding members of the Mundial Upheaval Society discussion group. Sahlins, Service, Wolf and Rappaport joined the Michigan department and formed an axis with Columbia where Harris was developing the concepts of etics and emics. Harris defended materialism and was a leader in the 1968 campus uprisings at Columbia. Cultural ecology later morphed into human ecology concerned with the relationship of people, culture, and nature, and subsequently developed into political ecology that combined political economy and historical ecology to historicise the social-ecological basis of production.

Following the turmoil of the 1960s, there were two different calls to critically reinvent anthropology. The political economy model of critique referred to the political (materialist), as against the interpretive (mentalist) model of critique that referred to literary criticism. The political economy and interpretive debate was a time of passionate opinions. The contrast was between anthropology as a pure science scholarly enterprise that left political involvement to the private individual, and an anthropology that spoke to political concerns for which it had special expertise.

The Cold War profoundly affected anthropology with decolonisation and the emergence of new states. Area studies programs, which expanded in universities, research institutes and think tanks were controlled by political scientists but included the local-level fieldwork of anthropologists. This work was dominated by modernisation theory that revived unilinear evolutionism combined with the expectation that traditional society would inevitably transform into modern society. Anthropologists used modernisation theory in the 1950s and 1960s, but by the Vietnam War, modernisation theory became anathema to many critical anthropologists who were concerned about the way it viewed decolonisation, underdevelopment and development programs in the Third World. Critique of modernisation theory and the study of peasant protest and revolution became a focus for many anthropologists, and they were stimulated by the emergence of Marxist approaches in anthropology (Silverman, 2005).

It was through the economist Andre Gunder Frank that dependency theory entered anthropology. Frank argued that it was not a unilineal evolution sequence from underdevelopment to development; rather these were opposite sides of the same coin that manifested the internal contradictions of capitalism (Frank, 1966; 1967). The asymmetrical relations between regions found in dependency theory included concepts of metropolis/satellite relationships, enclaves, internal colonialism, and uneven development that informed anthropologists about how the areas of their ethnographic interest were constructed. Dependency processes that engaged disparate and separated regions led anthropologist to think globally. Anthropologists readily adopted the language of world system introduced by the influential historical sociologist Immanuel Wallerstein with the publication of *The Modern World-System* (1974). World system and dependency offered the core and periphery, while anthropologists provided accounts of diverse ethnographic realities in the satellite regions (Silverman, 2005).

The publication of *Reinventing Anthropology* edited by Dell Hymes (1969), was influential and the authors shared a common view of anthropology as "unavoidably a political and ethical discipline" (Hymes, 1969: 48). The essays made a fivefold plea for relevance, responsibility, study of cultures of power, human experience and reflexivity. Gerald Berreman, for example, addressed the sterile scientism of anthropology that failed to confront human issues and Bob Schulte proposed a critical phenomenological approach in place of scientism. Although the goal was to revise, not to repudiate, the book set off vitriolic debate in America and Britain. Kaplan (1974) accused the re-inventors of rejecting objectivity and value-free science.

Diamond, Scholte and Wolf (1975: 870), contributors to *Reinventing Anthropology*, asserted their position as "critical scientists in the Marxist tradition" and focused on structures of power based on relations of production. Diamond founded the Marxist journal *Dialectical Anthropology*, Scholte situated the phenomenological approach within Marxism and Wolf used Marxist political economy to inform his *Europe and the People Without History* (1982), which attended "to the local differences and processes within the world economy and to the articulation of capitalism with other modes of production" (Silverman, 2005: 319). Harris' vulgar materialism was rejected for studies of inequality, rebellion and critical politics.

In the 1970s, the gap widened between "materialism, Marxism and political economy, on the one hand, and those of idealism, symbolism and interpretivism, on the other" (Silverman, 2005: 321). Symbolic anthropology was developed by Geertz as an interpretive anthropology in search of meaning, rather than a science in search of explanation and he labelled his method 'thick description'. Symbolic anthropology was also shaped by Claude Levi-Strauss from France and Victor Turner, Mary Douglas and Edmond Leach from Britain. Since the 1970s the Fordist era has been replaced by the postmodern flexible accumulation shift from production of commodities to consumption. The definitive response to postmodernism was represented by the appearance of two important texts — *Anthropology as Cultural Critique: An Experimental Moment in the Human Sciences* (Marcus and Fisher, 1986) and *Writing Culture: The Poetics and Politics of Ethnography* (Clifford and Marcus, 1986). These texts situated ethnography at the core of anthropology with critique as experimentation in writing. As with *Reinventing Anthropology*, these texts came under fierce attack with the rejoinders were equally impassioned (Silverman, 2005). The malaise between materialist and mentalist anthropology continued and by the 1990s had been mainstreamed.

The American Congress in 1953 adopted a policy of 'termination' that continued to reinforce the settler colonial logic of elimination. The termination policy intended to make Indigenous nations confined within America subjected to the same laws and entitled to the same privileges and responsibilities as other US citizens. The policy resulted in several Indigenous nations being terminated by statute, subjected to state laws and having their lands sold (Behrendt, 2009). Meanwhile the Bureau of Indian Affairs encouraged Indigenous peoples to 'relocate' and grants were offered to leave reservations for metropolitan areas. Relocation created populations of Indigenous peoples in urban areas that were: "unemployed, poor and suffering from the problems that accompany entrenched poverty" (Behrendt, 2009: 11). Public Law 280, passed by the American Congress in 1953, extended state and criminal jurisdiction to reservations in some states, which facilitated state power on reservations and over Indigenous peoples. States were prevented from taxing Indigenous peoples property held in federal trust and from interfering with treaty hunting and fishing rights (Behendt, 2009).

The period of parasitic anthropological dependence on the study of Native Americans lasted into the 20th century. In *Reinventing Anthropology* (Hymes, 1972) Richard Clemmer called for replacing the study of Native Americans that had become obscured by modernisation theories of acculturation and culture change with anthropological research of current Indigenous resistance movements. The tumultuous 1960s–1970s marked the break-up of the old anthropology of Native America and the end of anthropologies self-appointed disciplinary proprietorship of Indians.

The establishment of the Red Power Movement during the social and political turmoil of the 1960s–1970s began a period of estrangement between anthropology and Native Americans. The Red power Movement promoted Indian pride, activism and resistance to white domination. In *Custer Died for Your Sins* (1969), Vine Deloria lampooned the obnoxiousness of white anthropologists. Native Americans found they had no need for anthropologists and anthropologists discovered they no longer needed Indians. By the end of the 20th century the study of Native

American had moved from the centre of anthropology to the margins of the discipline (Starn, 2011).

By the 21st century an engaged, activist positioning became a prerequisite for ethnography of Native America. Assimilation was rejected and the distinctiveness of Indigeneity was explored as a powerful form of cultural identification, political organising and being part of a global community of Indigenous peoples. Indigenous peoples were associated with struggle, resistance, and social movement. The quaint anthropological term Native North America was replaced in universities by Native American studies, Native studies or the more encompassing global orientation of Indigenous studies, only a few anthropologists became involved in these interdisciplinary programs (Starn, 2011).

The American Anthropological Association (AAA) went for over a decade without a section for Indigenous anthropologists. In what appears to be too little too late, the Association of Indigenous Anthropologists (AIA) was created as a section of the AAA in 2007. The expectation of the AIA was to advance the study of Indigenous peoples and encourage professional research that would benefit the discipline of anthropology and Indigenous communities. The rival independent Native American and Indigenous Studies Association (NAISA) was incorporated in 2009. NAISA is the more representative and prominent Indigenous professional association and it publishes an official refereed journal: *Native American and Indigenous Studies*.

Britain: Anthropology after Empire

Leach, the maverick anthropologist at Cambridge, was credited with the main theoretical shift in British anthropology at the end of the 1960s. He creatively bridged the passage from structural functionalism to the post-1970 period of structuralism. He placed modern abstract structuralism strongly on the anthropological agenda and applied it to social structure, art, architecture, nonverbal communication, terms of abuse, ritual, and myth. Leach's and Levi-Strauss's writings brought a sea change to British anthropology. However, as Barth (2005: 49) observed, the structuralism frame and vocabulary led to the exploration of cultural data that involved stating a binary opposition, applying it to some superficial body of data and leaving it at that; "there does not seem to be any agreement in current British anthropology on canons of just what such analyses need to contain and spell out".

As in the United States and the Continent, British anthropology around 1970 embraced feminism, which proved to be a fruitful and enduring theoretical perspective. There had been successful contributions from individual women scholars, but women's lives and gender relations had received little empirical attention. Ethnographies from a new generation of mostly women anthropologists remedied the theoretical neglect of feminism. The impetus for feminist research was based on scholarly curiosity as well as reformist zeal. Marilyn Strathern (1941–) became professor at Cambridge in 1993 with ethnographic experience in Papua New Guinea and theoretical interests in exchange, kinship and feminist issues. Under Strathern Cambridge continued to play a central role in the life of British anthropology. Feminist theory has made a significant and lasting contribution to British anthropology (Barth, 2005).

As in the United States and the Continent, British Anthropology around 1970 also embraced Marxism. Marxism had been represented in the Manchester School in the 1950s and 1960s. However, it was the oppositional climate of the early 1970s with Asad's (1973) book and the Vietnam War protesters that neo-Marxism established extra clout on British campuses. Maurice Bloch at the LSE had ethnographic experience in Madagascar and productively engaged in several phases of Marxism and structuralism. In Barth's (2005: 53) assessment however, there has been little lasting effect of neo-Marxism on British anthropology and the:

> "[…] tensions between the functionalist ideal of fieldwork, static theoretical models, and the fiction of unit societies made any hope for the use of British anthropology for practical purposes in the postwar world somewhat illusory, and the addition of Marxism and abstract structuralism hardly helped the matter."

Ethnographic fieldwork takes place outside the former British Empire. There is a major flow of ideas from the United States and from such French scholars as Pierre Bourdieu and Maurice Foucault and a brain drain from Britain to the US. Contemporary British anthropology has gained in diversity; including greater variety in policy engagements, advocacy and applied work. Ethnic and race politics on campus has translated into academic programs focused around minority and postcolonial studies and some anthropologists have taken part in these programs. The subsequent turn towards multiculturalism and migration, which largely excluded ethnic and race studies and developed independently of anthropologists, established a new home in cultural studies. British and North American traditions are merging into modern Anglophone anthropology (Barth, 2005: 56).

Canada: The End of Self Appointed Anthropology Proprietorship of Indigenous Nations

Despite evidence of prior claims by Indigenous nations, critical policy reviews in Canada failed to create equity or stability. The Trudeau government 1969 White Paper blamed reserves and their status rather than colonial land theft for Indigenous poverty and marginalisation, and labelled treaties anomalies unworthy of the name. The White paper was rejected by Indigenous nations and it served as a catalyst for Indigenous political mobilisation. The federal government claim policy of 1973 introduced the euphemism of "exchange" for "extinguishment". The *James Bay and Northern Quebec Agreement*, the first treaty concluded under the new policy, incorporated almost verbatim blanket extinguishment clauses. The *Northeastern Quebec Agreement* of 1978 and the *Inuvialuit Final Agreement* of 1984 contain similar extinguishment clauses. The *Living Treaties, Lasting Agreements* (Coolican) Report in 1985 recommended extinguishment be abandoned and suggested that, despite constitutional amendments in 1982, Canada's elimination of legal vestiges of Indigenous claims have increased. From the White Paper to the federal policy of recognising rights in order to extinguish them, there has been an implicit refusal to review Indigenous nation-state relationships (Green, 1995).

Even with the Coolican Report's recommendation to abandon extinguishment, it was reaffirmed in so-called 'self government' models advanced in the 1993 Federal Policy for the Settlement of Native Claims. The co-opting language of self-government stripped inherent political agency from 'bands' and rendered them mere administrators of federal government programs and services. Nunavut, for example, should not be confused as an example of Indigenous governance. Rather than an expression of the inherent right, Nunavut is public government and represents a significant northern evolution whereby jurisdiction ultimately rests with the federal government. Nunavut for the foreseeable future is predominantly Indigenous, but regardless of changing ethnic composition, Nunavut is constructed as a public government for all residents within its jurisdiction, not just Inuit people (Green 1995); settler colonialism dominates the:

> "...seizure of Aboriginal lands and resources, the exclusion or peripheralization of Aboriginal nations from their lands, and the creation of justificatory legal, religious, economic and political structures and doctrines to enforce this state is colonial. Nothing has changed: Aboriginal nations remain economically and politically marginalized and deprived of their land and resource base."
>
> (Green, 1995: 99)

The Charter of the Assembly of First Nations was adopted in July 1985 and provided for the representative voice of 630 First Nation communities through the Assembly of First Nations. The representative First Nation Chiefs meet annually and set policy and direction through resolution on areas such as Indigenous and treaty rights, economic development, education, languages, health, housing, justice, land claims and the environment. The Chiefs also use the Confederacy of Nations forum to meet every three to four months. The Chiefs-in-Assembly elect a National Chief every three years (Behrendt, 2009).

A policy of self-government for First Nations was introduced in 1995 by the Canadian Department of Indian and Northern Affairs. Negotiations with Indigenous peoples enabled them to self-govern their internal affairs by assuming greater responsibility and control over decision making affecting their communities. Self-government agreements allow for the structure and accountability of Indigenous governments, law-making power and responsibilities for providing programs and services. There is no uniform model for self-government agreements, therefore some treaties made 100 years ago are reinterpreted and new treaties are negotiated in areas where they did not previously exist (Behrendt, 2009).

Indigenous peoples continue to be engaged in conflicts centred on specific territories. There is a prevalence of land disputes between settler and Indigenous peoples involving government and corporate interests. Indigenous nations are culturally, spiritually and historically tied to their lands and to specific important sites and defend their differential relationships to the land. Indigenous land resistance mark places where Canadian settler colonial power is far from absolute. Canada economically remains reliant upon land and resources rightly belonging to Indigenous nations (Barker, 2009). The essence of settler colonialism that occurs within the boundaries claimed by the state is the appropriation of the land, resources and jurisdiction of the Indigenous nations, not only for the sake of resettlement and exploitation, but for the territorial foundation of the dominant society itself. Indigenous peoples pursue local and place-based resistance, while the importance of land motivates the colonial interests of Canadian settler society (Tully, 2000); the following provides background to recent conflicts between Indigenous peoples and the settler colonial state:

> "Lubicon Lake [in 1988] was due to lack of federal recognition for the existence of the Lubicon Cree as a First Nation, the effect of which was the opening of Lubicon territory to timber and oil interests. The Oka standoff [in 1990] is the most well known and documented contemporary conflict between Indigenous and settler people, centered on an attempt to build a golf course over a Mohawk burial ground near Oka, Quebec. The Ipperwash standoff [in 1991] is named for Ipperwash Park, an area of Stoney Point (Anishinaabeg) territory that had been appropriated by the federal government during World War II for military purposes and never returned. The standoff resulted in the death of Stoney Point member Dudley George, who was shot by the Ontario Provincial Police. The Caledonia standoff [in 2006] in southern Ontario is an ongoing conflict in which Haudenosaunee people of the Six Nations reserve have occupied and reclaimed tracts of land under development for subdivisions that the confederacy claims under the Haldimand Grant of 1784."
>
> (Barker, 2009: 350)

There is an assumption in settler discourse that without control and enforced order Canadian society cannot exist.

During this period there was significant engagement of Canadian anthropologists with Fourth World and First Nation issues. One of the first contributions was Hugh Brody's *Maps and Dreams: Indians and the British Columbia Frontier* (1981), which presented an innovative analysis of Beaver Indian resistance to an oil pipeline on their land. Noel Dyck's *Indigenous Peoples and the Nation-State: Fourth World Politics in Canada, Australia and Norway* (1985), which included contributions from Dyck on the Fourth World concept, Harvey Feit on Cree opposition to the James Bay hydro project, Robert Paine on the Saami and Sally Saunders comparison of Canada and Australia. According to *Native Studies Review* (1986): "this volume provides the reader with both the theoretical overview and sufficient case material to develop an understanding of the political issues facing the peoples of the Fourth World."

International legal solutions to Indigenous nation-state relations are found in the right of 'peoples' to self-determination, from free association with the encapsulating state to secession from it. Indigenous nations understand the historical treaties to be a freely negotiated and terminable organic relationship, with mutually agreeable recognition that indigenous jurisdiction "rests upon inherent right and not a revocable grant" (Lam, 1992: 608).

Kymlicka (1998) contrasts between Anglophone Canadian ideas about (con-federation) with Francophone Quebec's sense of 'nation' and extends the concept to the First Nation peoples in Canada. The nation-ness of the First Nations is an outcome of Canada's colonial society, both in its history and in its internal configuration of Indigenous nation-state relations. National identity is not monolithic within Canada. The Haudenosauee (Iroquois) of the Grand River Territory issue their own passports. The Assembly of First Nations is pluralistic and contains 630 chiefs representing 50 Indigenous nations. First Nations are nation peoples in the plural because they so define themselves and they take for granted a transnational insistence on Indigenous nation to state status in negotiating the relationship of the First Nations to the Canadian state and to other nations, states and international bodies (Darnell, 2010).

By the end of the 20th century, anthropologists were no longer ethnographically engaged with studies of Indigenous nation-settler colonial state relations; they:

> "found it expedient, if not necessary, to withdraw from making larger pronouncements concerning economic, political and other relations

within Indigenous societies and between these societies and the states within which they found themselves."

(Asch, 2003)

Canada, along with the settler colonial states of America, Australia and New Zealand, has had distinctive challenges confronting ethnographers of indigenous–state relations. The emergence of Native Studies, First Nations Studies and Indigenous Studies programs has shifted the location of Indigenous nation-state relations into the hands of Indigenous scholars.

Anthropological research into Indigenous land claims and constitutional developments has also been displaced by other disciplines such as political science, history, public administration and law. A troubling division within anthropology has distanced those who identify as traditional and mainstream anthropology and want nothing to do with "Native studies" (Dyck, 2006), while others have taken the mentalists non-activist stance of 'postmodernism.' Nader (1997: 134–135) likens the literary postmodern turn in anthropology as an alternative way of remaining politically engaged but disengaged on the sidelines. Anthropologists engaged in the materialist ethnographic study of political relationships and processes have invited interrogation by political figures concerning the fieldworker's purposes and allegiances and by virtue of the personal conduct of research, ethnographers are typically more accessible to interrogation by subjects of their studies (Dyck, 2006).

The Canadian government's arbitrary imposition of a regime of compulsory research ethics with human subjects based on biomedical models has generally discouraged the practice of ethnography, especially research into Indigenous–state relations. The Canadian Social Sciences and Humanities Research Council (SSHRC) proposal that funding for Indigenous research would require the inclusion of Indigenous scholars, elders, program employees, and board members:

> "[…] reads like an ironically inverted imitation of measures contained in old versions of the Indian Act that placed virtually all aspects of the lives of registered Indians under the "authority of the Minister"…The threat it poses to the practice of open, independent, and critical scholarship looms especially large for anthropologists who characteristically rely upon

working directly and ethnographically with people and organizations to carry out their studies."

(Dyck, 2006: 92)

Australia: Demise of the Old Anthropology of Classicist Persistence

With no treaties, Indigenous peoples had to rely on the Australian legal system of the colonial settlers, the Constitution, common law and legislation, to find ways to protect their rights. For Indigenous peoples the Australian Constitution as originally drafted symbolised their marginalisation; founding of the state without their involvement, lack of recognition of their position as traditional owners of the country and silence about rights left them vulnerable to exploitation and the breach of their human and collective rights (Behrendt, 2009).

The 1967 referendum enjoyed bipartisan support and was endorsed by over 90% of voters and approved by all states. When voting 'yes' in the 1967 referendum it was to make two changes to the Constitution:

- to allow for Indigenous people to be included in the Census; and
- to give federal parliament the power to make laws in relation to Indigenous people

The 'yes' vote did not give citizenship to Indigenous people, nor did it give them the right to vote. There was a misplaced expectation that granting of additional powers to the federal government would herald in an era of non-discrimination for Indigenous people. Indigenous people quickly became disillusioned by the lack of changes that followed from the referendum and they rejected the assimilation/elimination notion for the idea of equal rights and equal opportunities for Indigenous people (Goodall, 2006).

Indigenous activism highlighted how the 1967 referendum failed to change Constitutional recognition of the unique status and place of Indigenous people and continued to leave recognition and protection of Indigenous rights to the benevolence of government. An example of Indigenous vulnerability to the whims of government policy can be seen in the 1997 High Court case of *Kruger v the Commonwealth*. The plaintiffs claimed a series of human rights violations, including the right to due process and equality before the law, freedom of movement and freedom of religion, by the effects of the Northern Territory Ordinance that allowed for the removal of Indigenous children from their families, but they were unsuccessful. Policies like child removal have a disproportionate high impact on Indigenous peoples and the *Kruger* case highlights the general silence about rights in the Australian Constitution and how the rights many Australians would assume are protected by the legal system are not (Behrendt, 2009).

Indigenous activism for social justice and protection of their rights includes the agenda for Constitutional reform. *Securing a Bountiful Place for Aboriginal and Torres Strait Islanders in a Modern and Tolerant Australia* (Brennan, 1994), highlighted three areas that regularly arise for Constitutional reform that included acknowledging the unique place of Indigenous peoples in Australia, providing stronger protection for human rights and engaging in building Indigenous nation-setter colonial state relations. Other possible options for Constitutional change in relation to Indigenous people included the recognition of Indigenous peoples entitlement to self-determination, recognition of self-government in remote communities and recognition of the inherent sovereignty of Indigenous peoples (Brennan, 1994).

Dispossession of Indigenous land has been the hallmark of settler colonialism and reclaiming the land has been the focus of the Indigenous sovereignty movement. The hallmark of settler colonialism in Australia was dispossession of Indigenous land, while the Aboriginal sovereignty movement focussed on reclaiming the land, classicist persistence of anthropology used the ethnographic present to erase history and reinforce popular conceptions of Aboriginal peoples as belonging in the past (Cowlishaw, 2017).

The Indigenous land rights struggle is more than a desire to reclaim soil; it represents the desire to exercise traditional obligations to the land as the source of life and sustainability. When Indigenous people claim land through either native title or land rights regimes it is for the goals of self-determination as well as cultural significance (Behrendt, 2009).

The landmark *Mabo* case in 1992 found that Australia was not unoccupied on colonial settlement and that Indigenous peoples had and continue to have legal rights to their traditional lands unless they had been validly extinguished. The then Keating Government passed the *Native Title Act 1993* and established the National Native Title Tribunal; native title was defined in section 223:

> "(1) The expression native title or native title rights and interests means the communal, group or individual rights and interests of Aboriginal peoples or Torres Strait Islanders in relation to land or waters, where:
>
> - (a) the rights and interests are possessed under the traditional laws acknowledged, and the traditional customs observed, by the Aboriginal peoples or Torres Strait Islanders; and
> - (b) the Aboriginal peoples or Torres Strait Islanders, by those laws and customs, have a connection with the lands or waters; and
> - (c) the rights and interests are recognised by the common law in Australia.
>
> (2) Without limiting subsection (1), rights and interests in that subsection includes hunting, gathering, or fishing, rights and interests."

The Indigenous Land Corporation was established in 1995 as the second part of the government's native title response to administer a fund to buy land for those Indigenous people impacted by settler colonialism and unable to prove they had maintained a native title interest over their traditional land. A third response promised a social justice package that was never delivered (Behrendt, 2009).

The subsequent Howard Government in 1996 was hostile towards Indigenous rights. It made the registration of native title claims more difficult for Indigenous claimants and reduced the right of native title holders to negotiate with respect to mining interests. Other questions of native title were settled by several court decisions. In *Wik Peoples v Queensland* 1996, the High Court established that the exercise of native title could still exist with other interests such as pastoral leases, but if there was a conflict the native title would be extinguished. In *Yanner v Eaton* 1999, native title was extended in some circumstances to hunting and fishing rights. In *Commonwealth v Yamirr* 2001, native title could extend to the sea and seabed beyond the low water mark. Judges, not Indigenous people, have the larger role in recognising the existence and defining the content of native title (Behrendt, 2009).

The federal government passed legislation for a land rights regime in the Northern Territory, the *Aboriginal Land Rights (Northern Territory) Act* 1976 vests 'scheduled' areas of land in Aboriginal Land Trusts. Land right legislation has been passed in some states. In South Australia the *Pitjantjatjara Land Rights Act* 1981 vested land in Indigenous communities, previously reserves had been turned into perpetual leases. Victoria legislated to vest land in Indigenous communities such as the *Aboriginal Land (Manatunga Land) Act* 1992. Queensland had vested reserves into a form of freehold, but later introduced limited land rights based on customary affiliation through the *Aboriginal Land Act* 1991 and the *Torres Strait Land Act* 1991. The *Aboriginal Lands Act* 1995 in Tasmania vested 12 areas in the ownership of a land council in trust for Indigenous people. The New South Wales *Aboriginal Land Rights Act* 1983 is the most generous land rights regime established in Australia. Western Australia has not passed land rights legislation (Behrendt, 2009).

Native title and land rights both recognise Indigenous people's right to land but differ socio-politically and legally. Dissimilar political motivations informed the enactment of native title and land rights legislation. Native title legislation had its impetus in the courts based on judicial recognition of *Mabo* in 1992. Native title was not a political recognition of Indigenous rights to land, it was a judicial recognition. Land rights legislation in the various Australian jurisdictions was enacted in response to a broad social and political movement that had grown from the 1960s to the 1990s to include Indigenous and non-Indigenous people (Behrendt, 2009).

Regimes of neoliberal audit culture in the university threaten ethnographic research with Indigenous peoples. Anthropologists do not feel they are being served by ethics committees whose origins are in clinical research that has swallowed up new disciplines and methodologies. Anthropologist David Trigger (2014) maintains that ethical considerations are confounded by identity politics in research in Indigenous communities. He finds that Indigenous research cannot go ahead with propositions that:

- the research investigator must have some Indigenous ancestry
- the research guarantees positive outcomes for participants

- the research represents stealing culture, and
- the research requires all those in the study group to agree.

Indigenous scholars Michelle Trudgett and Susan Page (2014) criticise anthropologists that ironically debate research ethics and identity politics, while presuming to challenge the authenticity of Indigenous academics and their ability to represent Indigenous communities. Anthropologist Emma Koval notes that ethics guidelines are framed as protecting Indigenous Australians from research (Wynn, 2014).

Indigenous academics now teach and research in university-based Aboriginal and Torres Strait units. Indigenous scholars in law, education, political science and health manage and run significant national bodies such as the National Congress for the Association of First Peoples, as well as the Association of Indigenous Governance Institute, the National Centre for Indigenous Studies and the Australian Institute of Aboriginal and Torres Strait Islander Studies. Indigenous 'Peoples' enables and legitimates a formal political voice and allows for the new *National Congress of Australia's First Peoples* to act as a representative body. The *National Congress of Australia's First Peoples* is independently owned, controlled by membership and incorporated as a company in 2010. The new national body for Aboriginal and Torres Strait Islanders had their first congress in 2011.

New Zealand: Estrangement between Anthropology and the Maori Political Movement

From the early 1900s, the Maori political movement has been characterised by the recovery of lost sovereignty. Maori politicians attempted land recovery through representative democratic processes with little success against the indifferent settler majority. Maori religious-political leader T.W. Ratana internationalised the Maori political movement by travelling with a large delegation to London to petition King George over the breaking of the Treaty of Waitangi, but he was denied access. Ratana then sent a portion of his delegation to Geneva to the League of Nations and arrived later himself in 1925 but was again denied access (PFII, 2011). Maori have consistently challenged the proposition that in signing a treaty with the British their leaders ceded sovereignty over their lands.

Socio-economic order in New Zealand is realised around a hegemony based on the notion that Indigenous sovereignty was ceded and on images of benign settler colonialism. On the centenary of the signing of the treaty in 1940, the settler colonial majority boasted of having the 'best race relations in the world' (Huygens, 2011). Settler decolonisation activists still operated within an eliminationist-assimilationist approach in the 1960s. There were widespread protests in 1960 against rugby union acquiescing to a 'white' All Blacks team to tour South Africa from Maori organisations and settler decolonisation activists, including university staff. The long-standing Maori movement for self-determination and the ratification of the Treaty of Waitangi, the Kotahitanga Movement, was revived in 1967 in response to land alienation. In 1968, the Maori newsletter *Te Hokioi* and the newly formed Maori Organisation on Human Rights revealed ongoing settler colonial oppression and cultural loss (Huygens, 2011).

The Maori movement to gain self-determination was similar to movements by Indigenous nations in other settler colonial states in the late 1960s. Maori anthropologists including Robert Mahuta, Pita Sharples, Hugh Kawharu, Pare Hopa, Hirini Mead, Pat Hohepa and Ranginui Walker, enjoyed an influential national presence and, like Ngata before them, applied their anthropological expertise for revitalisation of Maori culture and language (Henare, 2007:103).

In 1975, the Treaty of Waitangi Act established the Waitangi Tribunal requiring it to settle differences by examining the 'principles' or spirit of the Treaty, especially where the two texts are different (Behrendt, 2009). By the 1970s, the media was broadcasting Maori protest marches and occupations contesting loss of land and culture to mostly complacent settler coloniser viewers. Books appeared that challenged the self-serving views of settler history (Scott, 1975; Simpson, 1979). A minority of settler decolonisation activists acknowledged that oppression was happening in their country. Maoris' worked on cultural restoration and asserted legal and constitutional claims. A Maori Land March against land alienation arrived at the New Zealand Parliament in 1975 proclaiming 'Not an Acre More'. Other historical claims of land alienation occurred in the late 1970s with widely televised Maori occupations at Bastion Point and Raglan golf courses (Huygens, 2011).

In the 1980s, the Maori self-determination movement firmed around the Treaty as a dishonoured agreement between Indigenous and settler coloniser people (Awatere, 1984). Settler decolonialisation activists began joining the annual Waitangi protests with the Maori Action Committee and the Koahitanga Movement protesting 'The Treaty is a Fraud'. The Maori Council of Churches challenged Waitangi Treaty House celebrations that claimed to offer national unity but delivered dominance and oppression. In 1984, it was resolved to respect the Maori ancestors who signed the Maori text in good faith and protest was refocused as 'Honour the Treaty' (Huygens, 2011).

In 1985, the powers of the Waitangi Tribunal were increased to investigate breaches dating back to 1840 and the Tribunal began hearing Maori claims of Treaty breaches and recommendations for compensation. Settler colonist and Maori debate is focused on the signed treaty text in the Maori language, *Te Tiriti o Waitangi* 1840, in which '*tino rangatiratanga*' (sovereignty) is retained by Maori, and '*kawanatanga*' (a more limited power of governorship) is granted to the British. The Maori consider their version of the Treaty, *Te Teriti o Waitangi*, guarantees Maori retention of self-constituted policies to which settler colonial institutions must relate (Huygens, 2011).

The Waitangi Tribunal heard a claim for the protection of the Maori language in 1983. In 1987, Maori became an official language of New Zealand, together with English. A Maori Language commission was also established in 1987. There is Maori language schools and Maori radio station and television channel broadcast in Maori language (Behrendt, 2009).

The Waitangi Tribunal has significantly recognised the fishing rights of the Maori people. Although the Treaty of Waitangi guaranteed Maori rights to fish, the government of the settler colonialists regulated commercial fisheries. In an interim agreement with the government, the Waitangi Tribunal transferred 10% of the fishing quota (60,000 tonnes). The Waitangi Tribunal provided the forum to evaluate and settle the claim. The settlement was finalised in 1992 and the Maori were allocated 23% of the fishing quota, 20% of any new species brought under the quota system, more shares in fishing companies and $18 million in cash (Behrendt, 2009).

Webster (1998) contends that Piddington influenced a 'culturalist ideology' that established a gap between Maori culture as presented by academic anthropology and by culture as reflected in the day-to-day lives of Maori people. A theory of culture was attributed to Piddington and his students that reified an essentialist and idealised vision of Maori culture (Henare, 2007: 103). Hanson (1989: 894) contentiously advanced the invention of two distinct idealised and reified images of Maori culture. One invention was to have occurred in the early 20th century to discover cultural similarities between Maori and Pakeha that enabled assimilation of Maori and creation of one culture. The second invention was to have occurred in the contemporary emphasis to locate cultural differences. It was argued that these cultural inventions enabled Maori to politically claim more power in a bicultural society of equal standing while retaining equal cultural distinctiveness.

Mentalist invention of tradition anthropology adherents were unable to "understand the lived reality, vitality, diversity and complexity of contemporary expressions of indigeneity" (Gagne and Salaun, 2012: 385). The contention that Maori culture was invented and therefore inauthentic was heatedly debated and the Maori were extremely angered over these claims (George, 2008). Cultural invention theory furthered the settler colonial trope of elimination of the native. The alleged gap between real and ideal images of Maori culture attracted political attention from politicians disagreeing with government initiatives singling out Maori for special treatment. Moreover, the idea that Maori should claim a separate identity at all came under vigorous attack (Henare, 2007: 105, 108). Anthropological discourse of cultural invention in the 1980s and 1990s "is perhaps an example of the danger of 'premature foreclosure' on an 'experimental moment' (Marcus and Fisher, 1986), whereby theories themselves become reified and objectified models embraced by academic mimics" (George, 2008: 58).

The Maori activist Titewhai Harawere challenged the right of non-Maori, especially academic anthropologists, to commentate on Maori issues (Henare, 2007:103). Indigenous scholar Vine Deloria in America had similarly critiqued the anthropological project in his book *Custer Died for Your Sins* (1969). Non-Maori researchers were challenged in regards to their participation in research on Maori. These developments contributed to the departure of Maori from anthropology (Henare, 2007: 104). In anthropology, the period of activism and ethnographic study of present-day Maori communities gave way to a redirection of research interests of many *pakeha* academic anthropologists, for whom the political climate made contemporary ethnography unfeasible and unsolicited.

Anthropology and Maori studies have separated across the universities of New Zealand. Anthropologists and Maori studies social scientists also have established their own professional associations. The New Zealand Association of Social Anthropologists started in 1975 and changed their name in 1997 to the Association of Social Anthropologists of Aotearoa/New Zealand (ASAANZ) (http://asaanz.science.org.nz/). The Maori Association of Social Science (MASS) started in 2006 as a permanent forum for Maori social scientists to interact (http://www.mass.maori.nz/). MASS aims to better network Māori social scientists to optimise their contribution to Māori development and advancement.

Conclusion

America

The period of parasitic anthropological dependence on the study of Native Americans lasted into the 20th century. The gap widened between materialist and mentalist anthropologists and some anthropologists continued to work on the side of settler colonial authorities to undermine the land rights of Indian nations, which contributed to the settler logic of elimination. The Red Power Movement promoted Indian pride, activism and resistance to white settler domination and there was an estrangement between Anthropology and Native Americans; few anthropologists became involved in university interdisciplinary Indigenous studies programs.

Britain

In Britain, ethnic and race politics translated into academic programs focused around minority and postcolonial studies and some anthropologists took part in these university programs. Subsequently, the turn towards multiculturalism and migration largely excluded ethnic and race studies and established a new home in cultural studies that developed independently of anthropologists.

Canada

The Assembly of First Nations consisted of 50 Indigenous nations represented by 630 First Nation chiefs. The importance of land motivated the settler colonial interests of Canadian society and First Nations pursued local and place-based resistance. First Nations studies and global Indigenous studies were initiated by some anthropologists, for example Dyck's (1985) research into nations, states and Fourth World politics. By the end of the 20th century, the location of nation-state relations was in the hands of Indigenous scholars. Most anthropologists were no longer ethnographically engaged with studies of nation-state settler colonial relations and a regime of compulsory research ethics based on biomedical models discouraged ethnographic research into nation-state relations.

Australia

The hallmark of settler colonialism was dispossession of Indigenous land, while the Indigenous sovereignty movement focussed on reclaiming the land. Indigenous people's right to land was through Native Title and Land Rights, which differed socio-politically and legally. Indigenous academics now teach and research in university-based Aboriginal and Torres Strait units and Indigenous scholars in law, education, political science and health manage and run significant national bodies.

New Zealand

From the early 1900s, the Maori political movement has been characterised by the recovery of lost sovereignty. In the Maori language *Waitangi* Treaty '*tino rangatiratanga*' (sovereignty) was retained by Maori, and '*kawanatanga*' (a more limited power of governorship) was granted to the British. Some mentalist anthropologists contended that Maori culture was invented and therefore inauthentic, which met with Maori anger and Anthropology and Maori studies subsequently separated across the universities of New Zealand.

CHAPTER 7

Civil–Military Intervention in Armed Conflict Among the People

Introduction

CANZUS: Settler Colonial Opposition to the Declaration on the Rights of Indigenous People

The Declaration on the Rights of Indigenous Peoples was adopted by the General Assembly on September 13, 2007 by a majority of 144 states in favour, 11 abstentions and four votes against that came from the settler colonial states of Canada, Australia, New Zealand and the United States (CANZUS). Indigeneity involved the counterpart non-Indigenous settler and a political regime exclusively controlled by settlers and their descendants. The Declaration however is no less than an anti-settler manifesto that challenges settler colonial societies.

Militarised Nations Against States

Fourth World geopolitics provided a ground-up portrait of international conflicts focused on ancient nations encapsulated within states. Anthropology largely ignored the national and international militant movement of ancient nations and failed to appreciate that global armed conflict has changed. The new wars in the world focus on the decolonised developing world and pit guerrilla insurgencies against state governments and states against ancient nations.

Nation Against State Armed Conflict Among the People

The Third World War project established that ancient nations resisting state military forces produced 75% to 80% of the wars being fought from the beginning of the Cold War to 1993. Armed conflicts became intrastate wars. The 121 intrastate wars as of 1993 included 97 nation against state armed conflicts, which involved a state government against a distinct nation such Burma versus Kachin. The comparative Minorities At Risk (MAR) project referred to nations as cultural and religious communal groups and ethnonationalists and identified 227 nations were in political protest and war from the beginning of the Cold War to 1990. The Ethnic Power Relations (EPR) project referred to nations as ethnonationalists and ethnics and identified 215 armed conflicts since World War II, which included 57 nation armed conflicts that were secessionist wars and 53 that were autonomy wars. The Uppsala Conflict Data Program (UCDP) project accounted for 248 armed conflicts from the beginning of the Cold War to 2011, with 153 locations that included 137 armed conflicts from 1989–2011. According to the UCDP, interstate armed conflict occurs between two or more states, intrastate armed conflict occurs between government and internal opposition forces, and internationalised intrastate armed conflict occurs between government and internal opposition forces; with the intervention from other states in the form of troops. In 2011, there were 15 (41%) state versus nation armed conflicts for control of territory, 13 (35%) state versus insurgency armed conflicts for control of government and nine (24%) intrastate internationalised interventions for control of government. Intrastate internationalised interventions emerged in the 21st century and accounted for 24% of armed conflicts.

CANZUS: Settler Colonial Opposition to the Declaration on the Rights of Indigenous People

Settler colonialism produces the categories of Indigenous and settler. Canada, Australia, New Zealand, and the United States (CANZUS) are united against the Declaration on the Rights of Indigenous Peoples because they were the settler colonial societies. Only CANZUS voted against the Declaration on the Rights of Indigenous People in 2007. Indigeneity involves the counterpart non-Indigenous settler and a political regime exclusively controlled by settlers and their descendants. The Declaration is no less than an anti-settler manifesto that challenges settler colonial societies (Veracini, 2012: 329–333). The CANZUS settler colonial polities voted against the Declaration, because in the relationship between Indigeneity and settler colonialism, settler polities are premised on the original dispossession of the Indigenous. Only in the settler colonial societies is there no locale that can be identified by the hegemonic settler as the political body's ancestral homeland.

The UN Declaration on the Rights of Indigenous Peoples was finally adopted by the General Assembly on September 13, 2007, with 143 states in favour, 11 abstaining, and the four settler colonial CANZUS states against. For Indigenous peoples, the right to self-determination is the cornerstone of the Declaration. The CANZUS settler colonial states considered the Declaration synonymous with decolonisation and a threat to territorial integrity and sovereignty of the state (Davis, 2008). Eventually CANZUS members signed the Declaration, because it functioned as a non-binding instrument for creating norms of behaviour by which states can be guided and was therefore thought to be a politically meaningless.

America

With the establishment of the Permanent Forum on Indigenous Issues (PFII) in 2000, it became the focal point for international Indigenous networking. In 2003, Miliani Trask, a former Pacific representative to the PFII, found that the CANZUS settler colonial states consistently blocked the unqualified right to self-determination for Indigenous peoples. The discursive positioning of the CANZUS settler colonial states against the Draft Declaration remained unchanged in resistance to collective rights, self-determination and control over natural resources (Davis, 2008). The CANZUS group of settler colonial states interjected and objected the most; the U.S. was the most frequent sole objector (David, 2008).

At the conclusion of the Indigenous Decade in 2004, the Draft Declaration on the Right of Indigenous Peoples was not ratified because of semantic battles with states; America contended that the Draft Declaration was not a reasonable evolution from existing human rights law and was too intrusive into state legal systems (Corntassel, 2007).

Canada

Despite the creation of the UN Permanent Forum on Indigenous Issues (PFII) in 2000, the UN failed to ratify the Declaration on the Rights of Indigenous Peoples during the first Indigenous decade (1995–2004). As observed by Corntassel (2007), a Tsalagi (Cherokee Nation) delegate to the WGIP and PFII, there were active international Indigenous networks for collective and individual rights, self-determination, globalization, colonization, and education during the Indigenous Decade, and co-option was also attempted to move Indigenous leaders away from their communities politically and ideologically, and towards the state.

The goal of the Indigenous Decade was to create the PFII and promote UN General Assembly ratification of the Draft Declaration by the end of 2004. At the conclusion of the first Indigenous Decade, the Declaration was not ratified because Indigenous peoples remained mired in semantic battles with states:

> "[…] Japan and the US contended that the Draft Declaration was not a reasonable evolution from existing human rights law and was too intrusive into national legal systems. Additionally at the 1995 meeting, Canada objected in principle to an Indigenous right to self-determination, the right to be identified as Indigenous and ten other key features of the Draft Declaration. These stalling tactics intensified in September 2003 when Canada and Australia were criticized by Indigenous delegates for derailing negotiations over the Draft Declaration. These two state governments proposed that fundamental rights over land and natural resources would be discussed between a state and its Indigenous population rather than being part of a universal declaration of rights of Indigenous people."
>
> (Corntassel, 2007: 150)

Indigenous delegates and states have consistently had semantic battles. The 2003 review of Mililani Trask found that every year the CANSUS states acted as a block objecting to the unqualified right to self-determination for

Indigenous peoples. These CANZUS states, and a few others, have insisted on redrafting the document.

On December 20, 2004, the UN General Assembly formally adopted a resolution proclaiming a Second Indigenous Decade commencing January 1, 2005. At the Fifth Session of the PFII Australia, New Zealand and America objected that the Draft Declaration could be misrepresented as conferring a unilateral right of self-determination threatening the political unity, territorial integrity, and security of existing UN Member States. The discursive positioning of the CANZUS settler colonial states remained virtually unchanged. Despite ongoing state resistance to language in the Draft Declaration recognising collective rights, self-determination and control over natural resources, Indigenous peoples were optimistic the Draft Declaration would be ratified during the Second Indigenous Decade (Corntassel, 2007).

When the UN Declaration on the Rights of Indigenous Peoples was finally adopted by the General Assembly on September 13, 2007, the CANZUS states initially refused to sign the Declaration. The Canadian Minister of Indian Affairs and Northern Development described the Declaration as unworkable in a Western democracy under a constitutional government. General Assembly President Sheika Haya warned that "even with this progress, Indigenous people's still face marginalization, extreme poverty, and other human rights violations. They are often dragged into conflicts and land disputes that threaten their way of life and very survival" (UN News Centre, 2007).

The Declaration significantly included nationality, self-determination, freedom from discrimination and the security of cultural and other practices. The acknowledgment of injustice, colonisation and dispossession are exceptionally important. Adoption of the Declaration by the General Assembly reconstructs the international Indigenous legal norm and shifts the discussion from domestic nations to international nations of Indigenous peoples.

The Declaration recognises Indigenous peoples strengthening their distinct political, legal, economic, social, and cultural institutions, while retaining their right to participate fully, if they so choose, in the political, economic, social and cultural life of the state. The Declaration stipulates that states shall provide mechanisms and redress for actions which dispossessed Indigenous peoples of lands and resources. Canada's reluctance to sign reflected a dismissal of Indigenous rights as a whole, not signing the Declaration served to perpetuate settler colonisation as a modern ideology and activity (Lindberg, 2010). On November 12, 2010 the Canadian government announced its endorsement of the Declaration. The decision reversed Canada's earlier opposition to the Declaration that it had pursued together with Australia, New Zealand, and America, which have all since endorsed the Declaration (IWGIA, 2010).

Australia

Indigenous people in Australia have internationalised their sovereignty claim. The WGIP resolved to create an international declaration on Indigenous rights during the fourth session in 1995. The five independent WGIP members formally undertook drafting the declaration, and the standard setting mandate enabled the active participation of Indigenous peoples. The final text of the Draft Declaration was concluded by the WGIP in 1993 and was followed by a technical review by the Secretariat. In 1995, the Commission on Human Rights set up a working group with broad Indigenous participation and observer status for Indigenous observers to elaborate the Draft Declaration. There was controversy between Indigenous observers and Member States over content and process (Davis, 2008).

WGIP Chairperson-Rapporteur Chavez was found by the Indigenous observers to be inconsistent and to extend excessive weight to the objections of the settler colonial CANZUS group in seeking consensus on the text. Indigenous observers found the CANZUS members to be particularly obstructionist to provisions relating to the right of self-determination and lands, territories, and resources. In 2002, Indigenous peoples were eventually invited to attend the private government informal consultations. Meanwhile, the notion of consensus was a continuing problem over the 11 years of the Draft Declaration working group. CANZUS interjected and objected the most (Davis, 2008).

An Indigenous 'no change' policy resulted in the rejection of any suggestions for amendment to the original text, which contributed to preventing progress on the declaration from 1995–2004. The first attempt to break the no change deadlock was offered by Mick Dodson, the Aboriginal and Torres Strait Islander Social Justice Commissioner, who attempted to shift the Indigenous position by:

> "[…] suggesting a negotiating framework upon which changes could be made to the text. This framework, which became known as the Dodson Principles, was predicated upon the standard-setting principles set out by the General Assembly in 1986. The Dodson Principles must be founded on the basis of a very high presumption of the integrity of the existing text."
>
> (Davis, 2008: 51)

Dodson's proposal failed, but eventually the no change position was abandoned, and Indigenous observers participated in amending the text. However, many Indigenous observers argued they had stronger legal rights by means of treaties, constitutional recognition and statutory recognition and remained unsupportive of redrafting the text. The Indigenous delegation from Australia was isolated from this discussion because they were encapsulated by a state without treaties, constitutional recognition, nor a charter of rights enshrining non-discrimination. Indigenous oral interventions frequently alluded to the state's failure to honour treaty agreements and referred to the wealth of many states, especially the settler colonial CANZUS group, which had been acquired through dispossession of Indigenous lands (Davis, 2008).

The Draft Declaration working group broke the impasse between Indigenous peoples and states in 2004. The Chairperson's text did not achieve consensus but a wide support. Sarah Pritchard, legal advisor to the Aboriginal and Torres Strait Islander commission, observed that although the WGDD created difficulties for some delegations, overall Indigenous participants demonstrated considerable skill in their interventions. Indigenous rights to consultation and rights to land, territories and resources were linked with dispossession and exclusion from institutions of the colonising state. Overall the power imbalance weighed in favour of Member States, but the strength of Indigenous interventions based on historic narratives powerfully influenced many states (Davis, 2008).

The Declaration is a non-binding instrument drafted to create norms of behaviour by which states can be guided. For Indigenous peoples, the right to self-determination is the cornerstone of the Declaration, but for many states, especially CANZUS, it was synonymous with decolonisation and a threat to territorial integrity and sovereignty of states. The Chairperson assuaged these fears by inserting the provision that limited Indigenous peoples' rights to internal aspects of self-determination, with rights to autonomy or self-government in matters relating to internal and local affairs. Similarly, rights of Indigenous peoples to conclude treaties and agreements are implemented within domestic legal and political systems. The Declaration recognises collective rights of Indigenous peoples, which is contrasted with the individual nature of Western human rights discourse. In Australia, collective Indigenous rights are already part of the domestic legal system through the *Native Title Act 1993*. Lands and resources are important to Indigenous peoples for survival of their culture and related to the militarisation of Indigenous lands, free and informed consent and principles of land conservation, restoration and protection of the environment. The CANZUS group believed the language was too broad and needed to be amended in light of their domestic land laws (Davis, 2008).

Shepherding the Declaration through the General Assembly was a massive achievement and testament to Indigenous representatives at the UN. It is also a triumph of the UN's demonstrated commitment to accommodating Indigenous peoples' issues within international law. According to Davis (2008), the international Indigenous movement prefers the Declaration to remain non-binding in international law and contend that a move toward a convention would be unlikely to attract enough signatures to become an international instrument. The Declaration will have political, moral, and educative value in Australia. Moreover, the Declaration will be an important source for the judiciary in providing an instructive set of standards that are increasingly practised by Member States, UN agencies and human right advocates. The underlying principles of the Declaration are about participation, engagement, and consultation and, in the absence of a treaty or constitutional recognition, the Declaration is the primary basis to conduct Indigenous nation-state affairs.

The Draft Declaration remained a controversial instrument for the entirety of the former Howard Government, which maintained a strict alliance with the other settler colonial CANZUS group in opposing the Declaration, and ultimately voted against it in the General Assembly in 2007. The Australian government, through defensive nationalism, has actively worked to contain Indigenous internationalisation. Indigenous transnational networking remains firmly rooted in localised attachments to place and have gained credibility and confidence through the emergence of the Declaration and Indigenous rights norms. There is a greater awareness of the pervasive nature of colonial dispossession that Indigenous nation-state relations are embodied in institutional structures of the state that can entrench settler colonial relations. At the basis of Indigenous demands for self-determination is the need for a holistic recognition on the part of the Australian government on their status as culturally distinct nations with unique histories, cultures, and rights constructed in relation to land (Gibson, 1999).

The Declaration on the Rights of Indigenous Peoples became the new international legal and norm-making instrument in 2007. In the Declaration on the Rights of Indigenous Peoples, the Indigenous political category acts as a bridge to global difference and solidarity and acts as a form of resistance against state colonialism. Indigenous people are legitimate actors on the transnational stage with a range of uniquely recognised rights and innovative politics of recognition. The Indigenous collectivity, and culture can only be sustained by a group (Holcombe, 2015).

New Zealand

The Maori internationalised their claim to self-determination by participating in the WGIP to assist in developing the Draft Declaration on the Rights of indigenous Peoples, which was referred to the Commission on Human Rights in 1993.

The term Indigenous became institutionalised in the UN as a specific category of people under domination. In UN discourse, the Indigenous claim for collective rights distinguishes them from minorities associated with demands for individual rights. Indigenous leaders in the UN have insisted on the plural Indigenous peoples, rather than Indigenous people (Gagne and Salaun, 2012).

Progress was slow because the New Zealand government, together with their fellow CANZUS group of settler colonial states, challenged provisions for Indigenous people's right to self-determination and the control of natural resources on Indigenous people's homelands. The WGIP met another 11 times to fine-tune the draft and finally referred the Declaration to the General Assembly, which voted on the adoption on September 13, 2007. CANZUS, with their settler majorities and remnant Indigenous populations, voted against (PFII, 2011).

The Maori movement for self-determination has presented a sustained challenge to the contemporary settler colonial social order. Although the General Assembly Declaration is not a legally binding instrument under international law, it does set out the collective rights of Indigenous peoples. In 2007, Parrekura Horomia, the Minister of Maori Affairs in the New Zealand government, found problems with four provisions of the Declaration, especially Article 26 that he said, "appears to require recognition of rights to lands now lawfully owned by other citizens, both indigenous and non-indigenous" (Scoop.co.nz, 2007). Maori Party leader, Pita Sharples, responded that it was "shameful to the extreme that New Zealand voted against the outlawing of discrimination against Indigenous people; voted against justice, dignity and fundamental freedoms for all" (Stuff.co.nz 2007). The New Zealand government announced in 2009 it intended to reverse their position and support the Declaration and, in April 2010, Pita Sharples announced at the UN that the government endorsed the Declaration.

The New Zealand government offered a rather strange form of support for the Declaration, with government members suggesting it would have no practical effect. Of particular concern to the New Zealand government were articles that related to self-determination, decision-making, and especially rights to land and resources (articles 26, 27 and 28), which were the same concerns used by the previous government to justify not endorsing the Declaration. Government support appears to be contingent on doing nothing differently and continuing unchanged with the Treaty of Waitangi claims settlement process, regardless if it is inconsistent with rights set out in the Declaration.

Militarised Nations Against States

Indigenous militancy has claimed a Fourth World (Varacini, 2012: 324). Under the leadership of Shuswap Chief George Manuel, the term Fourth World was born (Manuel and Posluns, 1974). The Fourth World spread during the 1970s as a result of intense Indigenous activism in Canada and America and of greater sensitivity to human rights and of the growing influence of NGOs (e.g., the World Council of Indigenous Peoples) in galvanising world opinion on the self-determination of peoples (Manuel and Posluns, 1974; Wilmer, 1993). Indigenous sovereignty and succession became increasingly debated in international arenas where the Indigenous nation transcends statehood. The Fourth World provided a ground-up portrait of international conflicts, focused on ancient nations encapsulated within states (Hipwell, 1997). Clay (1994) estimated that some 5000 ancient nations existed among the 192 states in the 1990s.

Beginning in the 1980s, publications appeared on the anthropological critique of the militarisation of ancient nations. Richard Lee and Susan Hurlich published *From Foragers to Fighters: South Africa's Militarisation of the Namibian San* (1982). In 1988, Robert Carmack edited *Harvest of Violence: The Maya Indians and the Guatemalan Crisis*. The author has critically discussed in depth case examples of states against ancient nations in the Philippines, Papua New Guinea, and West Papua, which include David Hyndman's *Organic Act Rejected in the Cordillera: Dialectics of a Continuing Fourth World War* (1991), *How the West (Papua) Was Won: Cystercicosis and Indonesian Counterinsurgency in a Continuing Fourth World War* (1987), *Resisting Ethnocide and Ecocide: Transnational Mining Projects and the Fourth World on the Island of New Guinea* (Bodley, 1988) and Stratigos and Hyndman's *Mining, Resistance and Nationalism in the Republic of Bougainville* (1993).

The geographer Bernard Q. Nietschmann produced seminal contributions to understanding the Fourth World in *The Third World War* (1987) and in *The Fourth World: Nations Versus States* (1994), which provide the most cogent scholarly theorising to explain the persistence of ancient nations, including those in the settler colonies of America, Canada, Australia and New Zealand. The Fourth World refers to the lack of international recognition of nations encapsulated in the states of the First, Second, and Third worlds. Nation refers to a self-identifying people with claims to a common cultural homeland. A 'nation', according to Nietschmann (1994: 226):

> "[…] refers to the geographically bounded territory of a common people as well as the people themselves…a community of self-identifying people who have a common culture and a historically common territory. Nations are bound by the three commonalities of identity, culture and common territory."

A 'state', not to be confused with the nation, refers to a populated area within internationally recognised boundaries under the sovereign authority of some form of combined civilian and military bureaucracy; Nietschmann (1994: 227) defines the 'state' as:

> "[…] a centralised political system within international legal boundaries recognized by other states. Further, it uses a civilian–military bureaucracy to establish one government and to enforce one set of institutions and laws. It typically has one language, one economy, one claim over all resources, one currency, one flag, and sometimes one religion. This system is imposed on many pre-existing nations and peoples."

The appearance of Indigenous nationalist movements has had profound implications for territorial assumptions of the state system as nations of the global Fourth World achieve some form of sovereignty over Indigenous lands, which has implications for the territorial assumptions of the state system (Hipwell, 1997).

Nation Against State Armed Conflict Among the People

Indigenous peoples are the subject peoples in territories of the settler colonial states. Anthropology in the settler colonial states has been asked to take the Other seriously. However, in largely ignoring the national and transnational movement of Indigenous nations, anthropology has failed to appreciate that global armed conflict has changed. The new wars in the world are focused on the decolonised developing world and pit guerrilla insurgencies against state governments and states against ancient nations. By the late 20th century, 75% to 80% of wars being fought were intrastate and involved Indigenous nations resisting state military forces (Clay, 1994: 24; Nietschmann, 1994: 237).

A Third World War has emerged over control of the state and state control over autonomous nations; wars that are mostly over territory, resources and identity, not East-West politics or North-South economics (Nietschmann, 1987). The Third World War project established that nations resisting state military forces produced 75% to 80% of the wars being fought from the beginning of the Cold War to 1993:

> "States and nations represent two seemingly irrepressive forces in collision: states, with their large army, expansionist ideologies and economics, and international state-support networks, and nations, with their historical and geographic tenacity anchored by the most indestructible of all human inventions-place-based culture."
>
> (Nietschmann, 1994: 236)

Armed conflicts have become intrastate wars. The 121 intrastate wars, as of 1993, included 97 nation against state armed conflicts, which involved a state government against a distinct nation, such as Burma versus Kachin. There were 15 insurgencies against state-armed conflicts for control of the state government, such as the Philippines versus the New Peoples Army. There were six nations against nation armed conflicts, which involved war between nations such as Muslim versus Christian sects (nations) in Lebanon. There were three nations against insurgency armed conflicts that involved left- or right-wing guerrilla forces against a nation such as Sandero Luminoso versus Aymara in Peru. The world at the end of the 20th century was in a state of continuing intrastate war, with the majority of the world's conflicts being fought over Indigenous nation geography (Nietschmann, 1994: 237).

There are nomenclature issues associated with the comparative Minorities at Risk (MAR) project, which is based around what Gurr (1993) refers to as cultural and religious communal groups and ethnonationalists. Nation peoples do not call themselves ethnic groups, minorities or ethnonationalists, or cultural and religious communal groups. Nation peoples have a name for themselves and their territories. When nation peoples take up arms against state invasion and occupation, they are referred to as rebels, separatists, insurgents, terrorists, fanatics, non-state actors, and communists, almost never by their real name and real places. A people within its homeland are a people, not an ethnic group or a national minority. Ethnic groups are placeless minorities within a state and minorities is the state term for a people and its nation. According to the United Nations, states, and most academics and journalists, nation peoples are minorities and ethnic groups that may keep their folklore, while the state takes their land and resources (Nietschmann, 1994).

The term "cultural and religious communal groups" was replaced by "nations" in the MAR project, which identified there were 227 nations in political protest and rebellion from the beginning of the Cold War to 1990 (Gurr, 1993). These nations (communal groups) each shared a distinctive and persistent collective cultural identity. Virtually all post-colonial state-building has meant nation-destroying through policies aimed at assimilation, restraining collective autonomy, and extracting nation resources and labour for use of the state (Gurr, 1993). In the 1980s, nation (communal) rebellion was greater in non-democratic states. Democratic Spain saw a decline in the intensity of Basque and Catalonian separatism; whereas democratisation in Latin America coincided with rising activism by Indigenous peoples and their advocates. The return to autocratic rule in Sudan in the mid-1980s contributed to the resumption of nation against state-armed conflict and continuing nation-against-state war contributed to democratic decline in Sri Lanka, Lebanon, and Pakistan. Whether expansion of Third World socialist states as in Burma, Laos, Algeria, Guinea, Ethiopia, and Nicaragua, or expansion of non-socialist states as in the Philippines, Sri Lanka, Mali, Sudan, and Zambia; the state efforts to control resources stimulated resistance by adversely-affected nations (communal groups):

> "Most of the negative impact of state expansion is felt among ethnonationalists [nations] and Indigenous peoples whose autonomy and resources are being subjected to central control. Given their situations, regional rebellion is a more feasible strategy than urban protest."
>
> (Gurr, 1993: 185)

In the Ethnic Power Relations (EPR) project Wimmer, Cederman and Min (2009) referred to ethnonationalist/ethnic rather than nation wars and found that nations accounted for 75% of the wars since the Cold War ended. The EPR data set built on the MAR project to identify empirically observable mechanisms linking nations (ethnicity) to conflict. The EPR project statistically confirmed that 215 armed conflicts were fought from the beginning of the Cold War to 2005, 110 of which were nation (ethnic) conflicts and 105 were non-nation conflicts. The EPR project differentiated between secessionist and non-secessionist nation (ethnic) wars, which generated four kinds of nation conflict, which included secessionist armed conflicts, autonomy (non-secessionist) armed conflicts fought by nations (excluded groups), secessionist infighting and non-secessionist infighting fought by state power sharing nations. Of the 215 armed conflicts, 57 nation (ethnic) armed conflicts were secessionist rebellions and 53 were autonomy (non-secessionist) rebellions (Wimmer, Cederman and Min, 2009).

The Uppsala Conflict Data Program (UCDP) project accounted for 248 armed conflicts from the beginning of the Cold War to 2011 in 153 locations worldwide, which included 137 armed conflicts from 1989–2011 (Themner and Wallensteen, 2012). According to the UCDP, interstate armed conflict occurs between two or more states, intrastate armed conflict occurs between government and internal opposition forces, and internationalised intrastate armed conflict occurs between government and internal opposition forces; with the intervention from other states in the form of troops. Warring parties are governments of states in interstate conflicts, whereas warring parties in intrastate conflicts include the government of a state and insurgents and/or nations (Themner and Wallensteen, 2012).

In 2011, there were 15 (41%) state versus nation armed conflicts for control of territory, 13 (35%) state versus insurgency armed conflicts for control of government, and nine (24%) intrastate internationalised interventions for control of government. Although nation against state armed conflicts dropped from 80% of wars in the late 20th century to 41% of wars in the early 21st century, they have been persistent and still account for the majority of armed conflicts in 2011. Intrastate internationalised interventions emerged in the 21st century and accounted for 24% of armed conflicts in 2011 (Themner and Wallensteen, 2012).

Materialist anthropology relates to contemporary political struggle, but current fieldwork with Indigenous peoples is more politically challenging than the time of *Reinventing Anthropology* (Hymes, 1969). The native point of view is a continuing, protracted, and sustained adversarial resistance to the discipline and praxis of anthropology not as textuality, but as an often direct agent of political dominance.

There is almost a total absence of considering imperial intervention of settler colonial states as a factor affecting theoretical discussion. For some anthropologists they can only continue on one side of the imperial divide, there to remain as a partner in domination and hegemony (Said, 2001). The ethnographic affinity required for successful participant observation leaves anthropologists sympathising with their informants and unlikely to assist in their subjugation and even contributing to their resistance (Darling, 2014).

However, in the early 21st century, there have been other anthropologists who have returned to nation against state armed conflict areas long abandoned by ethnographers and whether as experts, reporters or witnesses, are themselves becoming actors bearing witness to violence and injustice (Marcus, 2010). Some anthropologists have developed programs of scholarly research with Indigenous nations under one or another rubric such as applied anthropology, advocacy anthropology or community-based social justice research and have exhibited determinedly independent and critical stances.

Conclusion

CANZUS: Settle Colonial Opposition to the Declaration on the Rights of Indigenous People

The Declaration on the Rights of Indigenous Peoples was adopted by the General Assembly on September 13, 2007 by a majority of 144 states in favour, 11 abstentions, and four votes against that came from the settler colonial states of Canada, Australia, New Zealand and the US (CANZUS). Indigeneity involves the counterpart non-Indigenous settler and a political regime exclusively controlled by settlers and their descendants. The Declaration however was no less than an anti-settler manifesto that challenged settler colonial societies.

Militarised Nations Against States

Indigenous militancy has claimed a Fourth World, which has provided a ground-up portrait of international conflicts focused on ancient nations encapsulated within states. Anthropology has ignored the national and international militant movement of ancient nations focussed on WGIP and DRIP in the United Nations. Consequently, anthropology failed to appreciate that global armed conflict had changed. The new wars in the world are focused on the decolonised developing world and pit guerrilla insurgencies against state governments and states against ancient nations.

Nation Against State Armed Conflict Among the People

The Third World War project established that nations resisting state military forces produced 75% to 80% of the wars being fought from the beginning of the Cold War to 1993. Armed conflicts have become intrastate wars. The 121 intrastate wars as of 1993 included 97 nation against state armed conflicts, which involved a state government against a distinct nation such Burma versus Kachin. The comparative Minorities at Risk (MAR) project identified 227 nations in political protest and war from the beginning of the Cold War to 1990. The Ethnic Power Relations (EPR) project identified 215 armed conflicts that included 57 nation armed conflicts that were secessionist wars and 53 that were autonomy (non-secessionist) wars. The Uppsala Conflict Data Program (UCDP) project identified 248 armed conflicts from the beginning of the Cold War. In 2011, there were 15 (41%) state vs nation armed conflicts for control of territory, 13 (35%) state versus insurgency armed conflicts for control of government and nine (24%) intrastate internationalised interventions for control of government.

As military campaigns shifted away from war between states to occupations of regions identified as tribal and Indigenous, the ABCA Armies have sought anthropological cultural intelligence to understand the shifting characteristics of enemies and inform engagement with such adversaries. Internationalised armed conflicts and disasters in the early 21st century have become embedded in the same global logic of interventionism, which is based on the temporality of emergency and the conflation of military and humanitarian operations used to justify a state of exception.

CHAPTER 8

Cultural Intelligence in the ABCA Armies

Introduction

Unstructured open ended qualitative interviews were conducted with ABCA Army officers on anthropology and cultural intelligence (Flower, 2012). Content analysis coding categories were derived from the text data. The voices of ABCA Army officers constituted the basis for cultural narratives. The expanded cultural narrative **'Human Terrain System: Crush, Suppress, And Smother Resistance'** was compared between the ABCA Armies.

Cultural Narratives

ABCA Interoperability: 'More Cultural Commonality than Standardisation'

ABCA Armies were recognised as a doctrine working group.

> "American military operations were based on winning the war and were structured around force on force."
>
> (American Army Officer interview, 2012)

ABCA Army interoperability started with standardisation, but should become more about 'cultural commonality'. For the New Zealand Army, ABCA 'interoperability meant Hilux's not Humvees'.

In the American Army, people from the south seemed better at cross-cultural engagement because they were folksy and family was important, whereas people from the north were more contractual and focused on outcomes.

In the British Army, 'Empire epitomised use of cultural intelligence':

> "For the British Army the Empire epitomised use of cultural intelligence. British officers had language skills and were fluent in the language of the occupied area, while the Empire was policed with locals."
>
> (British Army Officer interview, 2012)

Expeditionary forces were sent to intervene in alien cultures and the British Army was very comfortable with and understood culture.

The British Army were recognised as having more cultural experience in handing over power to a decolonised population. Believing they were good with people and culture; the British Army thought they had a better understanding of Northern Ireland, but they did not. The British Army considered that British society was more multiculturally integrated than Australia and that the Army reflected its society, which was 20% non-white.

ABCA Armies represented 'cultures that could work together':

> "From the Canadian Army perspective ABCA represented diversity, conversation and similar cultures that could work together."
>
> (Canadian Army Officer interview, 2012)

The Canadian Army culture was reshaped by the Somalia peacekeeping experience into being easier going with lots of jokes, but professional. As reflected by the size of the force, the American Army by comparison, was not considered to be fun; it was seen as very strict, very demanding and very professional. The Canadian Army observed American soldiers acted like cowboys in Kandahar Afghanistan, it was like being in the Wild West. American soldiers would not patrol as small as a platoon, they patrolled with a company or even a battalion and they drove through staying in their trucks. Rogue American soldiers even burnt the Quran, which caused mass unrest.

Colleagues in the ABCA Armies 'prompted awareness of the values of the Australian Army'.

> "Being part of the ABCA Armies prompted awareness of the values of the Australian Army."
>
> (Australian Army Officer interview, 2012)

The Australian Army was considered more like the American Army, it was Americanised in its mind set and focused on force protection. Aussies used vehicles with blackened windows, while Kiwis always had windows down because they believed it was necessary to have locals see you as a human being smiling, waving and talking; Australian soldiers were believed to take longer to warm to people and they were risk averse and undertook risk analysis to do anything.

A New Zealand Army soldier related that 'I am Scottish but I have a *marae*' and acknowledged that without Maori culture, the New Zealand Army would be Poms at the end of the world.

> "The *marae* helps recruits realise everyone belongs to the tribe: I am Scottish but I have a *marae*."
>
> (New Zealand Army Officer interview, 2012)

The New Zealand Army was a big family; when in Bougainville, for example, the whole deployment went to the *marae* together. The New Zealand Army became increasingly aware of their distinctive culture and that they were really a tribe:

> "The New Zealand Army opened their *marae* in 1995 to keep Maori culture alive in the Army. Rangatira was the chief of the Army Morae. Maori were the original people of this place, they were warriors. In society the Maori have a strong Indigenous voice influencing politics and treaty. I am Scottish but I have a *marae*. There was learning about

Maori history at the *marae* for two days and nights. The *marae* helped recruits realise everyone belongs to the tribe. Once you understood culture it was more appreciated."

(New Zealand Army Officer interview, 2012)

Like society, the New Zealand Army viewed themselves as a multicultural Pacific people. The New Zealand Army believed that they were an independent broker able to mediate and that they were good at engaging right down to the private level because it was in their DNA to be empathetic. The relationship of New Zealand society with Maori was not like the relationship of Australian society with Australian Aborigines and peoples in the Southwest Pacific know it. The New Zealand Army was considered to be much more similar with the Canadian Army because of the positive relationships they had with Indigenous peoples.

Compared to New Zealand soldiers, the average American soldier had no idea about the country in which they were deployed. There was no equivalent to the banter that existed between Pakeha and Maori, when walking around Bagram in Afghanistan, segregation between ethnic groups was seen in the American Army. The vast majority of American soldiers did not display cultural awareness, they did not think there were any good Afghans; at local bazaars they were very disrespectful. Although American soldiers thought they were better than everyone, they were actually hated.

While on a visit to Guam, a New Zealand Army officer went out to experience local culture and was surprised to learn that American troops had been in Guam for three years and had never got off the base. American troops were very passionate about politics, whereas Kiwis and Aussies were more disrespectful of politics and politicians — Kiwi and Aussie soldiers could joke on the same lines and pull the piss out of each other, but American soldiers found it offensive. Australian Army soldiers in East Timor were observed to be similar to New Zealand Army soldiers in their ability to interact with locals. Overall, New Zealand Army soldiers clicked with the British soldiers more than with Australia.

Deployment Culture Training: 'Cultural Empathy Creates Pussycats'

The ABCA Armies trained primarily on kinetic force encounter with the enemy and created 'lions'; whereas deployment cultural intelligence training created 'pussy cats':

> "[...] training, which was primarily in the use of kinetic, force on force encounter with the enemy, created 'lions', whereas military training that embraced cultural empathy created 'pussycats'."
>
> (New Zealand Army Officer interview, 2012)

The value of cultural intelligence training was questioned, because 'you cannot train someone to be a lion and tell them to be a pussycat'.

It was difficult to incentivise cultural factors in the American Army especially, because only the language incentive program offered extra pay.

A pilot cultural intelligence training course was delivered through Cranfield, the British Army staff college:

> "A pilot cultural training course offered in the British Army in 2010 featured anthropological aspects of political and economic organisation, beliefs, and values and kinship, but British Army soldiers were left thinking 'so what'."
>
> (British Army Officer interview, 2012)

The British Army complained that academic cultural intelligence could become unfocused and a more useable product was needed. Although there was no regular provision of training, there were three levels of exposure to cultural intelligence. Everybody received one day's training, one week was provided for selected soldiers who were to have more contact with locals, and a few soldiers were chosen for a month at Cranfield, which included two weeks of social science training and two weeks on Afghanistan.

In the Canadian Army, some effort was taken to understand culture, particularly in 'war amongst the people'. Learning was by trial and error, which was considered inadequate.

> "The Canadian Army received cultural intelligence training for war in Kandahar Afghanistan in 2009; the orientation was to kinetic operations even though it was 'war amongst the people.'"
>
> (Canadian Army Officer interview, 2012)

The Canadian Army developed a lesson learned centre to debrief soldiers and create a database.

In 2006, the Canadian Army began the Wainwright Training Centre, which produced Language Cultural Advisors (LGAs). LGAs were selected from Canadian citizens trained for one week, cleared security and deployed with Canadian Army Officers.

Australian Army soldiers, like the American soldiers, could 'give a shit' about cultural intelligence, primarily because they were not picked for being culturally sensitive.

> "The Australian Army delivered cultural intelligence training, but the 'soldiers gave a shit.'"
>
> (Australian Army Officer interview, 2012)

In the New Zealand Army, cultural intelligence was thought to be more than 'kicking around a ball with kids', and it needed to be done more scientifically.

> "In the New Zealand Army, cultural intelligence was not considered a capability, because it was "just kicking around a ball with kids."
>
> (New Zealand Army Officer interview, 2012)

The New Zealand Army was considered to lack a technological edge; therefore, they always had to act face-to-face. For deployment culture training to Afghanistan the New Zealand Army provided CDs on Sharia Law, copies of the Five Pillars of Islam and background on women in society. The quality of the information received from diaspora refugees was judged to be mediocre. Only two one-hour sessions provided just a modicum of cultural intelligence training. What was needed was how to build up a generic study of culture and how to think about culture in general, rather than consider each unique culture.

Culture in Conflict among the People: 'Couldn't Tell Me Who to Whack'

An American soldier in Afghanistan wanted some kills was disappointed the cultural advisor "couldn't tell me who to whack".

> "I asked my cultural advisor who the enemy was and they couldn't tell me who to whack."
>
> (American Army Officer interview, 2012)

War this century no longer pitted state versus state in armed conflict, and has instead been replaced by conflict among the people. It was commonly misunderstood in the American Army that cultural intelligence was to be used in conflict among the people for understanding the population, not for the targeting of insurgents. An American Army Officer deployed in Afghanistan found that it took about six months to understand Jalalabad, even with an interpreter and cultural advisor who had been there for two years. Cultural intelligence prioritised lower casualties and observance of how one looked to the other side, appearing in full battle gear left nowhere to go.

Cultural intelligence was imprecise and used in the British Army 'only when all else failed'.

> "Since the military liked things definite and certain, culture, politics and economics were overridden. Cultural intelligence was considered insignificant."
>
> (British Army Officer interview, 2012)

British soldiers demonstrated varying degrees of cultural sensitivity. Afghanistan girls enrolled in school was a measure of success, even though they were culturally unaware that the girls were only going to school for food. Afghans were not referred to as rag heads; it was understood that taking weapons off Afghan men insulted them, their manhood was linked to their rifle and to take their weapons was emasculating.

A Canadian soldier in Afghanistan was focussed on the enemy and openly hostile towards cultural intelligence because he did not want to be part of a Provincial Reconstruction Team and 'eat with those monkeys'; instead he occupied the battlespace and 'wanted to kill people'.

> "A Canadian Army soldier remarked that he did not come to Afghanistan to be part of a Provincial Reconstruction Team; he was in the battle group, wanted to kill people and he didn't want to eat with those monkeys."
>
> (Canadian Army Officer interview, 2012)

When deployed to Bosnia the Canadian Army had access to country handbooks and developed a degree of cultural awareness, each platoon built their own houses and lived with the people. In Afghanistan cultural intelligence in the Canadian Army was on the periphery, there was no formal system of cultural analysis. HUMINT counterinsurgency intelligence was found to be deficient, but anthropologists were not engaged in HUMINT activity because it used a stream of intelligence to target insurgents.

The New Zealand Army understood the significance of 'conflict amongst the people' meant the enemy was concealed in complex environments and needed to hide in the population; therefore, it was important to have cultural intelligence to understand the population.

> "For the New Zealand Army, it was 'guitars not guns' in the Bougainville Pacific Way intervention because it was 'conflict amongst the people.'"
>
> (New Zealand Army Officer interview, 2012)

The separation between humanitarian space and battlespace influenced the New Zealand Army missions in recent times, which were not only about killing, but included development and peacekeeping, as well as prevention and reduction in conflict among the population. It was absolutely essential to ensure aid was seen as coming from local government and police to avoid linking aid with cooperation. Officers were too busy with other things to get down with local cultural understanding. It was the lowest ranks that needed cultural intelligence, because they are the ones who spent the most time with the locals. Action against the enemy was not considered as important as action with the population, 'because who do the bad guys look like, they look like the people'.

The New Zealand Army took the lead in 'Pacific Way' non-threatening interventions. Appropriately, the first to land in the Bougainville Bel Isi operation were the Maori Cultural Group, it was 'guitars not guns' that facilitated genuine engagement and interaction in Buin, the New Zealand base in Bougainville. The New Zealand Army patrolled in the daytime with Australians in Bougainville, but they never engaged with Australian uniformed HUMINT counterinsurgency personnel.

For deployment in East Timor, the New Zealand Army was presented with a large package on cultural intelligence that emphasised Melanesian and Portuguese influence but failed to address internal cultural factions and the diversity of languages that included English, Portuguese, Indonesian and Tetum. Maori represented 30% of the New Zealand Army personnel in recognition of the multiculturalism in East Timor. Focus was placed on improving cultural intelligence to ensure proportional response, 'flying Russian Choppers created a 120 KNT down drought that destroyed local houses and using them represented a cultural intelligence failure'.

Cultural Intelligence and Counterinsurgency: 'Take them by the Balls and their Hearts and Minds Will Follow'

Soldiers in the American Army who advocated the concept of 'take them by the balls and their hearts and minds will follow' indiscriminately utilised population-centric and insurgency-centric intelligence to advance kinetically related operational objectives.

> "Take them by the balls and their hearts and minds will follow."
>
> (American Army Officer interview, 2012)

In the American Army, recognition of local tribes and tribal leaders were identified through anthropological 'structural functional research'. Although HTS maps named who was related to whom, the maps should not be used for counterinsurgency targeting. The population and the insurgents were seen in binary opposition, anthropology was population-centric, whereas counterinsurgency was insurgency-centric. The American Army Institutional Review Board (IRB) supported kinetically related operational objectives and provided counterinsurgency intelligence with its own IRB.

Provincial Reconstruction Teams (PRT) in Iraq and Afghanistan did not ethically question being part of a combined cultural and counterinsurgency intelligence hearts and minds campaign. PRTs received $25,000 per month through the 'Commanders Emergency Response Program' to address the reconstruction of the Afghan population, but complained that the population could not culturally and politically absorb the large amount of money. PRTs did not heed the caution from the New Zealand Army that is was absolutely essential to ensure aid was seen as coming from the local government and police to avoid linking aid with cooperation.

In the British Army, anthropology was seen as descriptive, whereas 'psychology understood how people worked irrespective of culture'.

> "[...] anthropology was merely descriptive whereas psychology, by comparison, was seen as trying to help and to understand how all people work irrespective of culture."
>
> (British Army Officer interview, 2012)

As the American Army actively tried to learn about culture, the British Army felt left behind on understanding culture. 'Patterns of life analyses' provided through anthropological research contributed an important cultural intelligence function to the British Army.

As a result of engaging the Afghans, they became more trusting, but interpreters became targets, and the Canadian Army 'created their own counterinsurgents'.

> "In Afghanistan, the Canadian Army realised that their interpreters became high valued targets and they had 'created their own counterinsurgents' through their actions."
>
> (Canadian Army Officer interview, 2012)

Being fearful of the Afghans and keeping away from them was the worst scenario for the Canadian Army. The Canadian Army was convinced that the Afghanistan population protected the insurgents but focusing on insurgents, rather than on the population, was problematic. Counterinsurgency in the Canadian Army was seen as the opposite of conventional kinetic force. Medals were given for bravery in battle, but not for not fighting, which for counterinsurgency was more valuable to mission success. The approach in conventional force was reactive, whereas counterinsurgency involved taking locals onside and making the insurgents reactive.

The Australian Army taught how counterinsurgency in Afghanistan was 'created for targeting Taliban leaders'.

> "Counterinsurgency had a kinetic focus in the Australian Army and it lent itself to more quantitative measures like Fusion Analysist Cell Intelligence, which was created for targeting Taliban leaders."
>
> (Australian Army Officer interview, 2012)

In the Australian Army, counterinsurgency intelligence was considered to be more quantitative, compared to cultural intelligence that was more qualitative. In 2008 in Afghanistan, HTS cultural intelligence appeared to lack depth and academic rigor and it was in need of a textbook.

In the New Zealand Army, 'anthropologists know people' and cultural intelligence brings a completely different lens; to understand the culture of the population was to understand the problem.

> "In the New Zealand Army political scientists know policy but anthropologists know people."
>
> (New Zealand Officer interview, 2012)

The New Zealand Army considered it rude to go to a country and not respect their culture. East Timor was recognised by the New Zealand Army to be culturally diverse and friendly, and community engagement patrols were conducted.

Ethical Challenges of Anthropological Research: 'Find, Fix, and Finish the Enemy'

Too many American Army officers controversially used anthropological research as a stream of intelligence to support targeting to 'find, fix and finish the enemy':

> "Too many American Army Officers believed the primary value of cultural intelligence was to find, fix and finish the enemy."
>
> (American Army Officer interview, 2012)

Research supporting cultural intelligence has been challenged by Gonzales (2009), because ethically research should do no harm, be transparent, and be based on voluntary informed consent. Ethically, the American army should not allow HUMINT collectors to go out with cultural research missions, but Special Ops has cultural aspects included in doctrine decisions about using kinetic force.

Anthropological ethics was considered to be 'political correctness' in the British Army.

> "In the British Army, anthropological ethics was considered political correctness."
>
> (British Army Officer interview, 2012)

War was nasty and savage and did not lend itself to the modern application of culture.

The anthropology ethic code was violated when the HTS in the Canadian Army was not doing research but instead, was writing intelligence.

> "The Canadian Army HTS field teams did not operate as anthropologists, because they were 'not doing research but writing intelligence'."
>
> (Canadian Army Officer interview, 2012)

The Canadian Army was thought to have good ethics. It was better to be comfortable in your illusion then uncomfortable in your reality; the moral high ground was lost when war could be bloodless for your side.

The Australian Army officer had ethical concerns that contractor research anthropologists were not subject to the Uniform Code of Military Justice.

> "The Australian Army had ethical concerns with contractor anthropologists conducting culturally specific propaganda campaigns supporting assassinations."
>
> (Australian Army Officer interview, 2012)

The dual trap of cultural research came when New Zealand Army officers demanded specific information, which could be used for 'reconstruction or killing'.

> "The New Zealand Army understood that dual use of cultural research could not be stopped; cultural research could be used for 'reconstruction or killing.'"
>
> (New Zealand Army Officer interview, 2012)

It was problematic in the New Zealand Army to treat cultural research as intelligence, because it was not to be used for targeting. Cultural research was for understanding the cultural environment, identifying king makers, determining who is loyal to who and demonstrating how the religion functions. Anthropologists were supposed to be unbiased and neutral observers, and having an ethics code for culture research was essential. In the New Zealand Army, conduct of cultural research guidelines could be made more specific to avoid misinterpretation and to protect participants; the AAA code of conduct could be observed along with informed consent and not lying or spying.

Expanded Cultural Narrative

Human Terrain System: 'Crush, Suppress, and Smother Resistance'

Between July 2005 and August 2006, the American Army assembled the controversial 'HTS' program as part of the broader counterinsurgency effort designed to 'crush, suppress, and smother' resistance in Iraq and Afghanistan.

"The Human Terrain System was considered part of the broader counterinsurgency effort designed to "crush, suppress, and smother resistance in Iraq and Afghanistan."

(American Army Officer interview, 2012)

HTS was a Program of Record in the American Army with an administration and a budget. In 2010, there were 31 teams, with the bulk of people based in Fort Leavenworth in Kansas, and HTS teams were deployed to Iraq and Afghanistan. At GS15, military personnel rank anthropologists earned $70,000 when on deployment, the contractor BAE Systems Corporation had previously promised $310,000, and by comparison, an American university postdoc typically received $32,000. Former intelligence people who were previously research managers became HTS social scientist trainers, with some subject-matter knowledge but no experience working on a team. HTS personnel needed training to be more mission focused. International studies, political science, and anthropology were equally considered social scientists, and the prevailing notion in the American Army was to indiscriminately 'plug and play'.

Three levels of HTS cultural intelligence included: (1) description of cultural awareness for basic familiarity, (2) explanation of behaviour and cultural understanding and prediction from cultural intelligence, and (3) drivers of behaviour that shaped theatre-level decision-making. Few HTS personnel were able to perform at the third level of cultural intelligence. The practice of purging hard-won knowledge jeopardised establishing a reachback system.

There was emphasis on leadership in the HTS, but the skill set was questionable when the primary task was the use of kinetic force. HTS had to earn trust in order to be relevant; however, trust took valuable time. When the HTS experienced deployment fatigue, the personnel did not care about culture anymore; they just wanted to survive.

The American Army commonly misunderstood that cultural intelligence was to be used in conflict among the people for understanding the population, not for targeting insurgents. An American Army Officer deployed in Afghanistan found that it took about six months to understand Jalalabad, even with an interpreter and cultural advisor who had been there for two years. The population and the insurgents were seen in binary opposition; anthropology was population-centric, whereas counterinsurgency was insurgency-centric and were used to advance kinetically related operational objectives.

British Army Cultural Advisors (CULADS) worked with HTS but considered it to be overly scientific.

> "British Army Cultural Advisors (CULADS) from the Defence Cultural Specialist Unit (DCSU) worked closely with HTS."
>
> (British Army Officer interview, 2012)

The chain of command in the British Army complicated the use of HTS cultural research reports, because the observer was disconnected from the decider. The HTS failed to offer enough value judgments, and the British Army was more comfortable with pictures and graphs as the cultural way of understanding the world.

The Canadian Army found systematic HTS research could not be done in an operational environment, because there was only five minutes available to ask one question.

> "Security led to time criticality; it took time to develop trust and get reliable reports and there was 'only five minutes available to ask one question.'"
>
> (Canadian Army Officer interview, 2012)

The American Army attached HTS to the Canadian Army in 2010, but the Canadian Army did not want HTS teams; the preference was for individuals. It was not possible to confirm risks to informants. Cultural intelligence in the Canadian Army was on the periphery. In Afghanistan, there was no formal system of cultural analysis.

The Marine Corp posted in Anbar, Iraq, was observed by the Canadian Army to be anti-HTS, they told them to 'sit in an office and eat donuts'. Security was tight, but Iraqis knew the difference between civilian HTS and the Marines and Army. The Marines insisted on weapons training and handling, but at least one female HTS member indicated she never carried a gun. HTS talked with Marines to corroborate data and test reliability.

HTS personnel were issued an American Army uniform, but they were not made to wear them.

HTS had logistic issues; they did not have assets such as cars or helicopters. HTS had no idea what was expected of them; there was no training on how to work with ABCA and coalition partners or other service branches. HTS operated outside the chain of command; HTS was not about being an academic, but how to insert into the chain of command. HTS and command needed to come halfway to understand one another. HTS anthropologists were appreciated for having their own ethics and for having a stronger culture of listening, but directions were provided from command and HTS had to sort out their role. Anthropologists were not deployed to write academic reports. The 100 out of 10,000 reports actually circulated in the ABCA Armies dealt variously with energy drinks, respiratory problems when running in sandstorms, Iraqi men being trained by 19- to 23-year-old marines and questioning why Iraqi women could not take up nursing training.

When HTS showed their notepads, it was supposed to express interest in the people. HUMINT intelligence collectors were not to go out with HTS 'cultural research' missions, but Special Ops included cultural intelligence in doctrine decisions about using kinetic force. Too many officers in the American Army controversially used anthropological 'cultural research' as a stream of intelligence to support targeting to 'find, fix and finish the enemy'.

Supporters in the Australian Army HTS believed 'cultural research' outputs from the theatre of conflict had positive feedback as a 'gentler form of counterinsurgency'.

> "The five-person HTS teams were considered to be a kinder, 'gentler form of counterinsurgency.'"
>
> (Australian Army Officer interview, 2012)

HTS computer simulations with heightened graphics and incidents were available to the Australian Army. Supporters claimed HTS reduced kinetic operations in Afghanistan, even though no data was provided in support of such a claim. The HTS was conceptualised and developed while fighting two wars, there was not time to embed the cultural knowledge into the ABCA Armies. An initial issue for the HTS was recruitment contracted through the BAE Systems Corporation. In the Australian Army, psychology with western frameworks predominated over anthropology, but social psychology interview protocols were reviewed by cultural specialists. In 2008 in Afghanistan, HTS cultural intelligence appeared to the Australian Army to lack depth and academic rigor and it was in need of a textbook. The anthropology ethic code was violated because was 'not actually doing research but writing intelligence'.

From the perspective of the New Zealand Army, the American Army had to create the HTS system because they simply did not recognise culture.

> "The New Zealand Army observed during peacekeeping in Sinai that the American bar was for Hispanics only on Tuesday, Blacks only on Wednesday and White rednecks only on Thursday, which begged the question if the 'American's had no internal cultural understanding', how could there be cultural understanding with others?"
>
> (New Zealand Army Officer interview, 2012)

Since the Americans had no internal cultural understanding, how could there be cultural understanding with others. Multiculturalism was integrated in the New Zealand society and Army, and it was a valued cultural asset, even if not perfect. The New Zealand Army was surprised by the HTS use of anthropology in military space and was sceptical about military personnel undertaking HTS cultural research. American HTS personnel were not armed, wore civvies and used females in the team. Moreover, the New Zealand Army had no interaction with HTS reports. There was a big lag in the American HTS system between 'cultural research' and supplying reports that subsequently flowed through to ABCA Armies. HTS reporting alone was not the answer; the cultural context of the data was needed. HTS was like trying to make a science out of an art. HTS was seen as great technology, but it was questionable that the 'cultural research' changed understanding enough to act on it. How long did the New Zealand Army have to be immersed in culture for HTS to change the outcome? The head of USAID said the HTS approach was over the top and unachievable, and the focus should rather be on narratives of people and how they were likely to behave.

The dual trap of 'cultural research' came when officers demanded specific HTS information, which could be used for 'reconstruction or killing'. 'Cultural research' treated as intelligence in the New Zealand Army would be problematical because it was not to be used for targeting. 'Cultural research' was for understanding the cultural environment, identifying king makers, determining who is loyal to who and demonstrating how the religion functions. Anthropologists were supposed to be unbiased and neutral observers and an ethics code for 'culture research' was essential. In the New Zealand Army conduct of 'cultural research' guidelines could be made more specific to avoid misinterpretation and to protect participants; the AAA code of ethics should be observed along with informed consent and not lying or spying.

Conclusion

The ABCA Armies trained primarily on kinetic force encounter with the enemy and created 'lions'; whereas deployment cultural intelligence training created 'pussy cats'. A pilot cultural intelligence training course provided the British Army with anthropological aspects of political and economic organisation, beliefs, and values and kinship, but the participants were left thinking 'so what'. In the Canadian Army, some effort was taken to understand culture, particularly in 'war amongst the people'. Australian Army soldiers, like American soldiers, could 'give a shit' about cultural intelligence, primarily because they were not picked for being culturally sensitive. In the New Zealand Army, cultural intelligence was thought to be more than 'kicking around a ball with kids', and it needed to be done more scientifically.

War this century has no longer pitted state versus state in armed conflict, it has been replaced by conflict among the people. Cultural intelligence was imprecise and used in the British Army 'only when all else failed'. A Canadian soldier in Afghanistan was focused on the enemy and openly hostile towards cultural intelligence because he did not want to be part of a Provincial Reconstruction Team and 'eat with those monkeys'; instead, he occupied the battlespace and 'wanted to kill people'. The New Zealand Army understood the significance of 'conflict among the people' meant the enemy was concealed in complex environments and needed to hide in the population; therefore, it was important to have cultural intelligence to understand the population.

Soldiers in the American Army who advocated 'take them by the balls and their hearts and minds will follow' indiscriminately utilised population-centric and insurgency-centric intelligence to advance kinetically related operational objectives. In the British Army, anthropology was seen as descriptive, whereas 'psychology understood how people worked irrespective of culture'. As a result of engaging the Afghans they became more trusting, but interpreters became targets and the Canadian Army 'created their own counterinsurgents'. The Australian Army taught how counterinsurgency in Afghanistan was 'created for targeting Taliban leaders'. In the New Zealand Army, 'anthropologists know people' and cultural intelligence brings a completely different lens; to understand the culture of the population was to understand the problem.

Many American Army officers controversially used anthropological research as a stream of intelligence to support targeting to 'find, fix and finish the enemy'. Anthropological ethics was considered to be 'political correctness' in the British Army. In the Canadian Army, the HTS violated the anthropology ethic code because it was not doing research but writing intelligence. The Australian Army had ethical concerns that contractor research anthropologists were not subject to the Uniform Code of Military Justice. The dual trap of cultural research came when officers in the New Zealand Army demanded specific information, which could be used for 'reconstruction or killing'.

Between July 2005 and August 2006, the American Army assembled the controversial 'HTS' program as part of the broader counterinsurgency effort designed to 'crush, suppress, and smother' resistance in Iraq and Afghanistan. The American Army viewed the population and the insurgents in binary opposition; anthropology was population-centric, whereas counterinsurgency was insurgency-centric, and they were used to advance kinetically related operational objectives. British Army Cultural Advisors (CULADS) worked with HTS but considered it to be overly scientific. The Canadian Army found systematic HTS research could not be done in an operational environment, because there was 'only five minutes available to ask one question'. Supporters in the Australian Army believed HTS 'cultural research' outputs from the theatre of conflict had positive feedback as a 'gentler form of counterinsurgency'. From the perspective of the New Zealand Army, the American Army had to create the HTS system because they simply did not recognise culture. The New Zealand Army was surprised by the HTS use of anthropology in military space and was sceptical about military personnel undertaking HTS cultural research.

CHAPTER 9

Case Studies

OPERATION OUTREACH: THE AUSTRALIAN ARMY DOMESTIC CIVIL–MILITARY INTERVENTION IN THE NORTHERN TERRITORY

Introduction

Globally, there are two types of borders; the obvious is the state border that separates different states, less obvious is a nation and a state border that separates two realities that coexist within the same global space. Aboriginal people, without consultation, were forced to comply with the domestic Northern Territory (NT) civil–military Intervention. Operation Outreach guided the civil–military NT Intervention and consisted of 600 soldiers, including 400 'green skins' from 'Australia's Indigenous Army'. Unarmed soldiers in the Operation Outreach campaign crossed the Aboriginal cultural border into 73 Aboriginal owned communities, established military operational space and launched the 'chaperone system', 'permissive environments', 'safe houses' and 'insertion of governance', which provided a system of security, protection and civil policing to manage hostile reception in the Aboriginal owned communities.

The Commonwealth 'Operational Centre' established humanitarian operational space in Darwin on non-Aboriginal land in the settler state. Whole-of-Government (WoG), non-governmental organizations (NGOs), and volunteers were integrated into an on-ground 'taskforce'. An Aboriginal man referred to the taskforce staff chaperoned by soldiers to Aboriginal-owned land as 'snowing white'. Aboriginal people regarded national emergency governance to create new sociocultural spatial institutions and to change the sociocultural spatial order as 'negative humbugging'; not from kin as Major-General Chalmers suggested, but from the taskforce.

Operation Outreach Military Operational Space

A decade has passed since the June 2007 release of the '*Little Children Are Scared*' report on child sexual abuse in Aboriginal communities in the Northern Territory (NT). The then Howard government announced the Northern Territory Emergency Response, commonly known as the NT Intervention, to protect Aboriginal children from abuse. Urgency masked the menacing civilising settler colonial intentions of the state (Howard-Wagner, 2012: 222). The report had actually called for empowerment of the essentially self-governing Aboriginal communities since the 1970s to lead them out of the malaise, but Aboriginal people, without consultation, were forced to comply with the NT civil–military Intervention. The securing of title over traditional land, that had enabled Aboriginal communities to establish settlement patterns appropriate to family and kin structures, came under threat with the NT Intervention.

Aboriginality associated with remote traditional communities in the self-determination era provided the then Howard government with a geographic object to introduce the NT Intervention. The primary object of settler colonialism is the land itself (Wolfe, 2006). Aboriginal self-determination and rights to land challenged the prevailing settler state and provoked a conservative backlash.

The domestic military campaign in the NT Intervention was infelicitously codenamed Operation Outreach. The Department of Families, Housing, Community Services and Indigenous Affairs (FaHCSIA) took the lead in the Whole-of-Government (WoG) inter-agency taskforce (CJOPS 2007/8). Major-General Dave Chalmers was the uniformed field commander controlling and coordinating WoG efforts (CJOPS 2007/8). Domestic placement of the Army was under the Defence Assistance to the Civil Community (DACC) Category 6 type arrangements that was not to include law enforcement tasks. The Army raised Joint Taskforce (JTF) 641 on June 27, 2007 and Defence provided an operational budget of $15,000,000 (CJOPS 2007/8).

Operation Outreach consisted of a force of 600 soldiers based on the Army's North West Mobile Force (NORFORCE), which was formed in 1980 with 600 regulars and reservists and included 60% Aboriginal soldiers (Hancock, 2010: 68). NORFORCE conducts surveillance and intelligence in the remote north of the Northern Territory and Kimberly region of Western Australia, which is exposed to drug smugglers, illegal fishermen and terrorists (Hancock, 2010: 68). Operation Outreach included 400 Aboriginal soldiers from NORFORCE, known as 'Australia's Indigenous Army' (Ashby-Cliffe, 2008). Operation Outreach afforded NORFORCE the opportunity to re-engage with the Aboriginal people of Southern and Central NT.

In the view of Indigenous leader Pat Dodson (2007), deploying armed forces to seize control of 73 'proscribed' communities on Aboriginal-owned land effectively established a form of martial law. Metaphors typical of Australia's external civil–military Provincial Reconstruction Team (PRT) interventions, as in Timor-Leste, were deployed to rationalise the severity of the domestic NT civil–military Intervention (Howard-Wagner, 2010). The Commonwealth government was "deploying troops into the Northern Territory to fight against the community problem" and "troops [were] seizing control of Aboriginal communities" (Brough, 2006). Indigenous townships and town camps were equated to 'refugee camps' and 'war zones' (Howard-Wagoner, 2012: 222). As Mal Brough, ex-army officer and then Howard government minister responsible for the NT Intervention put it: 'stabilise, normalise, exit' (Morris and Lattas, 2010). The execution of Operation Outreach included Phase One — *stabilization* — for protection of Aboriginal child health; Phase Two — *normalization* — for safer and healthier Indigenous communities; Phase Three — *enduring support* — to minimize degradation of Indigenous community reform and Phase Four —*regeneration*— for post-operational remediation (CJOPS 2007/8).

Operation Outreach, through NORFORCE, was expected to provide FaHCSIA and other WoG bureaucrats with the logistic and security support needed to 'protect' Aboriginal children from abuse, suspend Land Rights title in prescribed areas for five years, manage 73 Aboriginal communities, supervise community stores and welfare payments, prosecute criminals, and remedy social degradation of Aboriginal communities (CJOPS 2007/8).

For the targeted Aboriginal people, the NT Intervention created a strange and mixed message. For example, Aboriginal poet Ali Cobby Eckermann (2015) was living with her kinship family at Titjikala on the edge of the Simpson Desert and she was an eyewitness to the intimidating methods used to implement the NT Intervention. Eckermann (2015) observed NORFORCE Aboriginal soldiers 'protect' bureaucrats to deliver mandatory 'sex checks' on all children residing in the 73 Aboriginal owned communities and noted that extreme wages were paid to interventionists, including to doctors from interstate who were paid $5,000 per week with benefits due to their 'perilous task'. Eckermann (2015) witnessed alcohol restrictions, quarantining of money from all families and Aboriginal residents, changes in land tenure to 40- to 90-year leases held by the Commonwealth government in return for essential services, suspension of the Land Council permit system controlling access to Aboriginal communities, and abolition of the Community Development Employment Project.

Unarmed soldiers in the Operation Outreach campaign crossed the Aboriginal cultural border in 73 Aboriginal owned communities to establish military operational space. New laws scrapped the permit system that allowed Aboriginal people to determine entry to their community by government officials, media, researchers, and tourists. Child Health Check Teams (CHCTs) was expected to 'protect' the interests of Aboriginal children but ordered mandatory 'sex checks' for all children residing in the Aboriginal owned communities. Operation Outreach coordinated Aboriginal owned communities to assist health and social workers to operate in 'permissive environments' (CJOPS 2007/8) to extend emotional, physical, and military support to CHCT personnel from visiting agencies working in unfamiliar environments (Snowden, 2008). NORFORCE directly surveyed six Aboriginal-owned communities per week, and reform operations commenced one week after the site survey of Aboriginal-owned communities. Aboriginal soldiers in NORFORCE set an example and brought their own children in for sex checks from the Aboriginal owned communities targeted for CHCT inspection (CJOPS 2007/8).

In the 19th century, Aboriginal troopers and police were recruited by government and settlers to attack their Aboriginal enemies (Rosser, 1991; Fels, 1988) thus they fought the colonised at the same time they colonised themselves (Pels, 1997). In the NT Intervention, soldiers in Australia's Indigenous Army recruited for the Operation Outreach campaign brought their own children in from the Aboriginal owned communities targeted for 'sex checks', thus they engaged with colonised communities at the same time they occupied military operational space and colonised themselves.

Operation Outreach provided a 'chaperone' system for the CHCT to complete 73 Aboriginal owned community surveys and child health checks, including multiple re-visits. Personnel contracted to the former Department of Health and Ageing DoHA received reception and delivery to staging areas, accommodation and life-support, cultural and environmental awareness training, movement to and from Aboriginal owned communities and community liaison by NORFORCE. The 'chaperone' system was calculated to establish an atmosphere of security and trust for the CHCT DoHA workers to operate in the military operational space in remote Aboriginal owned communities and the Army extended the implied authority and sense of security that their mere presence provided (CJOPS 2007/8).

Operation Outreach delivered and installed welfare related temporary 'safe house' accommodation in three remote Aboriginal owned communities (CJOPS 2007/8). A violent clash erupted between rival clans In Yuelamu on August 9, 2007 and NORFORCE patrolled to secure the safely of a CHCT team operating out of the community health clinic until the Northern Territory Police (NTPOL) arrived (CJOPS 2007/8). As the community CHCT 'sex checks' were completed, Operation Outreach instigated an 'insertion of governance' that involved significant planning and deployment for NTPOL, including expansion into 11 Top End Aboriginal communities. Operation Outreach, through 'insertion of governance', purchased, delivered, installed, and commissioned NTPOL containerised workplace and custodial accommodation across 18 Aboriginal communities (CJOPS 2007/8). An Australian soldier who had returned from duty in Afghanistan questioned "why had he built schools for girls in Uruzgan Province, but come back to the Northern

Territory to build police stations as part of the NT Intervention" (Triggs, 2015: 2).

Humanitarian Operational Space

The Commonwealth 'Operational Centre' established humanitarian operational space in Darwin (FaHCSIA, 2008) on non-Aboriginal land located in the Australian settler state. National emergency jurisdiction governance integrated WoG, NGOs, and volunteers into an on-ground 'taskforce'. An Aboriginal man remarked that when Indigenous soldiers chaperoned the taskforce from non-Aboriginal land to Aboriginal owned land it was 'snowing white', an interesting metaphor for the Top End (Altman, 2007). Aboriginal people regarded the attempt to implement neoliberal technologies of governing to create new sociocultural spatial institutions and to change the sociocultural spatial order as 'negative humbugging'; not from kin as Major-General Chalmers suggested, but from the taskforce (Altman, 2007).

The settler state envisaged Aboriginal organisations, Land councils and the NT government as a 'failed state' that required federal intervention as the answer. Aboriginal owned communities were constructed as failed social enclaves allowing for new disciplining practices. Viable economies and entrepreneurial culture were to become the new norm and failed apparatuses of welfare were to be dismantled (Howard-Wagner, 2010).

New laws changed land tenure arrangements put in place under the Commonwealth Aboriginal Land Rights Act (Northern Territory Act, 1976) and special leases from the Northern Territory government. The existing model of self-governance and Aboriginal communal land ownership was suspended. Aboriginal owned townships were acquired through five-year leases to establish individual private property ownership by building houses and introducing market-based rents (Howard-Wagner, 2010). Exception became the norm and federal legislation brought into effect a 'new model of governance' whereby vesting of inalienable freehold land trusts on behalf of traditional owners was resituated in new modes of occupancy (Howard-Wagner, 2012: 230). The move away from community-based approach to land management and ownership was replaced by a system of market-based rents and long-term lease tenancy. Central to amending land-tenure was the 'commoditisation of land', despite Aboriginal people not regarding land as an economic commodity (Howard-Wagner, 2010).

Aboriginal communities had a 'culturalised border' and Aboriginal people became 'citizen residents' of land rather than owners of the land (Howard-Wagner, 2012: 232). The suspended operation of the *Racial Discrimination Act 1975* did not protect Aboriginal people who were at risk of losing their land or being discriminated against in relation to their welfare payments (Behrendt, 2010). The NT civil–military Intervention underpinned the settler colonial logic of replacement, particularly in housing and land tenure reforms (Howard-Wagner, 2012: 231). There were changes to land tenure to lease holds by the Commonwealth in exchange for essential services. Private ownership of land and welfare reform were unrelated to effective approaches to dealing with systemic problems of violence and abuse and Aboriginal control over land and resources were undermined (Behrendt, 2010). The declared state of emergency suspended statutory laws and legal norms as well as the rights of Aboriginal peoples who lived there (Howard-Wagner, 2010).

The state reinforced a 'zone of exception' by quarantining welfare payments and stipulating what the money could be spent on. Quarantining the welfare payments of families to ensure their children attended school was a punitive measure considering that the government failed to adequately provide funding for teachers and classrooms in many Aboriginal owned communities in the NT and there was no evidence that linking welfare to behavioural change was effective. Moreover, the quarantining applied to anyone who lived in an Aboriginal owned community designated as a prescribed area. To achieve this:

> "The federal government prevented the Racial Discrimination Act from applying, suspended protections and rights of appeal under the Northern Territory anti-discrimination legislation, and suspended the rights to appeal to the social security appeals tribunal. It took away the rights of the most marginalised within our community to complain about unfair treatment of, or unfair impact on, just about anyone."
>
> (Behrendt, 2010: 203)

Modernising and economic objectives of settler colonial and neoliberal agendas worked hand in hand; there was a move away from community-based land management and ownership to individual housing and leasehold tenure (Howard-Wagner, 2012: 234). Housing in the community sector was the responsibility of then Minister for Housing Tanya Plibersek, while Jenny Macklin, then Minister for Indigenous Affairs, was concerned with Indigenous housing:

> "Plibersek supports the transfer of the title of public housing *from* state and territory housing authorities *over to* the community housing sector so they can provide housing. Macklin...is insisting that the title of the land on which community housing is built must be transferred *from* the Aboriginal community *to* state housing authorities through a long-term lease (from 40 to 99 years)".
>
> (Behrendt, 2010: 205)

Aboriginal people questioned why their land rights must be surrendered for accessing housing money, when other Australians gained access without any such guarantee. In the opinion of Walpiri Elder Harry Nelson Jakamarra:

> "The NT Intervention housing programme has not built any new houses at Yuendumu. We are just being blackmailed. If we don't hand over our land we can't get houses maintained, or any new houses built. We have never given away any Walpiri land and we are not going to start now".
>
> (Behrendt, 2010: 205)

The $800 million housing programme in the NT Intervention failed to deliver a single house in 18 months.

Culturalisation of Political Conflict

'Culturalisation' of political conflict, as in the NT civil–military Intervention, was part of a global trend that rendered cultures ineligible for tolerance (Howard-Wagner, 2012: 223). Bureaucrats shifted discourse from government failure onto Aboriginal people ineligible for tolerance. There was an ideological use of ethnographic and anthropological theory by politicians, public servants, military, and the public (Lattas and Morris, 2010). Government and media narratives constructed violence and sexual abuse as a feature of Aboriginal culture. Then minister for FaHCSIA, Mal Brough, implied that child abuse in Aboriginal owned communities was related to cultural values of patriarchy and declared that 'paedophile rings' were working behind a veil of customary law (Brough, 2006). Aboriginal leader Mick Dodson (2007) acknowledged, in a speech before the National Press Club, that while there was violence and sexual abuse in Indigenous communities, they were not and never were part of Aboriginal tradition:

> "[…] a disjunction had occurred between Indigenous representation of family violence, child abuse and neglect, and federal government and media representations, which tended to attribute blame for them to Indigenous culture or to inherent failure of Indigenous society itself."

The alleged paedophile rings never materialised (Altman, 2017).

Peter Sutton and other senior anthropologists produced selective ethnographic data that normalised the NT civil–military Intervention and supported welfare dependency having deep cultural roots in Aboriginal ritual, ceremonial and kinship obligations. Aboriginal culture was identified as a significant part of the 'Aboriginal problem' in the culture wars of the Howard years. Sutton argued that the progressiveness of the self-determination era was responsible for the hyper marginality of remote communities that were culturally maladapted to late modernity (Altman, 2017). Sutton, in *"The Politics of Suffering"*, judged Aboriginal parents incapable of responsibly caring for their children, therefore the settler state must exercise the 'right to intervene' to prevent the suffering of women and children. Sutton (2009: 9–10) called for the NT civil–military Intervention into the 73 Aboriginal owned communities to intimidate paedophiles, drug addicts and corrupt oligarchs: "women and children needed reassurance that the state was on their side…They got it with the Army, the state incarnate, a particularly apt symbolic statement."

The NORFORCE model for Aboriginal cultural connection is the concept of "skin" groups to differentiate clans. As Warrant Officer Ross Sneath puts it: "I am green skin; you are green skin" (Hancock, 2010: 69). Lt-Col Richard Parker, former NORFORCE CO, indicates that "the green skin of NORFORCE is something they understand in their culture…when we come together we form our own group-the green-skin group. It's a very effective way of doing business" (Hancock, 2010: 68). As Lt-Col Parker puts it: "we try to work closely with our Indigenous soldiers and accommodate Indigenous culture" (Hancock, 2010: 69). Under command of Major-General Chalmers, 'green skin' Aboriginal soldiers in Operation Outreach occupied military space in the 73 Aboriginal owned communities.

Since the early 1990s, many members of the Army have studied and qualified in a Defence sponsored cross-cultural awareness course at Nungalinya College in Darwin (ABC News Online, 2007). Major General Chalmers believed the important thing Aboriginal people could do for their future was to preserve their culture:

> "Over time, we as a society have undervalued Indigenous culture and in many places it's been lost. And where it's been lost people have lost their compass, they've lost their framework of life. It's not being replaced by a mainstream Australian framework and people are in limbo. We need to be paying a lot more attention to traditional healers and traditional lawmakers, the role they played and play, in people's lives."

(Toohey, 2008)

Major General Chalmers identified Aboriginal cultural as essentially associated with established ancestral traditions. The ethnographic present was a technique of classicist persistence that erased history and reinforced Aboriginal people as belonging to the past (Cowlishaw, 2017). Major Chalmers agreed with Sutton's position of abandoning self-determination, limiting Aboriginal control over recently acquired land, taking direct control over community governance and attributing difficulties in remote Aboriginal communities to liberal policies that abandoned assimilation and encouraged cultural continuity (Cowlishaw, 2017).

The Army recognised that Aboriginal movement and observation skills in the bush cannot be taught by even the best military instructors. Therefore, NORFORCE selected Aborigines with a bush knowledge background to become 'green skins', because "their talents are 'instinctive', a product of thousands of years of accumulated knowledge of landscapes, the seasons and the weather that the NORFORCE 'green skins' put to use protecting the remote north" (Hancock, 2010: 68).

Identifying Aboriginal knowledge of the bush as an 'instinctive talent' belongs to 19th century evolutionary anthropology. Edward Curr, well known anthropologist, government officer and settler, published *The Aboriginal Race* in 1886. Furphy, Curr's biographer, discusses the notion of instinctive knowledge of the bush among the Banderang of Port Phillip:

> "The Banderang have a 'remarkable' ability to navigate in the bush. Curr stressed that admirable Aboriginal skills were innate and instinctive, rather than reasoned or logical. "The ability to find his way about the bush, wrote Curr, is more akin to instinct than to reason and comparable to similar ability in cattle." Curr could not perceive the method used by the Banderang, he assumed that the ability was "born with him in embryo". He was unable to attribute it to cultural knowledge passed from one generation to the next."
>
> (Furphy, 2013: 178)

'Instinctive talents' is a relic of 19th century evolutionary anthropology, while traditional culture, social pathologies and cultural dysfunctions were formerly suited to functionalist anthropology that enabled settler state concerns with the scientific administration of Indigenous peoples (Morris and Lattas, 2010). The NT Intervention became a social trial reminiscent of the 'assimilation experiment' (Altman, 2017) that masqueraded behind the lie that Aboriginal people must be protected from themselves, whether they like it or not (McMullen, 2012).

'Colonial necrophilia' is the love of Indigenous people after you have killed them socially and politically (Hage, 2010). A form of settler colonial resentment emerges when colonised Indigenous people simply refuse to 'politically die' (Hage, 2010). Aboriginal people in the NT civil–military Intervention refused to 'politically die', their complaint about being removed from the protection of the *Racial Discrimination Act* (RDA) was strongly condemned by the UN Committee for the Elimination of Racial Discrimination. The Commonwealth attempted to keep the emergency as a domestic concern, but Aboriginal resistance was internationalised through the United Nations Permanent Forum on Indigenous Issues (PFII). Special Rapporteur Professor James Anaya was invited to make a professional visit. Professor Anaya wrote a very critical report that found the NT Intervention to be in violation of Australia's honouring the Declaration on the Rights of Indigenous Peoples and other human rights covenants (McMullen, 2012). The experience of an Aboriginal man at the PFII led him to say, "we speak the same language in Geneva and do not have to justify why the Declaration on the Rights of Indigenous Peoples is important" (Triggs, 2015: 2).

Settler colonialists frustratingly ask the colonised "why don't you die so we can love you" (Hage, 2015). Sutton (2009) took exception to the commitment to what he termed the 'rights agenda', which entailed:

> "[…] a prioritisation of land rights and commitment to symbolic measures like a treaty and a national apology; a belief in Indigenous self-management, the view that the extension of civil rights is necessary to secure improvements in welfare; and the belief that rights are not just the properties of individuals but also collectives, [and] were initiated in the wake of the 1967 Referendum as self-determination began to overtake integration and assimilation, and were bound up with a new Indigenous assertiveness that…came to an end around 2000."
>
> (Whyte, 2012: 38)

Some senior anthropologist's addressed 'why all the hatred' and realigned Aboriginal voice and need with Commonwealth government manufacture of the practical being in opposition to Aboriginal political rights, they noted that the historical and sociocultural specificity of Aboriginal peoples made it inappropriate to apply universal human rights (Morris and Lattas, 2010).

The 'necrophilic desire' is prevalent among Australians who are still articulated to a settler colonial imaginary, look at the world with settler colonial eyes and feel increasingly insecure in their power to affect things in the world (Hage, 2010). Sutton 'moralised culture' and argued the more deeply culture was practiced the more disadvantaged were those Aboriginal people who practice it. Moralising culture in the NT civil–military Intervention supported the 'necrophilic desire' for offering human rights to women and children for their own good. Human rights to be free from abuse trumped culture and self-determination. The NT civil–military Intervention prevented suffering 'one individual at a time' and replaced concerns of self-determination and collective justice (Whyte, 2012).

The settler colonialist can only exploit the colonialised after they have 'politicised' them (Hage, 2015). The threat to Aboriginal land has very real implications for Australian governments blinded by 'quarry vision' and the reliance on minerals exploited from politicised Aboriginal lands (Pearce, 2009). Hage (2016: 6) notes that:

> "In Australia...we witness a 'free for all to see' connection between the endless desire of a powerful but troubled mining sector and the moves to further expropriate land from Indigenous people and shrink their spaces for autonomy."

'Politicide' entails the settler colonialist desire to kill the political will of the colonised (Hage, 2015). In Australia's settler colonial society, the Aboriginal people, as far as they have a political will, cannot exist in the eye of the settler colonialist. Their political will, the capacity to rule themselves, must be eradicated (Hage, 2015). Re-categorising land as leasehold and private property for economic development situated Aboriginal people and their land as part of the market economy and involved breaking down communal title into individual property rights (Howard-Wagner, 2012: 240). The compulsory acquisition of land obtained the ultimate object of settler colonialism, the land itself.

Two separate worlds co-existed within the same space in the NT civil–military Intervention; within the settler state national border the military considered Operation Outreach a success, as Lt-Col Mick Rozzoli indicated: "the people of the communities are now having better lives with more law and order, more accountability and the kids are back in school (Ashby-Cliffe, 2007)." Within the Aboriginal nation border Operation Outreach decisively instigated transformation of the Aboriginal socio-spatial order that were inconsistent with Aboriginal models of self-governance and self-determination. The call from Aboriginal owned communities for real autonomy was a threat to the settler state and represented politicide; the settler colonist desire to kill the political will of the colonised. Aboriginal politicide made way for 'colonial necrophilia', the love of the dead Other; you politically kill the other and you love them (Hage, 2015).

Prior to the domestic NT civil–military Intervention, the Army had participated with FaHCSIA in the Army Aboriginal Community

Assistance Program (AACAP). AACAP began in 1996 to provide infrastructure improvements to Indigenous communities by the Army's 19th Chief Engineer Works. Currently, AACAP collaborates with Department of Prime Minster and Cabinet and each joint project is funded up to $6 million. Projects have three components: construction, health, and training. On the 20th anniversary in 2016, 42 infrastructure projects had been completed in remote Indigenous communities (Defence Media, 2016). AACAP in 2007 was engaged with FaHCSIA in Doomadgee, Queensland in a parallel project to the NT Intervention (CJOPS 2007/8).

The Australian Army has deployed external Provincial Reconstruction Teams (PRTs) in support of civil–military post-conflict resolution in Afghanistan and Iraq and later in the Solomon Islands (Shephard, 2009), located in Australia's northern arc of instability. PRTs require consent from the central government of the host country before they are deployed in unstable areas with use of force strategies including combat, counterinsurgency, stability, reconstruction and security, and non-use of force in humanitarian and disaster assistance. PRTs facilitate local provincial populations to familiarise with and trust counterinsurgency in order to extend the reach and legitimacy of the central government (Bebber, 2008).

AACAP and the NT civil–military Intervention delivered Indigenous capacity-building projects for improvement in environmental health, housing, essential services, infrastructure, preventive medicine, and education on healthy living, and they have provided precedents for establishing domestic PRTs (Shephard, 2009). External and domestic humanitarian PRTs share the following similarities: securing permission from the state; the right to intervene compelling participation from local Indigenous people; joint civil–military operations; military, WoG and NGOs operating in separate military and humanitarian space; providing security, logistics, and extending the reach and legitimacy of the central government without the use of force. External PRTs use force for the local population to become familiar with and trust counterinsurgency.

In 2017, former Prime Minister Tony Abbott shockingly appealed for the use of Army defence powers to forcefully invade states and territories to take control of natural gas reserves for the federal government, which would compel states to increase gas exploration and supply, and enable the Commonwealth to take management of resources (Duncan, 2017). Operation Outreach provided an example of a domestic civil–military intervention imposed on Indigenous people in Australia. However, Liberal colleagues in Parliament dismissed Abbot's khaki solution because the use of force in counterinsurgency and policing functions would be highly controversial if applied domestically in Australia.

The NT civil–military Intervention represents the Army's largest domestic response to the most widespread humanitarian disaster in Australia. No Aboriginal person was detained by the military (Toohey, 2008). However, the role of the military in the NT civil–military Intervention was controversial because Operation Outreach necessarily included a civil policing function (Ashby-Cliffe, 2007). The Army, acknowledged there was risk of failures with the NT civil–military Intervention, which included adverse impact on Aboriginal perception of NORFORCE and the Army and compromised capacity to engage and recruit (CJOPS 2007/8). The Army preferred that in the long-term, the NT civil–military Intervention, emergency or not, should have been headed by a civilian official rather than a serving military officer (ABC News Online, 2007). The Army considered it was inappropriate that Major-General Chalmers had continued as head of the NT Intervention because of constitutional, professional and national-unity grounds (ABC News Online, 2007).

Major-General Chalmers was confident that Operation Outreach, which used military operational space to expedite social reform free of interference, was correct for the NT civil–military Intervention (Toohey, 2008). Operation Outreach was led by Major-General Chalmers until it concluded October 21, 2008 (Ashby-Cliffe, 2008). Major-General Chalmers left the military in October 2009 (Henderson, 2009) but took control of the NT Intervention in January 2010 as civilian Territory manager of FaHCSIA (Henderson, 2009).

The NT Intervention of 2007 continued as Stronger Futures laws from 2012, which extended the BasicCard regulation of expenditure and the Community Stores Licencing Scheme to deliver food security. Aboriginal people continued to be vulnerable to settler state rule without permission or invitation, the 'right to intervene' is reminiscent of the failed assimilation experiment (Altman, 2017). The shift from politics to morality in the NT Intervention legitimates discourse for state militarism.

Conclusion

The Operational Centre taskforce occupied the humanitarian operational space and labelled Aboriginal organisations, Land Councils and the NT government as a 'failed state' that required federal intervention as the answer. 'Aboriginal failure' validated the 'zone of exception' where neoliberal economies and entrepreneurial culture became the new norm and failed apparatuses of welfare were dismantled. The 'new model of governance' replaced Aboriginal-owned community-based management and ownership of land with 'commoditised land'. Aboriginal land became 'culturalised space' and Aboriginal people became 'citizen residents' of land rather than owners of the land. 'Moralised politics' placed care for suffering of victims over the demand for justice. The NT Intervention was an 'assimilation experiment' trial masquerading behind the lie that Aboriginal people must be protected from themselves, whether they liked it or not.

Culturalisation of political conflict in the NT Intervention was part of a global trend that rendered cultures ineligible for tolerance. Bureaucrats argued child abuse and 'paedophile rings' hid behind Aboriginal culture, but paedophile rings were never found. The 'Aboriginal problem' used Aboriginal culture to normalise the NT civil–military Intervention and support welfare dependency having deep cultural roots. The settler state maintained the 'right to intervene' because Aboriginal parents were judged culturally incapable of responsibly caring for their children and preventing the suffering of women and children.

'Colonial necrophilia' is the love of Indigenous people after you have killed them socially and politically. Aboriginal people in the NT Intervention refused to 'politically die'; the Commonwealth attempted to keep the emergency as a domestic concern, but Aboriginal people internationalised their resistance through the PFII. The 'rights agenda' argued that the historical and sociocultural specificity of Aboriginal peoples made it inappropriate to apply universal human rights. 'Moralised culture' contended the more deeply culture was practiced the more disadvantaged were those Aboriginal people who practice it. The 'necrophilic desire' offered human rights to women and children; being free from abuse trumped culture and self-determination. 'Quarry vision' was the settler state reliance on minerals exploited from politicised Aboriginal lands. Aboriginal politicide killed the political will of the colonised and made way for 'colonial necrophilia', the love of the dead other; you kill the other and you love them.

Major-General Chalmers believed the important thing Aboriginal people could do for their future was to preserve their culture:

> "Over time, we as a society have undervalued Indigenous culture and in many places it's been lost. And where it's been lost people have lost their compass, they've lost their framework of life. It's not being replaced by a mainstream Australian framework and people are in limbo. We need to be paying a lot more attention to traditional healers and traditional lawmakers, the role they played and play, in people's lives."
>
> (Toohey, 2008)

Major-General Chalmers identified Aboriginal people as essentially cultural and associated with established ancestral traditions. The ethnographic present was a technique of classicist persistence that erased history and reinforced Aboriginal people as belonging to the past (Cowlishaw, 2017).

Aborigines with a bush knowledge background were selected to become 'green skins', because "their talents are 'instinctive', a product of thousands of years of accumulated knowledge of landscapes, the seasons and the weather that the NORFORCE 'green skins' put to use protecting the remote north (Hancock, 2010: 68)." Identifying Aboriginal knowledge of the bush as an 'instinctive talent' belongs to 19th century evolutionary anthropology.

The NT civil–military Intervention represents the Army's largest domestic response to the most widespread humanitarian disaster in Australia. No Aboriginal person was detained by the military (Toohey, 2008). However, the role of the military in the NT civil–military Intervention was controversial because Operation Outreach necessarily included a civil policing function (Ashby-Cliffe, 2007). The Army preferred that in the long term the NT civil–military Intervention, emergency or not, should have been headed by a civilian official, rather than a serving military officer (ABC News Online, 2007). The Army considered it was inappropriate that Major-General Chalmers served as head of the NT Intervention because of constitutional, professional, and national-unity grounds (ABC News Online, 2007).

OPERATION BEL ISI: THE NEW ZEALAND ARMY PACIFIC WAY CIVIL–MILITARY INTERVENTION IN THE BOUGAINVILLE NATION VS PNG STATE CONFLICT

Introduction

A strong sense of cultural history, identity, land and matrilineality informed the impact of the Panguna mine on Bougainville in the Southwest Pacific. The Bougainville Revolutionary Army mobilised for armed conflict and closed the Panguna mine. An intrastate war among the people erupted between the Bougainville nation and the Papua New Guinea state from 1988–1997; it was the largest armed conflict in the southwest Pacific since World War II (Woodbury, 2015).

Panguna Mining Invasion of Bougainville

The Bougainville nation, including adjacent Buka Island, has 19 language/tribal groupings and a population of 160,000 to 200,000 (Wehner, 2001). Bougainville is materially and spiritually matrilineal. Women own the land, and authority and status is held by and inherited through the female line. These arrangements are grounded in place through land and matrilineal genealogy, the things that have value in negotiation between competing interests are land and fruits of the land, access to the sea and fruits of the sea and women and the children they bear (Rimoldi, 2009: 57).

Settled in the foothills and mountains that surround the Panguna mine on Bougainville are some 14,000 Nasioi (Wurm, 1982: 237);

the region has been their home since 1911 (Ogan, 1972: 13). Cash-cropping — of coconuts and cocoa among the men and market vegetables among the women — became the important economic innovation following World War II. Cash-cropping by the Nasioi (Ogan, 1972: 13) and the neighbouring Nagovisi (Mitchell, 1976: 1) was disastrous and provided low returns for labour input. Moreover, men passed on coconuts and cocoa trees patrilineally to their sons and cash cropping permanently tied up cultivatable land that created serious land shortages at the expense of subsistence production, which was based on access to shifting cultivation rights through matrilineal descent groups. Big-men (local political leaders) exchange among the Nasioi was conducted with kin or facilitated by putative kinship relations and was primarily a social activity; after cash-cropping big-men started competing for prestige through *bisnis* (Melanesian tok pisin for almost any cash-earning activity other than wage earner).

Cash-cropping and *bisnis* presented an acute crisis to established matrilineal kinship social relations of production among the tribes of southern Bougainville. They responded to the crisis with *kago* (Melanesian tok pisin for the cargo-cult belief that spiritual and material benefits can be obtained through ritual activity). *Kago* competed with bisnis and was used as a form of social protest. The German and Australian colonisers grew rich off paying cheap wages to Bougainville labourers and expropriating Bougainville land; *kago* became a social protest to redistribute the wealth.

Copper mineralisation on Nasioi land was confirmed by a geologist of the colonial Australian administration. The transnational Bougainville Copper Limited (BCL), an amalgamation of the Australia-based companies Conzinc Rio Tinto and Broken Hill Corporation began prospecting in 1963. Conzinc Rio Tinto gained permission for massive open cut copper mining at Panguna.

It was the women matrilineal landowners who led the early protests, removed survey pegs and attempted to block the advance of bulldozers with their bodies (Griffin, 2005). When BCL started test drilling in 1964, the Nasioi treated the prospectors as trespassers (Bedford and Mamak, 1977: 7–10). From 1969 to 1972, the colonial Australian administration granted BCL leases over 12,500 hectares for a mine site, access roads and waste disposal (Bedford and Mamak, 1977: 7–10). The Nasioi and their neighbours vigorously opposed all land acquisition.

No environmental impact study was required or carried out at the time the Panguna mine commenced production. The environmental destruction caused by mining seriously disrupted subsistence and cash-crop production, and expansion of cash-cropping became feasible only at the expense of shifting cultivation (Mitchell, 1971: 1; Ogan, 1972: 122–183; Ward, 1975: 97–101), which placed an even greater reliance on bisnis for cash earnings. Although compensation provided cash, it remained a very contentious issue because land appropriation and environmental degradation had severe consequences. The Australian colonial administration decision to flush all waste rock, silt, and chemical residue down the Karawong and Jaba Rivers was a social and ecological disaster. Until 1989, BCL was dumping about 135,000 metric tonnes of tailings daily into the Jaba River, the 35-kilometres-long valley was covered 30-metres deep and one-kilometre wide, and a 700-hecare toxic delta had accumulated in Empress Augusta Bay (Hughes and Sullivan, 1989: 37–38). Tailings were chemically contaminated with 800 to 1,000 parts per billion of copper, which killed all aquatic life and remobilised heavy metals ensured that such ecological damage would continue long after mining ended (Chalmers, 1985: 180).

In interviewing BCL chairman Don Carruthers (Griffin and Carruthers, 1990: 59), Professor Jim Griffin stated that Bougainvilleans had every reason to be resentful because "in 1966 then Minister for External Territories, Charles Barnes, visited Bougainville and told astonished villagers that, while their traditional land would yield astronomical riches, they themselves would have to be content with damage compensation and spin-off benefits, Minerals belonged to the State." BCL pushed for a fast-track development of the mine to catch a predicted up-turn in copper prices. The Australian colonial administration was determined that landowners would only receive occupancy fees, even though land 'occupied' by mining would be totally destroyed. Compensation was not standardised until 1980, when the Panguna Landowners Association (PLA) and a Road Mine Tailings Trust Fund (RMTL) was created. Actual compensation money was distributed very unevenly over a wide number of peoples and the sums made only a limited impact on people's lives (Connell, 1991).

Bougainvillean Mobilisation Against Mining

Because their rights as landowners were ignored, the Naisioi gave hostile and active resistance to the state and to the BCL exploration, construction and operation phases. According to Dove, Miruna and Togolo (1974: 182):

> "Land is our life. Land is our physical life — food and sustenance. Land is our social life; it is marriage; it is status, it is security; it is politics; in fact, it is our only world. When you take our land, you cut away the very heart of our existence. We have little or no experience of social survival detached from the land. For us to be completely landless is a nightmare, which no dollar in the pocket or dollar in the bank will ally; we are a threatened people."

Although 55% of the work force was Papua New Guineans when the construction phase peaked with 10,500 workers, among the landowners only eight percent of the adult Nasioi men worked at the mine (Moulik, 1977: 4). The Nasioi and their neighbours largely refused to accept mining employment (Bedford and Mamak, 1977: 8–10; Stent, 1970: 8).

Bouainvilleans despised the rapid urbanisation of their homeland. Arawa reached 15,000 and Panguna 3,500 by 1988. Leo Hannet, a former provincial premier, articulated Bougainvillean feelings toward rapid urbanisation created by BCL:

> "Arawa, in more ways than one, is everything else except a Bougainvillean town. Arawa is to most Bougainvilleans a strange town...[which] was born of an unholy wedlock between a multinational and a government that sacrificed Bougainvillean rights and well being in the names of expediency and the almighty dollar. Arawa is therefore seen as the single towering monument to the twin exploiters of Bougainville: copper and the Papua New Guinea Government."
>
> (Mamak and Ali, 1979: 73)

Bouainvilleans rejected personal financial gain in favour of self-determination and autonomous control over land and resources (Moulik, 1977: 83). The Bougainvillean competition that had taken place between cash-cropping, *bisnis* and *kago* was replicated when dissatisfaction with mining led to another major social protest movement. Napidokae Navitu, the Nasioi social protest movement for resources, autonomy, and identity, was born in a meeting to protest the resumption of the Arawa plantation in 1969. By 1972, Napidokae Navitu had attracted 8,000 followers and had become the social action focus for Bougainville secession and nationalism (Bedford and Mamak, 1977: 22; Griffin, 1982; Mamak *et al.*, 1974: 9).

The payback killing of two Bouanvillean civil servants in a car accident in the Highlands in 1973 (Griffin, 1982: 135) accelerated Bougainvillean calls for secession and repatriation of mainlanders (Hannett, 1975: 290). Labour unrest and interethnic hostilities culminated in a violent strike against BCL in 1975 in which infrastructure and production facilities were damaged. The self-governing Papua New Guinea administration then punitively withheld Bouainville investment royalties and Bougainville officially seceded only days before Papua New Guinea became a new state. Bougainvillean affiliation to the state was achieved when royalties were restored, and Bougainville was granted status as the North Solomons Province (not to be confused with the Solomon Islands) (Beford and Mamak, 1977: 88–89, 1979: 74–85). During these developments Napidokae Navitu continued to be focussed on Bougainvillean development, education and autonomy (Griffin, 1982; Oliver, 1973: 172–176).

The Emergence of the Bougainville Revolutionary Army

Throughout the 1980s Bougainvilleans realised they were economically neglected (Connell, 1991) and began to develop a distinctive Bougainvillean identity based on living close to their ancestral homelands, speaking Bougainvillean languages and placing great importance in their values, ceremonies and matrilineal-based kinship social relations of production (Nash and Ogan, 1990). The same period saw the BCL compensation money, which the Panguna Landowners' Association had received for family heads and for the RMTL Trust Fund, become a growing source of dispute among landowners.

For the women, another strong sense of cultural history that extends into the past was the new Panguna Landowners Association started in 1987. The new PLA, under the leadership of matriclan landowner Perpetua Serero, included younger, more educated Nasioi men and women who opposed the BCL mining operation. In 1988, Perpetua Serero and her brother Francis Ona claimed:

> "We don't grow healthy crops any more, our traditional custom and values have been disrupted and we have become mere spectators as our earth is being dug up, taken away and sold for millions. Our land was taken from us by force; we were blind then, but we have finally grown to understand what's going on."
>
> (Hiambohn, 1989: 18)

The new PLA protested against mining pollution, receiving such a small share of mining profits and they placed immediate demands on BCL. Filer (1990: 5) argued that the second generation of landowning communities developed a social time bomb relationship to the Panguna mining project.

In March 1988, the new PLA-organised 500 landowners and marched on BCL with a petition of demands for increased basic services, localisation of employment and greater control over environmental degradation and pollution (May 1990). Receiving no response, they closed the mine during a one-day sit-down protest two months later. BCL brought in Applied Geology Associates as consultants and in a public meeting of that year they used their report to refute Bougainvillean claims that the mine was responsible for loss of wildlife, declining agricultural production and a range of human illnesses. Francis Ona, one of the new PLA leaders, declared BCLs environmental inquiry to be a whitewash and stormed out of the meeting and landowners present at the meeting disagreed strenuously with BCLs conclusion (Connell, 1991).

Serero commented that from Richard West's book, *River of Tears: The Rise of the Rio Tinto Zinc Corporation, Ltd* (1972), 'we knew we could expect the worst.' A few days after the 'whitewash' public meeting, armed

Bougainvilleans took a large quantity of explosives from the BCL arsenal. In December, BCL shut down the Panguna mine as fires and explosions destroyed mine installations valued at K850,000. In a formal communication to North Solomons Provincial Premier Joseph Kabui, Ona indicated the people meant business and were prepared to die for their cause. In the following weeks Panguna mining installations were professionally blown up with the assistance of Bougainvillean Sam Kauna, an explosives expert trained in Australia who had left the PNG Defence Forces to join the armed struggle with Ona. Early in 1989, the armed Bougainvilleans began referring to themselves as the Bougainville Revolutionary Army.

Anthropologists Nash and Ogan (1990: 9–13) found that dealing with the Panguna mining project created Bougainvillean identity and nationalism:

> "Bougainvilleans have had to contend for years with very real violence to themselves and their way of life, committed by colonizers, by a multinational mining firm and presently by other Papua New Guineans, including riot police whose brutality under the guise of pacification is being investigated by the PNG government. Their creation of a Bouginvillean ethnic identity has precisely sustained collective cooperative efforts in self-defence against forces that might otherwise have overwhelmed them."

In May 1990, the BRA under Ona declared an independent republic of Bougainville. There was considerable media and academic focus on Ona and on state-controlled notions of legally defined conflict that ignored what the BRA were fighting for and the fact that the Bougainvilleans were united as a people.

Then Prime Minister Rabbie Namaliu misunderstood the nature of the conflict, ordered PNG Defence Force troops into the conflict and announced to the PNG parliament: "The priorities of the government are clear. First, we will rid Bougainville of this terrorist scourge. Second, we will restore peace to the island. Third, and vital for the entire nation, we will reopen the Bougainville copper mine," and a leaked cabinet document declared "cabinet is now firmly of the view that a state of insurgency exists." The armed conflict was a nation-against-state armed conflict over autonomous control of land and resources; not an insurgency to overthrow the PNG national government.

PNGDF unleashed counterinsurgency tactics; code named Operation Footloose, against the BRA and claimed more than 200 casualties (Senge, 1990: 12). The counterinsurgency reprisals generated greater Bougainvillean support for the BRA. During the campaign the PNGDF relocated civilians in strategic hamleting on the coast (Robie, 1989: 16). A Bougainville Resistance Force (BRF) was established among those relocated to strategic hamlets, but the BRA and PNGDF only succeeded in becoming armies of occupation.

Bougainvilleans form distinct zones of economic and political authority over human and material resources. They can also form moral zones where relations between people are firmly located and constrain who you are and where you are (Rimoldi, 2009: 58). People move about less freely, identity is fixed, and geography and politics are personal:

> "The care centres set up by the PNG military during the war in order to separate villagers from rebels were essentially entropic in nature. Those incarcerated within them were cut off from the resources of bush and sea unless they had a pass from the soldiers; many rules of social decorum and morality were broken in the forced living arrangements and the pressure on the legitimate landowners was an abuse of customary hospitality. Promises of payment to those who gave assistance to the PNG military in this manner, or by joining the resistance to fight alongside the PNG military against their own people, have added to the social alienation."
>
> (Rimoldi, 2009: 63)

According to Moses Havini (1990: 25), who designed Bougainville's first secession flag in 1975 and went on to act as North Solomons Province executive officer, Ona was hailed by Bougainvilleans as their new hero; his broadcasts were recorded and played constantly in homes, shops and villages. There was widespread support throughout Bougainville for Ona's three demands, namely: a better deal for the landowners affected by the mine (including compensation for environmental damage); a better deal for Bougainville (that is, the profits from the mine staying in Bougainville rather than going to the PNG government; and secession.

In an effort to create dialog and trust, PNG and the BRA signed the Endeavor Accord aboard a New Zealand warship on August 5, 1990. Within weeks of signing the accord the PNGDF launched Operation Cleric and sent troops into Buka in the north and a second phase was extended to Buin in the south. The plan was to woo Bougainvilleans back to PNG by resuming services that had been shut off (Bougainville Information Service, 1990: 3). Operation Cleric never reached Buin, nor was there success in reinvading Bougainville from Buka. The Republic of Bougainville and PNG signed the Honiara Declaration of Peace, Reconciliation and Rehabilitation on January 24, 1991. Bougainvilleans were represented by Joseph Kabui, the previous North Solomons Province premier, and PNG was represented by the then Foreign Affairs Minister Michael Samare. Neither side honoured the terms (J S C F A, D and T., 1999: 26).

The BRA consisted of 2000 armed with 500 modern weapons and several thousand WWII vintage and homemade weapons (Wehner, and Denoon, 2001). By this time, there were around 800 PNGDF, another 150 in the riot squad, together with 1,500 armed BRF (Londey, 2004) The BRF home guard militia, aligned with and armed by the PNGDF, secured the north and southwest of Bougainville and reoccupied Arawa, the provincial capital, in 1993 (J S C F A, D and T., 1999). Armed conflict continued until 1997. The Bougainville armed conflict was not a civil war, or an insurgency fought over control of government. It was an intrastate nation versus state armed conflict fought over territory and the right to decide for autonomy or independence. Both sides in the intrastate conflict invited intervention of unarmed peacekeeping troops from New Zealand, Australia, Fiji, and Vanuatu.

Guitars not Guns: The Maori Cultural Initiative

A BRA member participated in the UN WGIP in 1993, the Year of Indigenous Peoples when the author was there as an observer. The BRA worked to internationalise their conflict, but PNG worked with New Zealand and Australia for a regional approach (Field, 2002). The political arm of the BRA, the Bougainville Interim Government, and the moderate Bougainville Transitional Government advocated autonomy if not independence. Bougainville leaders attended talks in Cairns in September and December 1995, while on their return home the BRA was attacked by the PNGDF. Given Australia's position against mediation, their colonial past in PNG and their support for the PNG government in the crisis, the BRA wanted to exclude them from future participation in conflict resolution (Rolfe, 2001: 46).

In the New Zealand Army, "it was hugely important to realise that 'conflict amongst the people' was not state on state conflict; the enemy was concealed in complex environments and needed to hide in the population, so it was necessary to understand the population" (New Zealand Army Officer interview, 2012).

"Action against the enemy was not considered as important as action with the population, because who do the bad guys look like, they look like the people; it is the lowest ranks that need cultural research, because they are the ones who spend the most time with locals" (New Zealand Army Officer interview, 2012).

A truce and agreement to demilitarise Bougainville was made in mid-1997, with talks held in Honiara and Barnham in New Zealand. The Burnham Declaration called for reconciliation and demilitarisation on Bougainville. Burnham II brought the Bougainville factions together and added the PNG government and military representatives. Barnham I and II emphasised Maori cultural practices, for example each morning featured touching of noses (*hongi*) by participants. A New Zealand official commented:

> "The 'Pacific' style of welcome had allowed PNG officials at the meeting 'to shake hands, touch noses and exchange breath' with Bougainvilleans with whom they had been fighting for 10 years. The Pacific Way enabled participants to walk through glass walls without thinking about what they were doing."
>
> (Rolfe, 2001: 48)

> "The New Zealand Army preferred deployments in the Pacific over the interventions in Bosnia and the Middle East and they took the lead in 'Pacific Way' interventions because they were non-threatening."
>
> (New Zealand Army officer interview, 2012)

The term 'Pacific Way', coined in the 1970s by Raru Sir Kamisese Mara, advocates for Pacific solutions to Pacific problems (Rolfe, 2001).

A New Zealand Army officer (interview, 2012) believed that "without Maori culture we would be Poms at the end of the world." "The New Zealand Army is increasingly aware of their distinctive culture and that they are really a tribe":

> "The New Zealand Army opened their marae in 1995 to keep Maori culture alive in the Army. Rangatira is the chief of the Army Morae. Maori were the original people of this place, they were warriors. In society the Maori have a strong Indigenous voice influencing politics and treaty. I am Scottish but I have a marae. There is learning about history of Maori at the marae for two days and nights. The marae helps recruits realise everyone belongs to the tribe. Once you have an understanding of culture you can appreciate it more."
>
> (New Zealand Army Officer interview, 2012)

An unarmed Truce Monitoring Group (TMG) was created and led by the New Zealand Army, supported by Australia, Fiji, and Vanuatu (Londey, 2004). Ona withdrew to the BRA Panguna stronghold and Kauna and Kabui initiated peace talks with then PNG Skate government. The New Zealand Army led the 250–300 personnel in the TMG, which was unarmed and tasked to patrol, monitor, and build confidence in the peace process. Domination of the Maori with the New Zealand Army peace monitors was a deliberate and very effective choice for the New Zealand Army to project a closer family feel (Field, 2002).

The New Zealand Army was on the cutting edge of cultural awareness and most visible in the peace process (Field, 2002). The New Zealand Army noted that:

> "in Bougainville we had guitars not guns because we understood it was a 'conflict amongst the people' and appropriately, the first to land in Bougainville were the Maori Cultural Group who initiated genuine engagement and interaction in the base in Buin Bougainville."
>
> (New Zealand Army Officer interview, 2012)

Australian soldiers in the TMG had no music culture to contribute. New Zealand peace monitors and their Fiji and Vanuatu counterparts brought their own music, dancing, and singing, which contributed enormously to breaking the ice (Field, 2002).

The TMG divided into four teams, which typically included:

"Eleven New Zealand military, including eight Maori and some women; three Fijians including the team commander; two officers from Vanuatu and five Australian civilians from police, foreign affairs and defence… with perhaps three women."

(Rolfe, 2001: 50)

TMG teams engaged in patrolling, observing and participating in village life, being on patrol would consist of:

"[…] village stops, presentations to the villagers about the peace process and the TMG, discussions about the peace process and how it was holding out in the village area and answering questions; the aim was instilling trust in the peace process over the widest possible area."

(Rolfe, 2001: 50)

Bougainvilleans witnessed the level of involvement of Maori team members in the TMG and the degree of respect the New Zealand Army held for the Maori. Women had involvement in the TMG because they were already integrated into the New Zealand and Australian Armies. As the matrilineal land owners, women worked towards peace and advanced education, healthcare, and jobs.

"Like New Zealand society, the New Zealand Army viewed themselves as a multicultural Pacific people and it clicked that if you were a redneck you couldn't function in the New Zealand Army."

(New Zealand Army Officer interview, 2012)

A New Zealand Army Officer explained that the Army was a big family; there was regular banter between Pakeha and Maori and when in Bougainville the whole deployment went to the marae together. The New Zealand Army believed that:

"they were an independent broker able to mediate and they were good at engaging right down to the private level because it was in their DNA to be empathetic."

(New Zealand Army Officer interview, 2012)

The New Zealand Army participants in the TMG found the Australian soldiers to be culturally insensitive clods, while in the eyes of the Australians, the New Zealand soldiers performed good with guitars and war dances but were hopeless at soldiering (Field, 2002). The New Zealand Army:

> "indicated they would patrol with Australians in Bougainville, but they never travelled at night and never travelled with uniformed Australian HUMINT teams, we observed them going into a village, shaking hands and immediately after washing their hands with sanitary wipes and after watching the locals watching us eat steak, the New Zealand Army concealed their eating so as not to appear insensitive to the Bougainvillean's."
>
> (New Zealand Army Officer interview, 2012)

New Zealand could not sustain the costs in leading the TMG. The Lincoln Agreement was signed in January 1998 (Londey, 2004) and a Peace Monitoring Group under Australian control replaced the TMG. In contrast to New Zealand's approach, the Australian cultural approach was more institutionalised and concerned with outcome over process (Field, 2002).

There had been disputes over the TMG between New Zealand and Australia about size, military versus civilian presence and New Zealand leadership, as Australia wanted an Australian civilian in command. Australian advisers wanted to reassert what they saw as Australia's primary responsibility for the southwest Pacific (Field, 2002). According to the New Zealand Army,

> "the relationship of New Zealand society with Maori was not like the Australian society relationship with Australian Aborigines and peoples in the SW Pacific know it."
>
> (New Zealand Army Officer interview, 2012)

The New Zealand command in the TMG considered the Australians to be less trusted by the Bougainvilleans and therefore more of a risk (Field, 2002).

New Zealand arranged a study tour a year after the Lincoln Agreement for the Bougainville leaders to progress their discussions. As guests of another Pacific village the Bougainville leaders were exposed to:

> "Maori approaches to being a nation within a state, to dealing with a 'foreign' government and to dealing with internal tribal divisions. The process involved immersion in Maori culture and living under the same roof. The Bougainville leaders simply could not ignore each other."
>
> (Rolfe, 2001: 49)

Negotiations resumed and the Matakana and Okataina understandings were signed to promote reconciliation. The Bougainville nation began a reconciliation process in 2000 (Wehner and Denoon, 2001) and the BRA and BRF started disarming (Londey, 2004).

As Bougainville moves from an autonomous nation to an independent state, Rimoldi (2009: 47) observed new sociopolitical demands being placed on matrilineal kinship, land and negotiated alliances between traditional leaders. The trucks that go up and down the road each morning and night seem to carry more people than produce, which reflects the change to a bureaucratic and service economy (Rimoldi, 2009: 62). With the increased availability of administrative, government, NGO, hospital industry, and commercial jobs, more and more women with children have paid work outside the home village. "Solo mothers" have become a new social category; correspondingly with some husbands being referred to as "babysitting":

> "It seems grandmothers and sisters are less likely to want to look after the children of mothers who have paid work. Often the grandmothers and sisters have paid work as well. What initially might seem a positive innovation, a Western version of gender equality, could also be the first sign of kinship entropy with not enough human resources to do the work of kinship. In a kinship-based culture, this could quickly create social disorganisation."
>
> (Rimoldi, 2009: 63)

The traditionally high economic and social status of women as landowners and mothers in matrilineal Bougainville society was expressed through a system of kinship relations rather than an individualised Western concept of gender empowerment" (Rimoldi, 2009: 63).

In the armed conflict between Bougainville and PNG, there were over 300 PNGDF killed (Aspinall, Jeffrey and Reagan, 2013). Estimates of Bougainvillean deaths from the armed conflict have varied from upwards of 10,000 (Woodbury, 2015), to only 1,000 to 2,000 casualties (Braithwaite, 2010). The intrastate Bougainville nation versus PNG state war lasted from 1988 to 1997, and was the largest armed conflict in the southwest Pacific since World War II (Woodbury, 2015).

Conclusion

The term 'Pacific Way', coined in the 1970s by Raru Sir Kamisese Mara, advocated for Pacific solutions to Pacific problems (Rolfe, 2001). There was a peace agreement in 2001 that enabled the creation of an Autonomous Bougainville Government (Woodbury, 2015), with their own criminal law and police force reporting to the government of Bougainville. Ona remained in his Panguna stronghold, named himself 'king' of Bougainville, and died of malaria in 2005 (McLeod, 2005). Passage of the Bougainville Mining Act in March 2015 enabled the Bougainville government control of mining, but Panguna remains closed (Phillips, 2015). A referendum on independence will be held by 2020 (Braithwaite, 2010).

CHAPTER 10

Conclusion

Settler Colonialism

The states associated with the ABCA Armies, America, Britain, Canada, Australia, and New Zealand, share the legacy of Anglo-Saxon settler colonialism, which is based on the logic of elimination for the expropriation of Indigenous land (Wolfe, 2006). Colonial settlers dealt with Indigenous peoples through resistance, containment, appropriation, assimilation or attempted destruction. Settler colonialism vitally constructed the foundational myths and narratives of settler colonialism in the past, but also challenged and transformed public discourse in these countries today (Hodge, 2008). Past settler colonialism cannot be demarcated from colonial struggles in the present (Thomas, 1994). Two types of borders are produced by settler colonialism; the obvious is the state border that separates different states, less obvious is a nation and a state border that separates two realities that coexist within the same settler colonial space (Hage, 2016: 6).

Militarised Anthropology

In 1831, the US Supreme Court created the concepts of wardship and domestic dependent nationhood. Powell professionalised the study of Indigenous nations within an evolutionary interpretive framework

(Silverman, 2005) and with the ethnologists of the Bureau of American Ethnology carried out fieldwork on the militarised frontier. Professor Boas professionalised American anthropology and placed greatest importance on salvage ethnography. Professor Boas published "Scientists as Spies" in *The Nation* in 1919 as an ethical critique of unnamed people who used the cover of anthropological research to work as World War I government agents. Half of all American anthropologists applied their skills to the Second World War. The FBI's Special Intelligence Service and the Office of Strategic Services, the precursor to the CIA, embedded anthropologists to coordinate cultural intelligence. Several institutions functioned as a kind of militarised 'brain trust'. In the Vietnam War in 1968, the CORDS program linked counterinsurgency and rural development projects with the Phoenix program which eliminated the Viet-cong command structure and more than 35,000 Vietnamese civilians were killed. Militant opposition to counterinsurgency in the Vietnam War galvanised dissention in the universities and brought ethics to anthropology; the AAA's first Code of Ethics declared that anthropologists should not conduct covert research, not issue secret reports, use pseudonyms, and show primary loyalty to those they studied. With the emergence of the Cold War, anthropology ethically rejected militarised anthropology and shifted the discipline away from being a tool of domination. In America, the period of parasitic anthropological dependence on the study of Native Americans lasted into the 20th century. The Red Power Movement promoted Indian pride and activism and rejected anthropologists and the domination of settler colonialism. There was an estrangement between anthropology and Native Americans.

There was political and moral complicity between anthropology and the colonial enterprise and there are obvious connections between British 19th century evolutionism and the establishment of the British Empire. The move to social anthropology theory and fieldwork methods was more suited to Britain's colonial administrative need and foundation Professor Malinowski advocated a colonial strategy based on anthropological knowledge. World War II interests conflated with the interests of colonialism as anthropologists administered or defended outposts of the British Empire. Significant political critique was mounted against British structural functional anthropology in the 1930s to 1960s for accommodating to and enhancing the powers of Empire and becoming complicit in it. After the demise of Empire, some anthropologists took part in new British academic programs focused around minority and postcolonial studies.

By the 1880s, the Canadian Department of Indian Affairs became oriented to salvage ethnography. The National Museum in Ottawa held a dominant position in anthropological research in Canada prior to World War II and shared a settler colonial discourse that traditional lifeways of Indigenous people were irrelevant to life in the 20th century. More than 125,000 American draft dodgers and deserters came to Canada between 1964 and 1977; it was the largest political exodus in American history and over half stayed in Canada. Initially, there was significant Canadian anthropological research on nations, states and Fourth World politics, but it became more challenging as they gained ever greater control over their resources and acquired increased political autonomy. By the end of the 20th century, anthropology no longer ethnographically engaged with First Nations.

Terra nullius was the rationalisation and greed for land was the motive for settler colonialism in Australia. Applied anthropology aided Australian government control, development, and advancement of Aboriginal peoples and the Sydney anthropology department trained administrators and missionaries for Australia's overseas colonies. The battle for Australia was fought in colonial New Guinea and the Directorate of Research and Civil Affairs (DORCA) was established and directly recruited anthropologists to study the effects of the of World War II on Indigenous peoples in New Guinea. Counterinsurgency in the Vietnam War created similar political climates on Australian and American universities. A rancorous conflict by members of the anthropology department at the University of Sydney centred on counterinsurgency intelligence research conducted in Thailand. Classicist persistence of anthropology used the ethnographic present to erase history and reinforce popular conceptions of Aboriginal peoples as belonging in the past. The hallmark of settler colonialism in Australia was dispossession of Indigenous land, while the Aboriginal sovereignty movement focussed on reclaiming the land.

The 19th century was the beginnings of Maori participation as anthropological subjects as well as analysts of their own culture. Peter Buck

(Te Rangi Hiroa) was a Maori medical doctor and anthropologist. When World War I broke out, Buck, with other Maori MPs, recruited a volunteer Maori contingent; after fighting in Gallipoli, Buck was promoted to second in command of the Maori Battalion and he later became director of the Bishop Museum in Hawaii. Best, and the Maori anthropologists, Ngata and Buck, pioneered the Dominion Museum field-based anthropology. During World War II, New Zealand anthropologists were used by colonial governments in the Pacific and enlightened colonial rule was considered beneficial for Indigenous peoples. Maori participation in anthropology began to flourish again in the 1960s–1970s. Based on the Waitangi Treaty of 1840, Maori anthropologists were politically active and reasserted old claims to redress injustices during settler colonialism. Mentalist anthropologists, who contended that Maori culture was invented and therefore inauthentic, met with Maori anger and Maori studies subsequently separated from anthropology across the universities of New Zealand.

Nation Against State Armed Conflict Among the People

Paradoxically, by the end of the 20th century, most anthropologists were no longer engaged with Indigenous peoples in America, Canada, Australia, and New Zealand. Indigeneity involved the counterpart non-Indigenous settler and a political regime exclusively controlled by settlers and their descendants. Indigenous militancy had claimed a Fourth World (Varacini, 2012: 324). Under the leadership of Shuswap Chief George Manuel, the term "Fourth World" was born (Manuel and Posluns, 1974). Awareness of the Fourth World spread during the 1970s, as a result of intense Indigenous activism in Canada and America, and of greater sensitivity to human rights and of the growing influence of NGOs (e.g., the World Council of Indigenous Peoples) in galvanising world opinion on the self-determination of peoples (Manuel and Posluns, 1974; Wilmer, 1993). Indigenous sovereignty and succession became increasingly debated in international arenas where the Indigenous nation transcends statehood.

The first 30 years of the UN Working Group of Indigenous People (WGIP) escaped anthropological attention. The claim of internationalised nations for equal rights and freedoms did not allow for group rights to be claimed within state structures, and since most states have formed over unconsenting nations, recognition of them as a distinct people would jeopardise state territorial claims. The Declaration on the Rights of Indigenous Peoples (DRIP), which internationalised the claim of encapsulated nations for equal rights and freedoms, was actually actively fought against by the settler colonial states of America, Canada, Australia, and New Zealand (CANZUS). The Declaration is no less than an anti-settler manifesto that challenges settler colonial societies.

Global armed conflict has changed and is focused on ancient nations encapsulated within states (Hipwell, 1997). Armed conflicts became intrastate wars among the 'people'; Clay (1994) estimated that 'the people' included some 5,000 ancient nations encapsulated among the 192 states. By the end of the 20th century, new wars in the world focussed on the decolonised developing world and pitted guerrilla insurgencies against state governments and states against ancient nations.

The Third World War project identified that 75% to 80% of the intrastate wars being fought from the beginning of the Cold War to 1993 were ancient nations resisting state military forces. Of the 121 intrastate wars since 1993, 97 were nation against state-armed conflicts, which involved a state government against a distinct nation, such as Burma versus Kachin. The comparative Minorities At Risk (MAR) identified 227 nations in intrastate war from the beginning of the Cold War to 1990. The Ethnic Power Relations (EPR) project identified 215 armed conflicts since World War II to 2005, which included 57 nation intrastate armed conflicts for secession and 53 nation intrastate armed conflicts for autonomy. The Uppsala Conflict Data Program (UCDP) project accounted for 248 armed conflicts from the beginning of the Cold War to 2011. In 2011, there were 15 (41%) state versus nation armed conflicts for control of territory, 13 (35%) state vs insurgency armed conflicts for control of government, and nine (24%) intrastate internationalised interventions for control of government. Intrastate internationalised interventions emerged in the 21st century and accounted for 24% of armed conflicts.

An American soldier in Afghanistan wanted some kills, and was disappointed that the cultural advisor 'couldn't tell him who to whack'. In the British Army, anthropological research was considered to be just descriptive only, while psychology, by comparison, was seen as trying to help and to understand how all people worked irrespective of culture. The

Canadian Army took some effort to understand culture, particularly in the 21st century 'war amongst the people'. In the New Zealand Army, 'anthropologists know people' and cultural intelligence brought a completely different lens; 'to understand the culture of the population was to understand the problem'. The separation between humanitarian space and battlespace influenced the New Zealand Army missions in recent times, which were not only about killing, but included development and peacekeeping, as well as prevention and reduction in conflict among the population. Action against the enemy was not considered as important as action with the population, 'because who do the bad guys look like, they look like the people'.

Targeting: Crisis of Cultural Intelligence

Between July 2005 and August 2006, the American Army assembled the controversial HTS program as 'part of the broader counterinsurgency' effort designed to 'crush, suppress, and smother' resistance in Iraq and Afghanistan. Anthropological research as a stream of intelligence controversially supported targeting to 'find, fix and finish the enemy'. HTS in the American Army provided a population-centric approach to counterinsurgency, and 'success in cultural analysis was judged by body count'; the HTS skill set was of questionable value when the primary task was the use of kinetic force. The HTS had no idea what was expected of them and there was no HTS training on how to work with ABCA and coalition partners or other service branches.

Among the ABCA Armies, the HTS was both an operational and tactical 'tool of counterinsurgency' balanced between security and development tasks and between kinetic and non-kinetic effects. Cultural intelligence, termed 'research', controversially operated among the local population for 'cultural appreciation used in planning, execution and assessment of operations' (ABCA, 2011).

When the American Army advocated 'take them by the balls and their hearts and minds will follow', they utilised population-centric and insurgency-centric intelligence to advance kinetically related operational objectives. The American Army went to HTS because it was war among the people and they had to create the HTS system because they simply did not recognise culture.

The ABCA Armies trained primarily on kinetic force encounter with the enemy and created 'lions'; whereas cultural training created 'pussy cats'. A pilot cultural intelligence training course was delivered through Cranfield, the British Army staff college that included the anthropological cultural knowledge of political and economic organisation, beliefs and values, and kinship. However, the participants were left thinking 'so what'. The Australian Army and the American Army could 'give a shit' about cultural intelligence, primarily because they were not picked for being culturally sensitive. In the American Army recognition of local tribes and tribal leaders were identified through anthropological 'structural functional research'. The population and the insurgents were seen in binary opposition, anthropology was population-centric, whereas counterinsurgency was insurgency-centric. In the Australian Army, counterinsurgency intelligence was considered to be more quantitative compared to cultural intelligence, which was more qualitative.

Canadian Army cultural research was for understanding the cultural environment, identifying king makers, determining who is loyal to who, and demonstrating how the religion functions. The dual trap of cultural research came when officers demanded specific information which could be used for 'reconstruction or killing'.

Compared with traditional intelligence analysis, anthropological research was not supposed to support targeting. HTS research supporting culture as a stream of intelligence was anthropologically challenged in 2007, because ethically research should do no harm, be transparent and be based on voluntary informed consent (Gonzales, 2009). The American Anthropological Association (AAA) formally opposed the HTS and denounced it as 'an unacceptable application of anthropological expertise.' The AAA's Code of Ethics declared that anthropologists should not conduct covert research, not issue secret reports, use pseudonyms and show primary loyalty to those they studied.

Civil–Military Operations

As military campaigns shifted away from war between states to civil–military operations regions identified as tribal and Indigenous, the ABCA Armies sought anthropological cultural intelligence to understand the shifting characteristics of enemies and inform engagement with such adversaries (Price, 2011: 3). The urgency of the situation and the danger to victims from war and disaster justified the exception of intervention.

Operation Outreach: Unsuccessful Use of Cultural Intelligence

Aboriginal people, without consultation, were forced to comply with the Australian Army domestic NT civil–military Intervention in 2007. Operation Outreach guided the civil–military NT Intervention and consisted of 600 soldiers, including 400 'green skins' from 'Australia's Indigenous Army'. Unarmed soldiers in the Operation Outreach campaign crossed the Aboriginal cultural border into 73 Aboriginal owned communities, established military operational space and launched the 'chaperone system', 'permissive environments', 'safe houses' and 'insertion of governance', which provided a system of security, protection, and civil policing to manage hostile reception in the Aboriginal owned communities.

The Commonwealth 'Operational Centre' established humanitarian operational space in Darwin on non-Aboriginal land in the settler state. WoG, NGOs, and volunteers were integrated into an on-ground 'taskforce'. An Aboriginal man referred to the taskforce staff chaperoned by soldiers to Aboriginal owned land as 'snowing white'. Aboriginal people regarded national emergency governance to create new sociocultural spatial institutions and to change the sociocultural spatial order as 'negative humbugging'; not from kin as Major-General Chalmers suggested, but from the taskforce.

Major-General Chalmers believed the important thing Aboriginal people could do for their future was to preserve their culture:

> "Over time, we as a society have undervalued Indigenous culture and in many places it's been lost. And where it's been lost people have lost their compass, they've lost their framework of life. It's not being replaced by a mainstream Australian framework and people are in limbo. We need to be paying a lot more attention to traditional healers and traditional lawmakers, the role they played and play, in people's lives."

(Toohey, 2008)

Major-General Chalmers identified Aboriginal cultural as essentially associated with established ancestral traditions. The ethnographic present was a technique of classicist persistence that erased history and reinforced Aboriginal people as belonging to the past (Cowlishaw, 2017). Major Chalmers agreed with Sutton's position of abandoning self-determination, limiting Aboriginal control over recently acquired land, taking direct control over community governance and attributing difficulties in remote Aboriginal communities to liberal policies that abandoned assimilation and encouraged cultural continuity (Cowlishaw, 2017).

Aborigines with a bush knowledge background were selected to become 'green skins', because their talents are 'instinctive', a product of thousands of years of accumulated knowledge of landscapes, the seasons and the weather that the NORFORCE 'green skins' put to use protecting the remote north" (Hancock, 2010: 68). Identifying Aboriginal knowledge of the bush as an 'instinctive talent' belongs to 19th century evolutionary anthropology.

The NT civil–military Intervention represented the Army's largest domestic response to the most widespread humanitarian disaster in Australia. No Aboriginal person was detained by the military (Toohey, 2008) however, the role of the Army in the NT civil–military Intervention was controversial because Operation Outreach necessarily included a civil policing function (Ashby-Cliffe, 2007). The Army preferred that in the long term the NT civil–military Intervention, emergency or not, should have been headed by a civilian official, rather than a serving military officer (ABC News Online, 2007). The Army considered it was inappropriate that Major-General Chalmers served as head of the NT Intervention because of constitutional, professional, and national-unity grounds (ABC News Online, 2007).

Operation Bel ISI: Successful Use of Cultural Intelligence

A strong sense of cultural history, identity, land, and matrilineality informed the impact of the Panguna mine on Bougainville in the Southwest Pacific. The Bougainville Revolutionary Army mobilised for armed conflict and closed the Panguna mine. An intrastate war amongst the people erupted between the Bougainville nation and the Papua New

Guinea state from 1988 to 1997; it was the largest armed conflict in the southwest Pacific since WWII (Woodbury, 2015).

The term 'Pacific Way', coined in the 1970s by Raru Sir Kamisese Mara, advocated for Pacific solutions to Pacific problems (Rolfe, 2001). A truce and agreement to demilitarise Bougainville was made in mid-1997 with talks held in Honiara and Barnham in New Zealand. The Burnham Declaration called for reconciliation and demilitarisation on Bougainville. Burnham II brought the Bougainville factions together and added the PNG government and military representatives. Barnham I and II emphasised Maori cultural practices, for example each morning featured touching of noses (*hongi*) by participants. A New Zealand official commented:

> "The 'Pacific' style of welcome had allowed PNG officials at the meeting 'to shake hands, touch noses and exchange breath' with Bougainvilleans with whom they had been fighting for 10 years. The Pacific Way enabled participants to walk through glass walls without thinking about what they were doing."

(Rolfe, 2001: 48)

The New Zealand Army was invited by the Bougainvilleans and the PNG government to undertake a culturally based Pacific Way civil–military intervention. An unarmed Truce Monitoring Group (TMG) was led by the New Zealand Army and supported by Australia, Fiji and Vanuatu. Maori unarmed peace monitors referred to their TMG deployment as a time for 'guitars not guns' and understood it was a 'conflict amongst the people'. Appropriately, the first to land in Bougainville were the Maori Cultural Group who initiated genuine engagement and interaction in the base in Buin Bougainville (New Zealand Army Officer interview, 2012). The New Zealand Army arranged a study tour a year after the Lincoln Agreement in 1999 for the Bougainville leaders to progress their discussions. As guests of another Pacific village the Bougainville leaders were exposed to:

> "Maori approaches to being a nation within a state, to dealing with a 'foreign' government and to dealing with internal tribal divisions. The

process involved immersion in Maori culture and living under the same roof. The Bougainville leaders simply could not ignore each other."

(Rolfe, 2001: 49)

The Maori lived creatively within two types of borders produced by settler colonialism; the obvious was the state border that separated different states, less obvious was a nation and a state border that separated two realities that coexisted within the same settler colonial space (Hage, 2016: 6). The Maori internationalised claim of nations for equal rights and freedoms achieved group rights claimed within state structures. The Maori provided the Bougainvilleans with approaches to being a nation within a state and how to achieve recognition as a distinct nation without jeopardising state territorial claims. The New Zealand Army Maori Cultural Group demonstrated use of cultural knowledge that was successful in acquiring Bougainville reconciliation, voting for an Autonomous Bougainville in 2015 and securing the vote for independence by 2020.

ABCA Commonality

Anglo-Saxon history and heritage, common-law legal system, and similar institutions of political and bureaucratic governance provided the foundational bond that united the ABCA Armies in interstate and intrastate armed conflict and civil–military interventions. Interoperability within the ABCA Armies should be more about cultural commonality than standardisation. The ABCA Armies were recognised as a doctrine working group structured around force on force with military operations based on winning the war. In comparing culture between the ABCA Armies, the New Zealand Army was considered to be much more similar with the Canadian Army and the New Zealand Army clicked with the British Army; whereas the Australian Army was considered more like the American Army, it appeared to be Americanised in its mind set and focused on force protection.

The pursuit of cultural intelligence in the American Army, in comparison with the ABCA Army counterparts, was dominated by the HTS. The ABCA Armies endeavoured to create and maintain intellectual interoperability. This produced an environment whereby cooperation extended to the development of doctrine and future force development objectives, which were usually sensitive areas that often excluded the involvement of non-ABCA countries (Durrell-Young, 2003: 99). The use of cultural intelligence in the ABCA Army accords with Betz's (2008: 3) observation that the appreciation of Anglo-Saxon values and the diversity of national approaches have empowered: "ABCA Army members to fight with Americans, not as Americans".

References

Aboriginal Affairs and Northern Development Canada. 2010. Canada's Statement on support on the United Nations Declaration on the Rights of Indigenous Peoples, 12 November 2010. http://www.aandc-aandc.gc.ca/eng/1309374239861.html.
ABC News Online. 2007. Keeping it Civil in Cases of Controversy. *The Drum*, 2 October. http://ada.asn.au/commentary/opinion-articles/2007-09/northern-territory-intervention.html. <accessed 22/12/2016>.
ABCA. 2010. *Intelligence Analysis of the Operational Environment: Human Terrain Analysis*. ABCA Report Number 115, 1 November 2010. America, Britain, Canada, Australia and New Zealand ABCA Armies Program.
ABCA. 2011. *ABCA Security Force Capacity Building Handbook*. Edition 2, 1 July 2011. America, Britain, Canada, Australia and New Zealand ABCA Armies Program. Website, cited 17 May 2012, http://www.abca-armies.org/Default.aspx.
ABCA. 2012. http://www.abca-armies.org/, cited 16 February 2012.
Albro, Robert, George Marcus, Laura McNamara, and Monica Schoch-Spana. Eds. 2012. *Anthropologists in the Security Space*. Walnut Creek, CA: Left Coast Press.
Alfred, Gerald. 1995. *Heeding the Voices of Our Ancestors: Kahnawake Mohawk Politics and the Rise of Native Nationalism*. Toronto: Oxford University Press.
Alfred, Taiaiake. 2005. *Wasase: Indigenous Pathways to Action and Freedom*. Peterborough, ON: Broadview Press.
Alfred, Taiaiake. and Jeff Corntassel. 2005. Being Indigenous. *Government and Opposition* 40(4): 597–614.

Altman, Jon. 2007. *The Howard Government's Northern Territory Intervention: Are Neo-Paternalism and Indigenous Development Compatible?* Centre for Aboriginal Economic Policy Research. Topical Issue No. 16/2007. Canberra: Australian National University. http://caepr.anu.edu.au/sites/default/files/Publications/topical/Altman_AIATSIS.pdf. <accessed 28/11/2017>.

Altman, Jon. 2010. What Future for Remote Indigenous Australia? Economic Hybridity and the Neoliberal Turn. Jon Altman and Melinda Hinkson, eds. *Culture Crisis: Anthropology and Politics in Aboriginal Australia*, pp. 259–280. Sydney: University of New South Wales Press.

Altman, Jon. 2017. The Debilitating Aftermath of 10 Years of NT Intervention. *The New Matilda*, 28 July 2017. https://newmatilda.com/2017/07/28/the-debilitating-aftermath-of-10-years-of-nt-intervention/. <accessed 11/12/2017>.

Anderson, Athol. 1990. Edward Shortland. In W. Oliver (ed.), *Dictionary of New Zealand Biography*, Volume 1, 1769–1869. Allen and Unwin/Department of Internal Affairs, pp. 394–397.

Anderson, David. and David Killingray. 1991. *Policing the Empire: Government, Authority, Control, 1830–1940*. Manchester: Manchester University Press.

Asad, Talal, ed. 1973. *Anthropology and the Colonial Encounter*. London: Ithaca Press.

Asch, Michael. 1992. Aboriginal Self-Government and the Construction of the Canadian Constitutional Identity. *Alberta Law Review* 30(2): 465–491.

Asch, Michael. 2003. *Reflections on the Relationship between Theory Building and Engagement in the History of Canadian Anthropology*. Paper for "Historicizing Canadian Sociocultural Anthropology" conference. Trent University, Peterborough, ON, 21 February.

Ashby-Cliffe, Cpl Jane. 2008. Reaching the End. *Army: The Soldiers Newspaper*. 3 November. Canberra, ACT: Defence Newspapers.

Asia Pacific Civil–Military Centre of Excellence. 2010. *Strengthening Australia's Conflict and Disaster Management Overseas*. Australian Government, Asia Pacific Civil–Military Centre of Excellence.

Association of Social Anthropologists of Aotearoa New Zealand, (nd) Principles of Professional Responsibility and Ethical Conduct. http://asaanz.science.org.nz/ <accessed 15 February 2012>.

Atkinson, Rick. 2003. *An Army at Dawn: The War in North Africa*. New York: Henry Holt.

Australian National Research Council. 1923. *Proceedings, (Second) Pan-Pacific Science Congress (Australia)*. Melbourne: Government Printer.

Awatere, Huata D. 1984. *Maori Sovereignty*. Auckland: Broadsheet Magazine Ltd.

Barker, Adam. 2009. *The* Contemporary Reality of a Canadian Imperialism and the Hybrid Colonial State. *The American Indian Quarterly*, 33(3): 325–351.

Barnes, John. 1962. *African Models in the New Guinea Highlands.* Man n.s. 1: 158–175.

Barsh, Russel. 1995. *The* Aboriginal Issue in Canadian Foreign Policy, 1984–1994. *International Journal of Canadian Studies*, 12(Fall): 107–134.

Barth, Fredrik. 2005. Britain and the Commonwealth. Fredrik. Barth, Andrea Gingrich, Robert Parkin, and Sydel Silverman, eds., *One Discipline, Four Ways: British, German, French, and American Anthropology, The Halle Lectures.* Chicago: University of Chicago Press, pp. 1–57.

Bebber, Robert. 2008. The Role of Provincial Reconstruction Team's (PRTs) in Counterinsurgency Operations: Khost Province Afghanistan. *Small Wars Journal*, 10: 1–18.

Beaglehole, Ernest. 1937. New Zealand Anthropology Today. *The Journal of the Polynesian Society*, 46: 154–172.

Beaglehole, Ernest. 1938. Anthropology in New Zealand. *The Journal of the Polynesian Society*, 47(4): 152–162.

Beaglehole, John Cawte. 1944. The South Seas Regional Commission. *Journal of the Polynesian Society*, 53(2): 59–71.

Beckett, Jeremy. 1996. Introduction. Contested Images: Perspectives on the Indigenous Terrain in the Late 20th Century. *Identities: Global Studies in Culture and Power*, 3(1–2): 1–13.

Behrendt, Larissa. 2009. Indigenous Peoples. *Hot Topics: Legal Issues in Plain Language*, 68: 1–36.

Behrendt, Larissa. 2010. Asserting the Doctrine of Discovery in Australia, pp.187–206. Robert Miller, Jacinta Ruru, Larissa Behrendt and Tracy Lindberg. *Discovering Indigenous Lands: The Doctrine of Discovery in the English Colonies.* Oxford: Oxford University Press.

Belich, James. 1986. *The New Zealand Wars and the Victorian Interpretation of Racial Conflict.* Auckland: Penguin.

Bellesiles, Michael. 1966. The Origins of the Gun Culture in the United States, 1760–1865. *Journal of American History*, 83: 425–455.

Belshaw, Cyril. 1950. *Island Administration in the South West Pacific: Government and Reconstruction in New Caledonia, the New Hebrides, and the British Solomon Islands.* London: Royal Institute of International Affairs.

_____. 1957. *The Great Village: The Economic and Social Welfare of Hanubada, An Urban Community in Papua.* London: Routledge & Kegan Paul.

Betz, David (2008) ABCA: The Alliance you never Heard of. *Kings of War.* http://kingsofwar.org.uk/2008/06/353/.

Boas, Franz. 1919. Scientists as Spies. *Nation*, 109: 797.
Brennan, Frank. 1994. *Securing a Bountiful Place for Aboriginal and Torres Strait Islanders in Modern Free and Tolerant Australia*. Canberra: Constitutional Centenary Foundation.
Brough Mal. 2006. Mutitjulu Sexual Abuse Story. *Lateline*. Australian Broadcasting Corporation. 16 May 2006.
Cowlishaw, Gillian. 2017. Tunnel Vision: Part One — Resisting Post-colonialism in Australian Anthropology. *The Australian Journal of Anthropology*, 28: 324–341.
Brown, Richard. 1979. Passages in the Life of a White Anthropologist: Max Gluckman in Northern Rhodesia. *The Journal of African History*, 20(4): 525–541.
Buchanan, Colin. 2006. Canadian Anthropology and Ideas of Aboriginal Emendation. In Julia Harrison and Regna Danell, eds. *Historicising Canadian Anthropology*. Vancouver: UBC Press, pp. 93–106.
Burger, Julian. 1994. United Nations Working Group on Indigenous Populations: The United Nations and Indigenous Peoples. Lydia van der Fliert, ed. *Indigenous Peoples and International Organisations*, pp. 90–102. Tokyo: U.N. University Press.
Burke, E. (1796) *First Letter on a Regicide Peace* IV. London: H.D. Symonds.
Byrnes, Giselle. 1994. "The Imperfect Authority of the Eye": Shortland's Southern Journey and the Calligraphy of Colonisation. *History and Anthropology*, 8(1–4): 207–235.
Canada, Permanent Mission in Geneva. 1981. Response of the Government of Canada respecting Communication submitted by Mr. Alexander Denny on behalf of the people of the Mi'kmaq tribal society on September 30, 1980.
Canada, Permanent Mission in Geneva 1985a. Statement by the Canadian Observer Delegation to the 4th Session of the U.N. Working Group on Indigenous Populations; August 3, 1984.
Canada, Permanent Mission in Geneva. 1985b. Response of the Government of Canada respecting Communications dated February 14, 1984 and March 27, 1985 from Chief Bernard Ominayak and the Lubican Lake Band to the Human Rights Committee.
CBC News 2010. Canada Endorses Indigenous Rights Declaration, 12 November 2010. http://www/cbc.ca/news/politics/story/2010/11/12/indigenous-declaration.html.
Castaneda, Quetzil. 2005. The Carnegie Mission and Vision of Science: Institutional Contexts of Maya Archaeology and Espionage. *History of Anthropology Annual*, 1: 37–74.
Chilver, Sally. 1977. The Secretaryship of the Colonial Social Science Research Council. *Anthropological Forum*, 4(2): 239–248.

Clay, Jason. 1994. Resource Wars: Nation and State Conflicts of the Twentieth Century. In Barbara Johnson, ed. *The Sociocultural Context of the Environmental Crisis*, pp. 19–30. Washington: Island Press.
Clifford, James. and George Marcus 1986. *Writing Culture: The Poetics and Politics of Ethnography*. Berkeley: University of California Press.
Clout, Hugh, Cyril Gosme. 2003. The Naval Intelligence Handbooks: A Monument in Geographical Writing. *Progress in Human Geography*, 27(2): 153.
Connor, John. 2005. *The Australian Frontier Wars 1788–1838*. Sydney: University of New South Wales Press Ltd.
Corntassel, Jeff. 2007. Partnership in Action? Indigenous Political Mobilization and Co-option during the First UN Decade (1995–2004). *Human Rights Quarterly*, 29: 137–166.
Cranswick, George, and Ian Shevill 1949. *A New Deal for Papua*. Anglican Australian Board of Missions.
Crehan, Kate. 1997. *The Fractured Community: Landscapes of Power and Gender in Rural Zambia*. Berkeley: University of California Press.
Crosby, Alfred. 1986. *Ecological Imperialism: The Biological Expansion of Europe, 900–1900*. Cambridge: Cambridge University Press.
Curr, Edward. 1886. *The Australian Race*. 4 vols. Melbourne: John Ferres, Government Printer.
D'Andrade, Roy. 1995. Moral Models in Anthropology. *Current Anthropology*, 16: 399–418.
Darling, Eliza Jane. 2014. Gunships in the Night: David Price, Weaponizing Anthropology: Social Sciences in the Service on the Militarized State. *Critique of Anthropology*, 34(1): 113–120.
Darnell, Regna. 1998. Toward a History of Canadian Departments of Anthropology: Retrospect, Prospect and Common Cause. *Anthropologia*, 40(2): 153–168.
Davis, Megan. 2008. Indigenous Struggles in Standard-Setting: The United Nations Declaration on the Rights of Indigenous Peoples. *Melbourne Journal of International Law*, 9(2): 439–471.
Defence Media. 2016. Army Aboriginal Community Assistance Programme Celebrates 20 Years of Service to Indigenous Communities. *Indigenous.gov.au*, 22 August 2016. Department of Defence. http://www.indigenous.gov.au/news-and-media/announcements/department-defence-army-aboriginal-community-assistance-programme. <accessed 10/12/2017>.
Deloria, Vine. 1969. *Custer Died for your Sins*. London: Collier-Macmillan.
Deloria, Vine. 1989. Laws Grounded in Justice and Humanity: Reflections on the Content and Character of Federal Indian Law. *Arizona Law Review*, 31: 203–223.

Deloria, Vine. 2004. Philosophy and Tribal Peoples. In A. Waters, ed. *American Indian Thought*, pp. 3–12. Malden, WA: Blackwell Publishing.

Diamond, Stanley, Bob Scholte and Eric Wolf. 1975. Anti-Kaplan "Defining the Marxist Tradition". *American Anthropologist*, 77(4): 870–876.

Dodson, Patrick. 2007. An Entire Culture is at Stake. *The Age*, 14 July, p. 9. http://www.theage.com.au/news/opinion/an-entire-culture-is-at-stake/2007/07/13/1183833765256.html. <accessed 22/12/2016>.

Duncan, Sam. 2017. Tony Abbott makes explosive call to enlist the ARMY to invade states and seize their natural gas — but is quickly slammed by colleagues who say 'we're not interested in a khaki solution'. *Daily Mail*, 3 October 2017. http://www.dailymail.co.uk/news/article-4928036/Tony-Abbott-suggests-army-INVADE-states-natural-gas.html#ixzz4vY0J1LJu. <accessed 12/10/2017>.

Dunning, Robert. 1959. *Social and Economic Change among the Northern Ojibwa*. Toronto: University of Toronto Press.

Durrell-Young, T, (2003) 'Cooperative Diffusion through Cultural Similarity' in Goldman, E.O. and Eliason, L.C. eds. *The Diffusion of Military Technology and Ideas*, pp. 93–113. Stanford: Stanford University Press.

Dyck, Noel. (ed.) 1985. *Indigenous Peoples and the Nation-State: Fourth World Politics in Canada, Australia, and Norway*. St. John's: Memorial University of Newfoundland, Institute of Social and Economic Research.

Dyck, Noel. 2006. Canadian Anthropology and the Ethnography of "Indian Administration". In J. Harrison and Regna Darnell (eds.) *Historicizing Canadian Anthropology*. Vancouver: UBC Press, pp. 78–92.

Eckermann, Ali Cobby. 2015. The Northern Territory Emergency Response: Why Australia will not recover from the Intervention. *Cordite Review*, 1 February 2015. http://cordite.org.au/essays/the-nt-emergency-response/. <accessed 12/10/2017>.

Elkin, Adolphus P. 1943. *Wanted — A Charter for the Native Peoples of the South West Pacific*. Sydney: Australasian Publishing Co.

Embee, John. 1939. *Suye Mura: A Japanese Village*. Chicago: University of Chicago Press.

Evans-Pritchard, Edward Evan. 1940. *Political System of the Anuak of Anglo-Egyptian Sudan*. London: London School of Economics.

Evans-Pritchard, Edward Evan. 1940. *The Nuer: A Description of the Modes of Livelihood and Political Institutions of a Nilotic People*. Oxford: Clarendon.

Evans-Pritchard, Edward Evan 1946. Applied Anthropology. *Africa*, 16(2): 92–98.

Evans-Pritchard, Edward Evan. 1949. *The Sanusi of Cyrenaica*. Oxford: Oxford University Press.

Fabian, Johannes. 1983. *Time and the Other: How Anthropology Makes its Object.* New York: Columbia University Press.
FaHCSIA. 2008. Northern Territory Emergency Response: One Year On. Canberra: Commonwealth of Australia. https://www.dss.gov.au/sites/default/files/documents/05_2012/nter_review.pdf . <accessed 28/11/2017>.
Falk, Richard. 1992. *Explorations at the Edge of Time: The Prospects for World Order.* Philadelphia: Tempe University Press.
Farish, Matthew. 2005. Archiving Areas: The Ethnographic Board and the Second World War. *Annals of the Association of American Geographers,* 95(3): 663–679.
———. 2010. *The Contours of America's Cold War.* Minneapolis: University of Minnesota Press.
Fassin, Didier, and Mariella Pandolfi, eds. 2010. Introduction: Military and Humanitarian Government in the Age of Intervention. *Contemporary States of Emergency: The Politics of Military and Humanitarian Interventions.* New York: Zone Books, pp. 9–25.
Fels, Marie. 1988. *Good Men and True: The Aboriginal Police of the Port Phillip District 1837–1853.* Melbourne: Melbourne University Press.
Ferguson, Brian. 2012. Plowing the Human Terrain. Laura McNamara and Robert Rubenstein eds. *Dangerous Liaisons.* Santa Fe: SAR Press, pp. 101–126.
Feuchtwang, Stephen. 1973. The Colonial Formation of British Social Anthropology. Talal Asad, ed. *Anthropology and the Colonial Encounter,* pp. 71–102. London: Ithaca Press.
Field, Henry. 1962. *"M" Project for F.D.R. Studies on Migration and Settlement.* Ann Arbor, Mich: Edwards Brothers.
Firth, Raymond. 1957. Siegfried Frederick Nadel 1903–1956. *American Anthropologist,* 59: 117–124.
Firth, Raymond. 1929. *Primitive Economics of the New Zealand Maori.* London: Routledge.
Firth, Raymond. 1936. *We, the Tikopia: A Sociological Study of Kinship in Primitive Polynesia.* London: Allen and Unwin.
Forster, Peter. 1994. Politics, Ethnography and the 'Invention of Tradition': The Case of T. Cullen Young in Livingstonia Mission, Malawi. *History and Anthropology,* 8(1–4): 299–320.
Fortes, Meyer. 1945. The Impact of the War on British West Africa. *International Affairs,* 21(2): 209–219.
Fortes, Meyer. 1953. The Structure of Unilinear Descent Groups. *American Anthropologist,* 55: 17–41.

Fortes, Meyer. 1959. Descent, Filiation and Affinity: A Rejoinder to Dr. Leach. *Man*, 59: 193–197, 206–212.

Forte, Maximilian. (ed.) 2011. *The New Imperialism: Militarism, Humanism and Occupation*. Montreal: Alert Press.

Fosher, Kerry (2013) *Considerations for Practicing Anthropology in Military Organizations*. In Riall Nolan (ed.), pp. 237–246. London: Wiley-Blackwell.

Foster, George. 2000. *An Anthropologist's Life in the Twentieth Century: Theory and Practice at UC Berkeley, the Smithsonian, in Mexico, and the World Health Organisation*. In Suzanne Riess, Regional Oral History Office, Bancroft Library, University of California, Berkeley.

Frank, Gunder. 1966. The Development of Underdevelopment. *Monthly Review Press* (September): 17–31.

Frank, Gunder. 1967. *Capitalism and Underdevelopment in Latin America*. New York: Monthly Review Press.

Furphy, Samuel. 2013. *Edward Curr and the Tide of History*. Canberra: ANU E Press.

Gagne, Natacha., and Marie Salaun 2012. Appeals to Indigeneity: Insights from Oceania. *Journal for the Study of Race, Nation and Culture*, 18(4): 381–398.

Geddes, William. 1945. *Deuba: A Study of a Fijian Village*. Wellington, N.Z.: Polynesian Society, Memoirs of the Polynesian Society; v. 22.

George, Lily. 2008. Articulating the Intellectual: Turangawaewae of an Indigenous Anthropologist. *Conference Proceedings (2010) Critical Mass: Building a National Maori Association of Social Sciences*. Te Herenga Waha Marae, Victoria University, June 11–13 2008.

Gibson, Chris. 1999. Cartographies of the Colonial/Capitalist State: A Geopolitcs of Indigenous Self-Determination in Australia. *Antipode*, 31(1): 45–79.

Gluckman, Max. 1971a. The Tribal Area in South and Central Africa. Leo Kuper and M.G. Smith eds. *Pluralism in Africa*. Berkeley: University of California Press, pp. 373–409.

Gluckman, Max. 1971b. Tribalism, Ruralism and Urbanism in Plural Societies. Lewis H. Gaan and Peter Duignan eds. *Colonialism in Africa*. Cambridge: Cambridge University Press, pp. 127–166.

Gonzales, Roberto. 2007. Phoenix Reborn? The Rise of the 'Human Terrain System'. *Anthropology Today*, 23(6): 21–22.

Gonzales, Roberto. 2008. 'Human Terrain' Past, Present and Future Applications. *Anthropology Today*, Vol. 24, No. 1, February.

Gonzalez, Roberto. 2009. *American Counterinsurgency: Human Science and the Human Terrain*. Chicago: Prickly Paradigm Press.

Goodall, Heather. 2006. *From Invasion to Embassy: Land in Aboriginal Politics in NSW from 1770 to 1972*. Sydney: Allen and Unwin.

Gurr, Ted Robert. 1993. Why Minorities Rebel: A Global Communal Mobilisation and Conflict since 1945. *International Political Science Review*, 14(2): 161–201.
Graburn, Nelson. 2006. Canadian Anthropology and the Cold War. In Julia Harrison and Regna Danell, eds. *Historicising Canadian Anthropology*. Vancouver: UBC Press, pp. 242–252.
Gray, Geoffrey. 1994. Piddingtons Indiscretion: Ralph Piddington, The Australian Research Council and Academic Freedom. *Oceania*, 64(3): 217–245.
Gray, Geoffrey. 2005. Australian Anthropologists and World War II. *Anthropology Today*, 21(3): 18–21.
Gray, Geoffrey. 2006. The Army Requires Anthropologists: Australian Anthropologists at War 1939-1946. *Australian Historical Studies*, 37: 127, 156–180.
Gray, Geoffrey. 2012. H. Ian Hogbin: Official Adviser on Native Affairs. Geoffrey Gray, Doug Munro and Christine Winter, eds. *Scholars at War: Australasian Social Scientists, 1939–1945*, pp. 73–93. Canberra: ANU E Press.
Gray, Geoffrey. 2012. W.E.H. Stanner: Wasted War Years. Geoffrey Gray, Doug Munro and Christine Winter, eds. *Scholars at War: Australasian Social Scientists, 1939–1945*, pp. 95–116. Canberra: ANU E Press.
Gray, Geoffrey., Doug Munro, Christine Winter. 2012. Introduction. In *Scholars at War: Australasian Social Scientists 1939–1945*. Canberra: ANU E Press, pp. 1–27.
Gray, Geoffrey., Christine Winter. 2012. The Australians. In Gray, Geoffrey., Doug Munro, Christine Winter, eds., *Scholars at War: Australasian Social Scientists 1939–1945*. Canberra: ANU E Press, pp. 29–34.
Green, Joyce. 1995. Towards a Detente with History: Confronting Canada's Colonial Legacy. *International Journal of Canadian Studies*, 12 (Fall): 85–105.
Grove, Richard. 1995. *Green Imperialism: Colonial Expansion, Tropical Island Edens and the Origin of Environmentalism, 1600–1860*. Cambridge: Cambridge University Press.
Haenn, Nora, and Richard Wilk. 2006. *The Environment in Anthropology: A Reader in Ecology, Culture and Sustainable Living*. New York: New York University Press.
Hage, Ghassan. 2010. Colonial Necrophilia. *Hage Ba'a*. 8 July 2010, blogspot. http://hageba2a.blogspot.com.au/2010/07/colonial-necrophilia.html. <accessed12/10/2017>.
Hage, Ghassan. 2015. Multiculturalism and the Islamic Question. *Processed Lives*. 22 June 2015, blog spot. http://processedlives.tumblr.com/post/122200204475/first-multiculturalism-despite-all-the-wonderful. <accessed 12/10/2017>.
Hage, Ghassan (2016) État de Siège: A Dying Domesticating Colonialism. *American Ethnology*, 43(1):1–22.

Headquarters Joint Operations Command. 2007/8. *CJOPS Post Operation Report (POR) — Operation Outreach*. Canberra: Australian Army General John Baker Complex. http://www.defence.gov.au/FOI/Docs/Disclosures/015_1718_Documents.pdf. <accessed 12/10/2017.

Hall, Anthony. 2003. *The American Empire and the Fourth World, Vol. 1: The Bowl with One Spoon*. Montreal: McGill-Queen's University Press.

Hall, Robert. 1991. Aborigines and Torres Strait Islanders in the Second World War, Desmond Ball, ed. *Aborigines in the Defence of Australia*. Canberra: Australian National University Press, pp. 32–63.

Hancock, David. 2010. Green Skin: Australia's Indigenous Army. *Australian Geographic*, 93 (Jan–Mar): 67–74.

Hancock, Robert. 2006. Toward a Historiography of Canadian Anthropology. In Julia Harrison and Regna Darnell (eds.) *Historicizing Canadian Anthropology*. Vancouver: UBC Press, pp. 30–43.

Hanks, Julien., and Jane Hanks. 1950. *Tribe under Trust: A Study of the Blackfoot Reserve of Alberta*. Toronto: University of Toronto Press.

Hanson, Allan. 1989. The Making of the Maori: Culture Invention and its Logic. *American Anthropologist*, 91: 890–90.

Henare, Amiria. 2007. Nga Rakua Te Pakeha: Reconsidering Maori Anthropology. In Jeanette Edwards, Penelope Harvey and Peter Wade; eds. *Anthropology and Science: Epistemologies in Practice*. New York: Berg Oxford, pp. 93–113.

Henderson, Anna. 2009. Chalmers Takes Charge of NT Intervention, again. *ABC News*, Wednesday, 28 October. http://www.abc.net.au/news/archive/?date=2009-10-28&page=10. <accessed 22/12/2016>.

Hinkson, Melinda. 2010. Introduction: Anthropology and Culture Wars. In Jon Altman and Melinda. Hinkson, eds. *Culture Crisis: Anthropology and Politics in Aboriginal Australia*. Sydney: University of New South Wales Press, pp. 1–13.

Hinton, Peter. 2002. The 'Thailand' Controversy Revisited. *The Australian Journal of Anthropology*, 13(2): 155–177.

Hipwell, William. 1997. Industria, The Fourth World and the Question of Territory. *Middle States Geographer*, 30: 1–10.

Hodge, Joseph. 2008. Recent Comparative Approaches to Imperial History and Settler Colonialism. *Journal of Southern African Studies*, 34(2): 451–470.

Hogbin, Ian. 1934. *Law and Order in Polynesia*. London: Christophers.

Hogbin, Ian. 1951. *Transformation Scene: The Changing Culture of a New Guinea Village*. London: Routledge Kegan Paul.

Hogbin, Ian., and Camilla Wedgwood. 1943. *Development and Welfare in the Western Pacific*. Canberra: Australian Institute of International Affairs.

Holcombe, Sarah. 2015. The Contingency of 'Rights': Locating Global Discourse in Aboriginal Central Australia. *The Australian Journal of Anthropology*, 26(2): 211–232.
Howard-Wagner, Deirdre. 2010. From Denial to Emergency: Governing Indigenous Communities in Australia. In Didier. Fassin and Mariella Pandolfi. *Contemporay States of Emergency: The Politics of Military and Humanitarian Interventions*. New York: Zone Books, pp. 217–239.
Howard-Wagner, Deirdre. 2012. Reclaiming the Northern Territory as a Settler-colonial Space. *Arena Journal*, 37/38: 220–240.
Huggins, Jackie. 1988. Firing on in the Mind: Aboriginal Domestic Servants. *Hecate*, 13(2): 5–23.
Huntsman, Judith. 2003. Raymond Firth 1901–2002. *American Anthropologist*, 105(2): 487–490.
Huygens, Ingrid. 2011. Developing a Decolonisation Practice for Settler Colonisers: Case from Aotearoa New Zealand. *Settler Colonial Studies*, 2(1): 53–81.
Hymes, Dell. (ed.) 1969. *Reinventing Anthropology*. New York: Random House.
International Work Group Indigenous Affairs (IWGIA). 2010. Canada Endorses UN Declaration on the Rights of Indigenous Peoples. International Work Group for Indigenous Affairs (IWGIA), 5 November 2010. http://www.iwgia.org/news/search-news?news?news_id=4.
Jorgensen, Joseph G, and Eric Wolf. 1970. A Special Supplement: Anthropology on the Warpath in Thailand. *The New York Review of Books*, November 19, 7pp.
Kaplan, David. 1974. The Anthropology of Authenticity: Everyman His Own Anthropologist. *American Anthropologist*, 76: 824–839.
Kennedy, Dane. 2005. *The Highly Civilized Man: Richard Burton and the Victorian World*. Cambridge MA: Harvard University Press.
Kilcullen, David. 2007. Two Schools of Classical Counterinsurgency. Small Wars Journal Blog, 27 January.
Kingfisher, Catherine, Jeff Maskovsky. 2008. Introduction: The Limits of Neoliberalism. *Critique of Anthropology*, 28(2): 4–9.
Kipp, Jacob *et al.* The Human System: A CORDS for the 21st century. Military Review, September–October.
Kirke, Charles (2005) Grappling with the Stereotype: British Army Culture and Perceptions, An Anthropology from within. Cranfield University. http://www.mngt.waikato.ac.nz/ejrot/cmsconference/2005/proceedings/recontextualising/kirke.pdf. <accessed 15 October 2013>.
Kirke, Charles (2009) A Soldier of the 71st — A Real Deal? An Ethnographic Approach to Authenticity. https://www.liverpool.ac.uk/media/livacuk/

schoolofmanagement/docs/abstracts/ethnography2009/Kirke.pdf. <accessed 15 October 2013>

Kirke, Charles (2010) Military Cohesion, Culture and Social Psychology. *Defense and Security Analysis*, 26(2): 143–159.

Kiste, Robert., Max Marshall. 1999. *American Anthropology in Micronesia: An Assessment*. Honolulu: University of Hawaii Press.

Kuper, Adam. 1986. An Interview with Edmund Leach. *Current Anthropology*, 27(4): 375–381.

Kymlicka, Will. 1998. *Finding Our Way: Rethinking Ethno-cultural Relations in Canada*. Toronto: Oxford University Press.

Lam, Maivan Clech. 1992. Making Room for Peoples at the United Nations: Thoughts Provoked by Indigenous Claims to Self-Determination. *Cornell International Law Journal*, 25(3): 603–622.

Lange, Matthew, James Mahoney, and Matthias vom Hau. 2006. Colonialism and Development: A Comparative Analysis of Spanish and British Colonies. *American Journal of Sociology*, 111(5): 1,412–1,462.

Leach, Edmund. 1951. The Structural Implications of Matrilineal Cross-Cousin Marriage. *Journal of the Royal Anthropological Institute*, 81: 23–55.

Leach, Edmund. 1954. *Political Systems of Highland Burma: A Study of Kachin Social Structure*. London: G. Bell.

Leach, Edmund. 1961. *Pul Eliya, a Village in Ceylon: A Study of Land Tenure and Kinship*. Cambridge: Cambridge University Press.

Leach, Edmund. 1977. In Formative Travail with Leviathan. *Anthropological Forum*, 4(2): 190–197.

Lindberg, Tracy. 2010. Contemporary Canadian Resonance of an Imperial Doctrine. In Miller, Robert, Jacinta Ruru, Larissa Behrendt and Tracy Lindberg. *Discovering Indigenous Lands: The Doctrine of Discovery in the English Colonies*. Oxford: Oxford University Press, pp. 126–170.

Lipset, David. 1980. *Gregory Bateson: The Legacy of a Scientist*. Englewood Cliffs, N.J., Prentice Hall.

Loizos, Peter. 1977. Personal Evidence: Comments on an Acrimonious Argument. *Anthropological Forum*, 4(2): 135–144.

Long, Jeremy. 1992. *The Go-Betweens: Patrol Officers in Aboriginal Affairs Administration in Northern Territory 1936–1974*. Canberra: North Australia Research Unit, Darwin.

Lyons, Oren. 1982. When You are Talking About Client Relations, You are Talking about the Future of Nations. *Rethinking Indian Law*. New York: National Lawyers Guild, Committee on Native American Struggles.

Macdonald, Judith. 2002. Sir Raymond Firth, 1901–2002. *Oceania*, 72(3): 153–155.

Maginnis, Robert (2005) ABCA: A Petri Dish for Multinational Interoperability. *Joint Services Quarterly*, 37: 53–57.

Mair, Lucy. 1948. *Australia in New Guinea*. London: Christophers.

Malinowski, Bronislav. 1922. *Argonauts of the Western Pacific: An Account of Native Enterprise and Adventure in the Archipelagos of Melanesian New Guinea*. London: G. Routledge and Sons.

Malinowski, Bronislav. 1929. Practical Anthropology. *Africa: Journal of the International African Institute*, 2(1): 22–38.

Martinez-Cobo, Jose. 1987. Special Rapporteur. Study of the Problem of Discrimination against Indigenous Peoples — Vol 5 — Conclusion, Proposals and Recommendations, p. 379. UNDocE/CN.4/Sub.2/1986/7/Add.4.

MASS, Maori Association of Social Scientists. (nd) http://www.mass.maori.nz/, <accessed 15 February 2012>.

McMullen, Jeff. 2012. Protector Macklin's Intervention. *Arena Magazine*. 20 April 2012. http://www.arena.org.au/2012/04/protector-macklin%E2%80%99s-intervention/.

McNamara, Laura and Robert Rubenstein, eds. 2011. *Dangerous Liaisons*. Santa Fe: SAR Press.

Manuel, George and Michael Posluns. 1974. *Fourth World: An Indian Reality*. Ontario: Collier-Macmillan Canada, Ltd.

Marcus, George. 2010. Experts, Reporters, Witnesses: The Making of Anthropologists in States of Emergencies. In Fassin, Didier, and Mariella Pandolfi, eds. 2010. *Contemporary States of Emergency: The Politics of Military and Humanitarian Interventions*. New York: Zone Books, pp. 357–378.

Marcus, George, and Michael Fischer. 1986. *Anthropology as Cultural Critique: An Experimental; Moment in the Human Sciences*. Chicago: University of Chicago Press.

Metge, J. 2000. Piddington, Ralph O'Reilly — Biography. *Dictionary of New Zealand Biography, Te Ara — the Encyclopaedia of New Zealand*. http://www.TeAra.govt.nz/en/biographies/5p28/1 <accessed 21/11/2011>.

Metge, Joan. 2013. The Politics of Knowledge: Anthropology and Maori Modernity in Mid-Twentieth-Century New Zealand. *History and Anthropology*, 24(4): 453–471.

Miles, Doug. 2008. Afternoon Light on the Thailand Controversy: An Afterward. *Asia Pacific Journal of Anthropology*, 9(3): 253–262.

Morgan, Lewis Henry. 1851. *League of the Ho-de-no-sau-ne, or Iroquois*. Rochester: Sage and Broa.

Morgan, Lewis Henry. 1870. *Systems of Consanguinity and Affinity of the Human Family*. Washington D.C.: Smithsonian Institution.

Morgan, Lewis Henry. 1877. *Ancient Society, or, Researches in the Lines of Human Progress from Savagery, through to Barbarism to Civilization.* New York: World Publishing.

Morris, Barry, and Andrew Lattas. 2010. Embedded Anthropology and the Intervention. *Arena Magazine.* http://www.arena.org.au/2010/09/embedded-anthropology-and-the-intervention/

Muehlebach, Andrea. 2001. "Making Place" at the United Nations: Indigenous Cultural Politics at the UN Working Group on Indigenous Populations. *Cultural Anthropology,* 16(3): 415–448.

Mulvaney, John. 1992. Donald Thomson's Report on the Northern Territory Coastal Patrol and Reconnaissance Unit 1941–43. *Aboriginal History,* 16(1): 1–57.

Munro, Doug. 2012. The New Zealanders. In Gray, Geoffrey., Doug Munro, Christine Winter. eds. *Scholars at War: Australasian Social Scientists 1939–1945.* Canberra: ANU E Press, pp. 163–170.

McFate, Montgomery. 2005a. Anthropology and Counterinsurgency: The Strange Story of their Curious Relationship. *Military Review,* 85(2): 24–38.

McFate, Montgomery. 2005b. The Military Utility of Understanding Adversary Culture. *Joint Force Quarterly,* 38: 42–48.

Nader, Laura. 1997. The Phantom Factor: Impact of the Cold War on Anthropology. In Noam Chomsky, Laura Nader, Immanuel Wallerstein, and Robert Lewontin (eds) *The Cold War and the University.* New York: New Press, pp. 107–146.

Nietschmann, Bernard. 1987. The Third World War. *Cultural Survival Quarterly,* 11(3): 1–16.

Nietschmann, Bernard. 1990. *The Unknown War: The Miskito Nation, Nicaragua and the United States.* New York: Freedom House.

Nietschmann, Bernard. 1994. The Fourth World: Nations versus States. In George Demko and William Wood (eds.), *Reordering the World: Geopolitical Perspectives in the Twenty-first Century.* New York: Seminar, pp. 225–242.

Oppenheim, Robert. 2008. On the Location of Korean War and Cold War Anthropology. *Histories of Anthropology Annual,* 4: 220–259.

Ortiz, Sutti. 2004. Sir Raymond Firth 1901–2002. *Proceedings of the American Philosophical Society,* 148(1): 129–133.

Parkinson, Louisa (2013) *Social Science and Cultural Awareness in Force Capability: Human Terrain, Influence Effects and Improving Human Centric Operations.* Defence Technology Agency Report 369. Auckland: New Zealand Defence Force.

Pearce, Guy. 2009. Quarry Vision: Coal, Climate Change and the End of the Resources Boom. *Quarterly Essay,* 33: 1–122.

Pels, Peter. 1997. The Anthropology of Colonialism: Culture, History, and the Emergence of Western Governmentality. *Annual Review of Anthropology*, 26: 163–183.

Pels, Peter., and Oscar Salemink. 1994. Introduction: Five Theses on Ethnography as Colonial Practice. *History and Anthropology*, 8(1–4): 1–34.

Peters, Emrys L. 1990. *The Bedouin of Cyrenaia: Studies in Personal and Corporate Power*. Cambridge: Cambridge University Press.

Pinkoski, Marc. 2008. Julian Steward, American Anthropology, and Colonialism. *Histories of Anthropology Annual*, 4: 172–204.

Pomeroy, John. 2012. A.P. Elkin: Public Morale and Propaganda. Geoffrey Gray, Doug Munro and Christine Winter, eds. *Scholars at War: Australasian Social Scientists, 1939–1945*, pp. 35–54. Canberra: ANU E Press.

Powell, Alan. 2003. *The Third Force: ANGAU's New Guinea War 1942–1946*. Melbourne: Oxford University Press.

Price, David. H. 2008. *Anthropological Intelligence: The Deployment and Neglect of American Anthropology in the Second World War*. Durham: Duke University Press.

Price, David. H. 2011. *Weaponizing Anthropology: Social Science in Service of the Militarized State*. Oakland: AK Press.

Radcliffe-Brown, Alfred Reginald. 1922. *The Andaman Islanders*. Glenkoe, Ill.: Free Press.

Radcliffe-Brown, Alfred Reginald. 1930–31. The Social Organisation of Australian Tribes. *Oceania*, 1: 34–63; 207–246; 322–341; 426–456.

Radcliffe-Brown, Alfred Reginald. 1952. *Structure and Function in Primitive Society*. London: Cohen and West.

Radcliffe-Brown, Alfred, and Daryll Forde., eds. 1950. *African Systems of Kinship and Marriage*. London: Oxford University Press.

Read, Kenneth. 1947. Effects of the War in the Markham Valley, New Guinea. *Oceania*, 18(2): 95–116.

Reid, Anthony. 1994. Early Southeast Asian Categories of Europeans. Stuart Schwartz ed. *Implicit Understandings: Observing, Reporting and Reflecting on the Encounters between Europeans and Other Peoples in the Early Modern Era*, pp. 268–294. Cambridge: University of Cambridge Press.

Riley, John, and Wilbur Schramm. 1951. *The Reds Take a City: The Communist Occupation of Soul*. New Brunswick, N.J.: Rutgers University Press.

Rivers, William Halse Rivers. 1906. *The Todas*. London: Macmillan.

Robinson, Kathy. 2004. Chandra Jayawarenda and the Ethical 'Turn' in Australian Anthropology. *Critique of Anthropology*, 24(4): 379–402.

Ronaasen, Sheree, Richard Clemmer and Mary E. Rudden. 1999. Rethinking Cultural Ecology, Multilinear Evolution, and Expert Witnesses: Julian Steward and the Indian Claims Commission, pp. 170–202. Richard Clemmer, David L. Meyers and Mary E. Rudden, eds. *Julian Steward and the Great Basin: The Making of an Anthropologist.* Salt Lake City: University of Utah Press.

Rosser, Bill. 1991. *Up Rode the Troopers: The Black Police in Queensland.* St Lucia: University of Queensland Press.

Rubenstein, Robert. 2008. *Peacekeeping under Fire.* Boulder: Paradigm Publications.

Scales, Robert. 2004. 'Army Transformation: Implications for the Future.' Testimony before US Armed Services Committee, 15 July. http://www.au.af.mil/au/awe/awcgatecongress/04-07-15scales-.pdf. <accessed 20/01/2018>.

Scoop.co.nz. 2007. Maori Party's head in the clouds. (http://www.scoop.co.nz/stories/PA0709/S00272.html) New Zealand government press release, via scoop.co.nz, 14 September 2007.

Scheper-Hughes, Nancy. 1995. The Primacy of the Ethical: Proposition for a Militant Anthropology. *Current Anthropology,* 36(3): 409–440.

Scott, Dick. 1975. *Ask that Mountain: The Story of Parihaka.* Auckland: Heinemann/Southern Cross.

Seligman, Charles Gabriel. 1910. *The Melanesians of British New Guinea.* Cambridge University Press.

Seligman, Charles Gabriel., and Brenda. Seligman., eds. 1911. *The Veddas.* Cambridge: Cambridge University Press.

Seligman, Charles Gabriel., and Brenda. Seligman. 1932. *Pagan Tribes of Nilotic Sudan.* Cambridge: Cambridge University Press.

Sheehan, Neil. 1988. *A Bright Shining Lie: John Paul Vann and America in Vietnam.* New York: Random House.

Shephard, Mark. 2009. *Australia's Nation Building: An Assessment of its Contribution to Regional Security in the Pacific, and a New Policy to Guide its Future.* Working Paper No. 413. Australian National University: Strategic and Defence studies Centre.

Shortland, Edward. 1851. *The Southern Districts of New Zealand: A Journal with Passing Notices of the Customs of the Aborigines.* London: Brown, Green and Longmans.

Simpson, Tony. 1979. *Te riri Pakeha: The White Man Anger.* Martinborough, NZ: Alister Taylor.

Simpson, Christopher. 1994. *Science of Coercion: Communication Research and Psychological Warfare.* New York: Oxford University Press.

Silverman, Sydel. 2005. The United States. In Fredrik Barth, Andre Gingrich, Robert Parkin, Sydel Silverman, *One Discipline Four Ways: British, German,*

French and American Anthropology. Chicago: University of Chicago Press, pp. 257–347.

Sluka, Jeff. 2010. Curiouser and Curiouser: Montgomery McFate's Strange Interpretation of the Relationship between Anthropology and Counterinsurgency. *PoLAR*, 33: 99–115.

Snowden, Warren. MP Minister for Defence Science and Personnel. 2008. Successful Conclusion to Operation Outlook. Canberra: *ParlInf*, Australian Government. https://www.aph.gov.au/Senators_and_Members/Parliamentarian?MPID=IJ4. <accessed 22/12/2016 >.

Spencer, Baldwin W., and Frank J. Gillen. 1899. *The Native Tribes of Central Australia.* London: Macmillan.

Sponsel, Leslie. 2006. Steward, Julian H., James Brix, ed. *Encyclopedia of Anthropology*, Vol. 5, pp. 2,128–2,130. Thousand Oaks CA: Sage.

Stanner, William Edward Hanley. (1949) Review of Australia in New Guinea. *International Affairs*, 25(3): 393–394.

Starn, Orin. 1986. Engineering Internment: Anthropologists and the War Relocation Authority. *American Ethnologist*, 13(4): 700–720.

Steward, Julian. 1936. The Economic and Social Basis of Primitive Bands. Robert Lowie, ed. *Essays on Anthropology in Honour of Alfred Louis Kroeber*, pp. 311–350. Berkeley: University of California Press.

Steward, Julian. 1955. *Theory of Culture Change: The Methodology of Multilinear Evolution.* Urbana: University of Illinois Press.

Stewart, Omar. 1985. The Shoshone Claims Case. Imre Sutton, ed. *Irredeemable America: The Indians' Estate and Land Claims*, pp. 187–206. Albuquerque: University of New Mexico Press.

Stocking, George. 1971. *What's in a Name? The Origins of the Royal Anthropological Institute.* Man (NS) 3: 369–390.

Stuff.co.nz. 2007. NZ indigenous rights stance 'shameful' — Maori Party. (http://www.stuff.co.mna/stuff/4202223a8153.html) Stuff.co.nz, 14 September 2007.

Sutton, Peter. 2009. *The Politics of Suffering: Indigenous Australia and the End of the Liberal Consensus.* Melbourne: Melbourne University Press.

Tambiah, Stanley. 2002. *Edmond Leach: an Anthropological Life.* Cambridge: Cambridge University Press.

Themner, Lotta and Peter Wallensteen. 2012. Armed Conflicts, 1946–2011. *Journal of Peace Research*, 49(4): 565–575.

Thomas, Nick. 1994. *Colonialism's Culture: Anthropology, Travel and Government.* London: Polity Press.

Thomson, Donald. 1953. War-Time Exploration in Dutch New Guinea. *The Geographical Journal*, 19(1): 1–16.

Toohey, Paul. 2008. *Soldier's Sympathy Intervenes*. The Australian, 22 November. http://www.theaustralian.com.au/archive/in-depth/soldiers-sympathy-intervenes/news-story/6e4e3a7dd1545331d73b13c9d3254c54. <accessed 22/12/2016>.

Tout. Dan. 2012. Stabilise, Normalise, Eliminate. *Arena Magazine*, 118: 40–43.

Trigger, David. 2014. Ethics and Politics. *The Australian Journal of Anthropology*, 25(3): 386–387.

Triggs, Gillian. 2015. *Northern Territory Intervention 2007*. Speech, Wednesday I July. Australian Human Rights Commission. https://www.humanrights.gov.au/news/speeches/northern-territory-intervention-2007. <accessed 22/12/2016>.

Trudgett, Michelle. 2014. When the Anths Come Marching In. *The Australian Journal Of Anthropology*, 25(3): 388–389.

Tully, James. 2000. The Struggles of Indigenous Peoples for and of Freedom. In Duncan Ivison, Paul Patton and Will Saunders (eds), *Political Theory and the Rights of Indigenous Peoples*. Cambridge: Cambridge University Press, pp. 36–59.

Tylor, Edward Burnett. 1871. *Primitive Culture: Researches into the Development of Mythology, Philosophy, Religion, Art and Custom.*, 2 vols. London: John Murray.

United Nations, 1990. Human Rights Committee, Fortieth Session. Summary Record of the 1,013th Meeting, U.N. Doc. CCPR/C/SR/205/.1013.

United Nations, 2007. United Nations Declaration on the Rights of Indigenous Peoples, UN GAOR, 61st sess.GA Res 61/295, UN Doc A/RES/47/1 (2007), http://www.un.org/esa/socdev/unpfii/en/drip.html.

United Nations, 2007. United Nations Declaration on the Rights of Indigenous Peoples, UN GAOR, 61st sess.GA Res 61/295, UN Doc A/RES/47/1 (2007), http://www.un.org/esa/socdev/unpfii/en/drip.html. <accessed 5/12/2011>.

UNPFII. United Nations Permanent Forum on Indigenous Issues. http://www.un.org./esa/socdev/unpfii/en/declaration.html. <accessed 5/12/2011>

UNPFII. 2011. *Declaration on the Rights on Indigenous Peoples*. United Nations Permanent Forum on Indigenous Issues. http://www.un.org./esa/socdev/unpfii/en/declaration.html <accessed 5/12/2011>.

Valentine, Douglas. 1990. *The Phoenix Program*. New York: Morrow.

Van Arsdale, Peter and Derrin Smith. 2010. *Humanitarianism in Hostile Territory*. Walnut Creek CA: Left Coast Press.

Veracini, Lorenzo. 2012. Settler Colonialism: A Global and a Contemporary Phenomenon. *Arena Journal*, 37/38: 322–336.

Wakin, Eric. 1992. *Anthropology Goes to War: Professional Ethics and Counterinsurgency in Thailand*. Center for Southeast Asia Studies, Madison WI: University of Wisconsin-Madison.

Wallace, Pamela. 2002. Indian Claims Commission: Political Complexity and Contrasting Concepts of Identity. *Ethnohistory*, 49(4): 743–766.
Wallerstein, Immanual. 1975. *The Modern World System, vol. 1: Capitalist Agriculture and the Origin of the European World-Economy of the Sixteenth Century.* New York: Academic Press.
Wax, Dustin. 2010. The Uses of Anthropology in the Insurgent Age. John Kelly, Beatrice Jaurequi, Sean Mitchell, Jeremy Walton, eds. *Anthropology and Global Counterinsurgencies*, pp. 153–167. Chicago: University of Chicago Press.
Webster, Donovan. 2003. *The Burma Road: The Epic Story of the China-Burma-India Theatre in World War II.* New York: Farrar, Straus and Giroux.
Webster, Steven. 1998. *Patrons of Maori Culture, Theory and Ideology in the Maori Renaissance.* Dunedin: University of Otago Press.
West, Andrew. 1994. Writing the Nagas: A British Officers Ethnographic Tradition. *History and Anthropology*, 8(1–4): 55–88.
Wetherell, David. 2012. Camilla Wedgwood: What are You Educating Natives for? Geoffrey Gray, Doug Munro and Christine Winter, eds. 2012. *Scholars at War: Australasian Social Scientists, 1939–1945*, pp. 117–132. Canberra: ANU E Press.
Weyler, Rex. 1992. *Blood on the Land.* Philadelphia and Gabriola Island: New Society Publishers.
Whyte, Jessica 2012. On the Politics of Suffering. *Arena Magazine*, 118: 37–39.
Wilmer, Franke 1993. *The Indigenous Voice in World Politics: Since Time Immemorial.* London: Sage.
Wimmer, Andreas, Lars-Erik Cederman and Brian Min. 2009. Ethnic Politics and Armed Conflict: A Configurational Analysis of a New Global Data Set. *American Sociological Review*, 74(April): 316–337.
Wolf, Eric. 1969. *Peasant Wars of the Twentieth Century.* New York: Harper & Row.
Wolfe, Patrick. 1994. "White Man's Flour": Doctrines of Virgin Birth in Evolutionist Ethnogenetics and Australian State-Formation. *History and Anthropology*, 8(1–4): 165–205.
Wolfe, Patrick. 1999. *Settler Colonialism and the Transformation of Anthropology: The Politics and Poetics of an Ethnographic Event.* London: Cassell.
Wolfe, Patrick. 2006. Settler Colonialism and the Elimination of the Native. *Journal of Genocide Research*, 8(4): 387–409.
Wolfe, Patrick. (2011). After the Frontier: Separation and Absorption in US Indian Policy. *Settler Colonial Studies*, 1: 13–51.
Worsley, Peter. 1970. The End of Anthropology. *Transactions of the Sixth World Congress of Sociology*, pp. 121–129. Madrid: International Sociological Association.
Wynn, L.L. 2014. Ethics Review Regimes and Australian Anthropology. *The Australian Journal of Anthropology*, 25(3): 373–374.

Index

AAA and the Australian Association of Social Anthropologists closed Australia debate 1972, 110

AAA denounced HTS as an unacceptable application of anthropological expertise, 8, 21, 217

AAA draft ethics Principles of Professional Responsibility, 95, 97

AAA Ethics Committee, 95, 108

AAA formal opposition to HTS, 8

ABCA 'alliance you never heard of', 4, 20

ABCA 'fight with Americans, not as Americans', 222

ABCA 'more cultural commonality than standardisation', 159

ABCA Anglo-Saxon alliance, 3–4

ABCA Anglo-Saxon foundational bond, 4

ABCA appreciation of cultural intelligence, 216

ABCA Armies, 4–6, 8, 10, 17, 21, 161, 163, 176, 217, 221

ABCA data analysis and ethical acceptability, 17

ABCA development of doctrine and future force development objectives, 222

ABCA force projection, 5

ABCA formalised arrangement, 4

ABCA interoperability, 159

ABCA relationship with intelligence and targeting, 10, 21

ABCA represented 'cultures that could work together' in Canadian army, 160

ABCA shared cultural affinities, 5

ABCA war-fighting, 5

Aboriginal 'proscribed' communities resembles martial law, 181

Aboriginal assimilation, 35, 38

Aboriginal forced compliance with NT civil–military intervention 2007, 218

Aboriginal frontier, 36–37
Aboriginal owned communities constructed as failed social enclaves, 184
Aboriginal people forced compliance with NT civil–military intervention, 181, 184–185, 187
Aboriginal small-scale fighting on the frontier, 37
Aboriginal spear tradition, 36
Aboriginals colonised without citizenship, political or civil rights, used in pursuit of war aims, 60, 75, 87
Alfred Haddon (1855–1940), 23, 29, 41, 55, 60, 83
Alfred Reginald Radcliffe-Brown (1881–1955), 50
Ali Cobby Eckermann, 182
America, Britain, Canada, Australia and New Zealand (see also ABCA), 3–5, 9–10, 18, 20, 86, 160, 174, 211, 216, 221
American and Australian Armies 'give a shit' about cultural intelligence, 217
American Anthropological Association (see also AAA), 8, 21, 46, 89, 93, 95–96, 108, 124, 171, 176, 217
American Applied Anthropology Unit (see also AAU), 43, 48
American Bureau of Indian Affairs (see also BIA), 43, 47–48, 123
American Museum of Natural History, 27
American WWII brain trust, 59, 61, 63, 87
American WWII FBI Special Intelligence Service (see also SIS), 59, 61, 65, 87, 212

American WWII M project, 59, 61–62
American WWII Office of Strategic Services (see also OSS), 59, 61, 66, 68, 87, 212
American WWII Office of War Information (see also OWI), 59, 61, 64
American WWII War Relocation Authority (see also WRA), 43, 61
Ancient Society (1877), 26
Andre Gunder Frank, 121
Anglo-Saxon history and heritage, 5, 20, 221
Anglo-Saxon settler colonialism, 10, 21, 211
Anglo-Saxon values, 222
Anthropological knowledge, 3, 19, 44, 50, 55, 57, 70, 75, 83, 98, 107, 212
Anthropologists in Canadian Army not engaged in HUMINT counterinsurgency intelligence, 166–167
Anthropology inside knowledge of the powerless, 110
Anthropology institutionalised in museums and government agencies, 27
Anthropology intervention 1970s between indigenous peoples and Canadian society, 106
Anthropology invented to support warfighting in the tribal zone, 7
Anti-Vietnam war teach-in, 93
Applied anthropology, 44, 48, 50, 52, 57, 70–71, 156, 213
Arawa, 199–200, 204
Armed conflict in the 21st century, 3, 5, 15, 20, 22

Index

Armed conflict prevention and peacemaking, 2, 19
Army Aboriginal Community Assistance Program (*see also* AACAP), 191–192
Arunta living savagery unaware conception result of sexual intercourse, 35
Assimilation experiment, 189, 194
Asymmetrical enemies, 5
Australia 'breeding them white', 24
Australia 1967 referendum, 131, 190
Australia classicist persistence of anthropology, 132, 213
Australia ethnocide, 24
Australia New Left political activism critiqued American Vietnam policy, 107
Australia *terra nullius*, 24, 36, 42, 213
Australia threatened by yellow peril communist menace, 90, 107, 112
Australian Army counterinsurgency in Afghanistan 'created for targeting Taliban leaders', 169, 177
Australian Army five-person HTS team a kinder, 'gentler form of counterinsurgency', 174, 178
Australian Civil–Military Centre (*see also* ACMC), 19
Australian New Guinea Administrative Unit (*see also* ANGAU), 73–74, 79, 81
Australian settler colonialism part of British global colonisation, 36
Autonomy, 15, 22

Barnham I and II emphasised New Zealand Army and Maori cultural practices, 205, 220

Battle-space, 8
Bernard Q Nietschmann (1941–2000), 151
Biomedical models of compulsory research ethics discourage practice of ethnography, 116
Bisnis, 197–198, 200
Boasians, 61, 117
Bougainville armed conflict continued until 1997, 204
Bougainville armed conflict involved cultural history, identity, land, and matrilineality, 196, 219
Bougainville Autonomous vote 2015 and Independence vote 2020, 221
Bougainville Copper Limited (*see also* BCL), 197–202
Bougainville materially and spiritually matrilineal, 196
Bougainville nation against state armed conflict, 196, 209–210
Bougainville nation reconciliation process 2000, 209
Bougainville Pakeha and Maori banter and deployment to marae together, 207
Bougainville Revolutionary Army (*see also* BRA), 196, 200, 202, 219
Bougainvillean identity, 200, 202
BRA in 1995 excluded Australia from future participation in conflict resolution, 204
BRA, 202–204
Breaks doctrine of sovereignty, 3
British 19th century evolutionism and Empire, 212
British anthropology 1930s–1960s, 89, 98, 112, 212

British Army Cultural Advisors
  (*see also* CULADS), 9, 173, 177
British colonialism, 11, 33, 99
British HTS chain of command
  disconnects observer from decider,
  173–174
British Intelligence monitored
  economic and ideological
  developments in West Africa, 68
British structural functional
  juggernaut, 98
Bureau of American Ethnology, 23,
  26, 41, 212
Burma ethnographic fieldwork
  frontier Kachin highlands 1939,
  69, 71
Burnham Declaration Honiara and
  Barnham in New Zealand
  reconciliation and demilitarisation
  on Bougainville 1997, 205, 220
Burnham II Bougainville factions
  together and added PNG, 205,
  220

Camilla Hildegarde Wedgwood
  (1901–1955), 80
Canada Anthropology Division of the
  National Museum, early 20th
  century, 34, 51
Canada cold war academic
  anthropologists into applied
  research and social conflict, 60, 72
Canada Confederation in 1867, 30
Canada Department of Indian Affairs
  1880s, 24, 41, 213
Canada eliminationist-assimilationist
  policy, 24, 32, 41
Canada indigenous land resistance,
  128
Canada oppression of assimilated and
  naturalised indigenous peoples,
  26, 31
Canada White Paper (1969)
  "exchange" for "extinguishment",
  126
Canada, Australia, New Zealand and
  the US (*see also* 'CANZUS') UN
  group, 16–17, 141–143, 145–150,
  156, 215
Canadian ethnographers investigated
  nation-state relations 1960s, 110,
  116
CANZUS united against the
  Declaration on the Rights of
  Indigenous Peoples, 141–143
Carleton Stevens Coon (1904–1981),
  61, 66
Cash-cropping and *bisnis* crisis,
  197
Cash-cropping, 197–198, 200
Chaperone system, 179, 183, 218
Charter of the Assembly of First
  Nations (July 1985), 127
Child Health Check Teams
  (*see also* CHCTs), 182–183
Chrysanthemum and the Sword, 65
Civil Operations and Revolutionary
  Development Support (*see also*
  CORDS), 7, 21, 89, 94, 111, 212
Civil–military management, 2
Civil–military occupations of tribal
  and indigenous peoples, 2, 19
Civil–military operations, 1–2, 17–18,
  192
Civil–military shifting characteristics
  of adversaries, 3, 19
Classicist persistence of Australian
  anthropology, 132

Closely associated with government, 52
Clyde K.M. Kluckhohn (1905–1960), 64
Cold War area-study programs, 64
Cold War to 1990 227 nations in political protest and rebellion, 154, 157
Cold War to 2005 110 nation against state conflicts, 155
Colonial necrophilia, 189, 191, 194–195
Colonial Social Science Research Council (*see also* CSSRC), 68–69, 85, 87, 100
Colonial strategy social anthropology, 212
Commanders Emergency Response Program, 168
Commoditisation of land, 185
Common-law legal system, 5, 20, 221
Commonwealth 'Operational Centre' humanitarian operational space for WoG, NGO and volunteers, 179
Commonwealth 'Operational Centre', 179, 184, 218
Community analyst program, 43, 48, 62
Complex insurgency, 5
Conflation of military and humanitarian operations, 3, 20, 157
Conflict amongst the people, 142, 152, 157, 166, 205–206, 220
Contractor research anthropologists not subject to Australian Army Uniform Code of Military Justice, 171, 177
"Couldn't Tell Me Who to Whack", 165, 215

Counterinsurgency balances security and development tasks, kinetic and non-kinetic effects, 8, 10, 20, 216
Counterinsurgency Vietnam War, 14
Counterinsurgency, 3–4, 8, 14, 20–21, 69, 89, 93, 95, 103, 106, 111, 167–169, 174, 177, 193, 203, 213
Creation of an Autonomous Bougainville Government 2001, 210
Crisis of state borders, 10
Cross Cultural Survey 1937, 63
Crush, suppress, and smother resistance, 159, 171–172, 177, 216
Cultural ecology, 117, 120
Cultural empathy creates pussycats, 163
Cultural field research among local population for planning, execution and assessment of operations, 8–9, 20–21, 216
Cultural intelligence advice to commanders, 9, 21
Cultural intelligence, 4, 17, 26, 61, 65, 71, 160, 163, 165, 167, 169, 172, 174, 177, 221–222
Cultural research as intelligence, 18, 64
Cultural research dual trap used for 'reconstruction or killing', 171, 176–177, 217
Cultural-centric counterinsurgency, 6
Culturalisation of political conflict, 186, 194
Culturalised border for Aboriginal citizen residents, 185
Culture defined, 6
Culture generally, 24, 29, 41
Culture was intolerant and censorious, 52
Cyril Shirley Belshaw (1921–), 83

David Hyndman, 19, 143
David Goodman Mandelbaum (1911–1987), 67
Declaration on the Rights of Indigenous Peoples (*see also* DRIP), 14–15, 17, 141, 144–145, 149, 156 190, 215
Defence in armed conflict phase, 2, 19
Defensive/liberator as opposed to offensive/occupier, 103
Derek John Freeman (1916–2001), 84
Directorate of Research and Civil Affairs (*see also* DORCA), 53, 60, 77–78, 86–87, 213
Discourses of 'culture' and 'ethnography' under and for colonial rule, 101
Displacing them from the land, 11
Diversity of national approaches, 222
Division of the Supreme Command for Allied Powers (*see also* SCAP), 91–92
Domestic dependent nations in America, 23, 211
Donald Finlay Fergusson Thompson (1901–1970), 74
Draft Declaration on the Rights of Indigenous Peoples 1994, 16, 149
DRIP anti-settler manifesto, 157
DRIP fought against by CANZUS, 167, 215
DRIP new international legal and norm-making instrument 2007, 157
DRIP not legally binding instrument under international law, 150
DRIP reconstructs the international indigenous legal norm, 145
DRIP sets out collective rights of indigenous peoples, 148, 150
DRIP shifts the discussion from domestic nations to international nations, 145
Dual trap of cultural research when used for 'reconstruction or killing', 171, 176–177, 217

Edmund Ronald Leach (1910–1989), 71
Edward Evan Evans-Pritchard (1902–1973), 67
Edward Burnett Tylor (1832–1917), 28, 33
Effects of the War in the Markham Valley, New Guinea, 80
Eliminating native nations, 11
Empire epitomised use of cultural intelligence for British Army, 160
Eric Wolf "*Europe and the People Without History*" (1982), 122
Eric Robert Wolf (1923–1999), 95, 120
Ethical clearances, 19
Ethnic Power Relations (*see also* EPR) project, 142, 155, 157, 215
Ethnocide informed evolutionary anthropology and settler colonialism, 24, 35
Ethnographic affinity, 156
Ethnographic Board (1942), 59, 61, 63, 87
Ethnography 19th century offshoot of colonial intelligence, 22–23
Ethnography production of meaning, 110
Evolutionary anthropologists 19th century part of settler colonial intelligence, 13, 22
Evolutionary anthropology recreated prehistory, 34

Felix M. Keesing (1902–1961), 85
Feminism, 125
Find, fix and finish the enemy, 170, 174, 177, 216
First nation title by 11 numbered treaties, 30
First Nations, 13, 30, 34, 90, 106, 116, 129, 140, 213
Fourth World ancient nations encapsulated within states, 141–142, 151–152, 157
Fourth World, 15, 106, 116, 129, 140, 141, 151–152, 157, 213–214
Francis Ona, 201
Fred Siegfried Nadel (1903–1956), 81
Fredrik Weybye Barth (1928–2016), 124
From Foragers to Fighters: South Africa's Militarisation of the Namibian San (1982), 151

Genealogical methodology, 29
George "Pete" Murdock (1930–2012), 63
Global ethnographic surveillance, 4
Goals of native title and land rights regimes, 132
Green skin talents considered 'instinctive', 188–189, 195, 219
Green skin, 179, 187–188, 195, 219
Gregory Bateson (1904–1980), 61, 66
Group rights claimed within state structures, 221

Haddon second Torres Strait expedition 1898, 23, 29, 41
Harvey Feit, 129
Haudenosauee, 129
Hegemonic settler colonial societies without ancestral homeland, 145

Herbert Hoover FBI Director, 65
Historical particularism, 43, 46
Honour the Treaty 1984, 137
HTS: A CORDS for the 21st century, 7
HTS anthropological research as a stream of intelligence supports targeting, 170, 174, 177, 216
HTS as operational and tactical tool of counterinsurgency, 6
HTS operational environment 'only five minutes available to ask one question', 173, 178
HTS people as geographical space to be conquered, 7
HTS people as territory to be captured, 7
HTS program counterinsurgency to 'crush, suppress, and smother' resistance, 216
HTS research in the Canadian Army for writing intelligence, 170
Hugh Brody *"Maps and Dreams: Indians and the British Columbia Frontier"* (1981), 129
Human ecology, 120
Human Relations Area Files (*see also* HRAF), 59, 61, 63, 87
Human Terrain System (*see also* HTS), 2, 6, 9, 18, 20, 159, 171–172
Humanitarian space, 166, 192, 216
Humanitarianising naturalises conflict, 3
Hybrid warfare, 5

1934 *Indian Reorganisation Act*, 46
Ian Priestly Hogbin (1904–1989), 60, 77, 79

Immanuel Maurice Wallerstein (1930–) "*The Modern World-System*" (1974), 121
Indian blood quanta, 49
Indian Claims Commission (*see also* ICC), 117–120
Indian New Deal, 48, 62
Indians, the original communist menace, 45
Indigeno-scape, 15
Indigenous allotment in America, 26, 45
Indigenous militancy claimed Fourth World, 151, 157, 214
Indigenous people of New Zealand: Maori, 13
Indigenous peoples Arctic Cold War frontline, 104
Indigenous peoples of America: Native Americans, Inuit and Hawaiians, 12
Indigenous peoples of Australia: Aboriginals, Torres Strait Islanders, 13
Indigenous peoples of Canada: First Nations, Metis and Inuit, 13
Indigenous removal in America, 25
Institute of Pacific Relations, 78, 83, 85
Institute of Social Anthropology (*see also* ISA), 1943, 59, 61, 64, 87
Internationalised conflicts, logic of interventionism and state of exception, 158
Internationalised intrastate armed conflicts and disasters, 3, 20, 142, 155
Interpretivism, 116, 122
Interveners and intervenes power inequalities, 3
Interventionism political innovation, 3

Intrastate internationalised interventions nine (24%) for control of government, 142, 155–156, 158, 215
Intrastate war, 153, 196, 215, 219
Invention of two distinct idealised and reified images of Maori culture, 138

Japanese Behavior Patterns, 65
John Fee Embree (1908–1950), 64
John Paul Vann (1924–1972), 94
John Wesley Powell, 26
Jorgensen and Wolf (1970), 108–109
Julian Haynes Steward (1902–1972), 64, 117

Kachin counterinsurgency tactics, 103
Kago, 197, 200
Karawong and Jaba rivers social and ecological disaster, 198
Kawanatanga (a more limited power of governorship), 117, 137, 140
Kenneth Read, 60, 77, 80
Kinetic tactics, 6
Korean War, 4, 91–92, 105

Land is our life, 199
Landowners only receive occupancy fees, 197–198
Late 20th century intrastate war fought over indigenous nation geography, 153
Levels of sociocultural integration, 118–119
Lewis Henry Morgan, 23, 26
Lincoln Agreement Peace Monitoring Group under Australian control 1998, 208
Little Children Are Scared (2007), 180

Local cultures, 24, 29, 41
London School of Economics, 49, 53, 67–69, 79–80, 83–85, 98
Lucy Philip Mair (1901–1986), 60, 77, 79

Major General Chalmers promotes Aboriginal culture as classicist persistence, 180, 184, 188, 193, 195–196, 218–219
Major-General Dave Chalmers uniformed field commander, 180
Mal Brough, 181, 187
Malinowski's colonial strategy, 44
Manuel and Poslurs (1974), 214
Maori 19th century anthropological subjects and analysts, 24
Maori activist Titewhai Harawere challenged academic anthropologists, 138
Maori anthropologists revitalised Maori culture and language, 136
Maori approaches to being a nation within a state, 220–221
Maori Cultural Group in Operation Bel Isi used 'guitars not guns', 204, 206
Maori Cultural Group successful cultural knowledge for Bougainville reconciliation, 221
Maori cultural practices, 205, 220
Maori fishing rights, 137
Maori movement to gain self-determination, 136
Maori musket wars 1807–1842, 38
Maori rejection of invention of tradition anthropology, 138
Marilyn Strathern (1941–), 125
Marshall David Sahlins (1930–), 93
Marxism, 116, 122, 125

Materialism, 115, 120, 122
Max Gluckman (1911–1975), 67, 70
Mead committee AAA, 96
Metis, 13, 32, 105
Meyer Fortes (1906–1983), 67–68
Mick Dodson, 147, 187
Militarisation of ancient nations, 143
Militarised anthropology ethical opposition, 10, 13, 17, 21–22
Military intelligence in Ethiopia, Libya, Sudan and Syria, 69
Military operational space in Aboriginal owned communities, 182–183
Military operational space, 179–180, 182–183, 193, 218
Minorities at Risk (*see also* MAR) project, 142, 153, 157, 215
Modernisation theory, 121
Montgomery McFate, 6–7
Moses Havini, 203
Multi-agency collaboration, 2
Multi-agency, WoG coordination in post-ceasefire peace phases, 180
Mundial Upheaval Society, 120

1993–1997 nation against state armed conflicts, 142
Napidokae Navitu, 200
Nasioi, 196–201
Nation against state armed conflicts, 24, 142, 152–155, 215
Nation and state borders coexist within same settler colonial space, 211, 221
Nation and state borders, 11, 21, 179, 211, 221
Nation and state coexist same global space, 11

Nation defined, 142
National Museum in Ottawa, 44
National Museum of the Smithsonian, 27
Native Title Act 1993, 133, 150
Negative humbugging, 180, 184, 218
Neutralisation, 7, 21
New Aboriginal sociocultural institutions and spatial order considered 'negative humbugging', 180, 184, 218
New model of governance, 184, 194
New PLA leadership of matriclan landowner Perpetua Serero, 201
New Zealand and Canadian Armies similar relationships with indigenous peoples, 146, 151
New Zealand Army 'I am Scottish but I have a marae', 161–162, 206
New Zealand Army 'interoperability meant Hilux's not Humvees', 160
New Zealand Army tribe opened their marae 1995, 161, 206
New Zealand Army use of cultural intelligence, 164
New Zealand Dominion Museum, 44, 55, 57, 214
New Zealand Wars 1845–1872 over Maori land, 24, 40, 42
No environmental impact study (BCL), 198
Noel Dyck "*Indigenous Peoples and the Nation-State: Fourth World Politics in Canada, Australia and Norway*" (1985), 129
Nonstate actor enemies, 5
NORFORCE 'Australia's Indigenous Army', 181

North West Mobile Force (*see also* NORFORCE), 181–183, 187–188, 193, 195, 219
Northern Research Coordination Centre (*see also* NRCC), 105
Northern Kachin Levies guerrilla forces against the Japanese, 72
Northern Territory Emergency Response, known commonly as NT Intervention, 180
Northern Territory Special Reconnaissance Unit (*see also* NTSRU), 60, 75, 87
Nunavut, 127

Office of War Information (*see also* OWI), 59, 61, 64
Omer Call Stewart (1908–1991), 119
Ona declares independent republic of Bougainville May 1990, 202
Operation Bel Isi 'Pacific Way' Pacific solutions to Pacific problems, 196, 219
Operation Outreach, 179–183, 188, 193, 218
Operation Outreach 'insertion of governance', 183
Operation Outreach controversial civil policing function, 193, 196, 219
Operation Outreach included 600 soldiers with 400 'green skins' from 'Australia's Indigenous Army', 179, 181, 183, 218
Organic Act Rejected in the Cordillera: Dialectics of a Continuing Fourth World War (1991), 151

Pacific Way, 166–167, 196, 205, 210, 220

Paedophile rings, 187, 194
Panguna labour unrest and interethnic hostilities, 200
Panguna Landowners Association (*see also* PLA), 200, 201
Panguna Landowners Association (1987), 198
Panguna mine, 196, 198, 202, 219
Parasitic anthropological dependence on Native Americans, 115, 123, 139, 212
Peabody Museum, 27, 66
Peasant Wars of the Twentieth Century, 93
Peasants, 93
Period from 1989–2011 included 137 armed conflicts, 142, 155
Permissive environments, 179, 182, 218
Peter Buck (Te Rangi Hiroa), 44, 54, 213
Phoenix program, 7, 21, 89, 94–95, 111, 212
'Plug and play' social scientists in American army, 172
Piddington in 1950s and 1960s trained new generation of anthropologists in New Zealand, 111
Piddington proponent of action anthropology empowering indigenous people, 111
PNG and the BRA signed the Endeavor Accord 1990, 204
PNGDF Operation Footloose counterinsurgency strategic hamleting tactic, 203
Political climate made contemporary Maori ethnography unfeasible and unsolicited, 139

Political ecology, 120
Political economy and interpretive debate, 120
Political exodus of 125,000 students for sanctuary in Canada during Vietnam War, 112
Political Systems of Highland Burma (1954), 71–72
Politically active Maori anthropologists, 91, 111, 113, 214
Politically die, 189, 194
Politicide, 191, 195
Population and insurgency-centric intelligence for kinetic operations, 167, 177, 216
Population-centric for the control of people, 7
Post-ceasefire peacekeeping and peacebuilding, 2, 19
Post-colonial state-building by nation-destroying, 154
Primitive Culture (1871), 28
Professor A. P. Elkin, U Sydney 1933–1956, 44, 52–53, 74
Professor A. R. Radcliffe-Brown, 44, 52
Professor Bronislaw Kasper Malinowski (1884–1942), 49, 67
Professor Franz Uri Boas salvage ethnography (1858–1949), 51
Professor Gerald Duane Berreman (1930–2013), 95, 122
Professor Julian Steward, 64, 117
Project Camelot (1964), 67, 93–94
Property in America starts where Indianness stops, 25
Provincial Reconstruction Teams (*see also* PRT), 168, 181, 192
Psy-op counterinsurgency, 95

Public Opinion and Sociological Research (*see also* PO&SR), 91

Quarry vision, 191, 195

Radcliffe-Brown structural functionalism orthodoxy, 97
Radical Caucus AAA, 95–96
Ralph Piddington (1906–1974), 52
Raymond William Firth (1901–2002), 52–55, 67–69
Red Power Movement, 115–116, 123, 139, 212
Referendum on independence by 2020, 210
Regimes of neoliberal audit culture, 134
Reinventing Anthropology by Dell Hymes (1969), 90, 99, 112, 121–123, 156
Republic of Bougainville and PNG signed Honiara Declaration of Peace, Reconciliation and Rehabilitation 1991, 204
Research Grant: 'Anthropology, Counterinsurgency and Civil–Military Relations for Stabilisation, Peace-building and Conflict Prevention' 2012–2013, 19
Research: case study analyses, 19
Research: content analysis, 17–19
Research: ethnography, 13, 17
Rhodes-Livingstone Institute (*see also* RLI), 70–71, 99–100
Richard Clemmer, 123
Richard Francis Burton, 14, 28
Richard Lee and Susan Hurlich, 143
Right to intervene, 187, 192–194

Right to self-determination cornerstone of DRIP, 143–144, 148, 150
Road Mine Tailings Trust Fund (*see also* RMTL), 198
Robert Paine, 129
Royal Anthropological Institute 1871, 28
Ruth Fulton Benedict (1887–1948), 64

Sally Saunders, 129
Salvage ethnography, 24, 33–34, 41, 43, 45, 51, 212–213
Sam Kauna, 202
Samuel Lothrop, 65
Sanusiya by Evans-Pritchard (1949), 102
School of Civil Affairs (later ASOPA), 53, 74, 78, 80–82
Scientists as Spies, 43, 46, 56, 212
Self-determination, 3, 15, 22, 30, 129, 132, 136, 144–145, 148–151 180, 187, 190, 195, 214, 219
Self-management, 15, 22
Settler colonial needs the native in order to remain privileged, 25, 31, 42
Settler colonial societies permanent state of exception, 11
Settler colonialism logic, 10
Settler colonialism produces indigenous and settler, 142
Settler culture, 10
Sex checks perilous task, 182–183
Shoshonean people, 119
Shuswap Chief George Manuel, 151, 214
Similar institutions of political and bureaucratic governance, 5, 20, 221

Sir Ian "Hugh" Kawharu, 90, 111, 113, 136
Smithsonian Institution, 59, 61, 63, 87
Snowing white, 180, 184, 218
Social anthropology useful to colonial administration, 49, 100
Social anthropology, 44, 49–51, 53, 56, 87, 99–100, 111, 212
Social time bomb, 201
Sovietisation, 91–92
Special Rapporteur Professor James Anaya, 189
'Stabilise, normalise, exit' for protection of Aboriginal child health, 181
State border that separates different states, 211
State border, 11, 21, 179, 211, 221
State defined, 142
State efforts to control resources stimulated resistance by adversely-affected nations, 154
State of exception, 3, 10–11, 20, 158
State vs insurgency armed conflicts 13 (35%) for control of government, 157, 215
State vs nation armed conflicts 15 (41%) for control of territory, 157
Strategic Hamlet Programs, 94
Structural functional research used in American Army to identify local tribes and tribal leaders, 167, 217
Structural functionalism as neutral research observer challenged, 108
Structural functionalism, 97, 100–101, 107–108, 124
Student Mobilization Committee (*see also* SMC), 95, 108
Sutton 'moralised culture', 190, 194

Sutton 'rights agenda', 190, 194
Sutton "*The Politics of Suffering*" (2009), 187
Sydel Finfer Silverman (1933–), 212

'Take them by the balls and their hearts and minds will follow', 167, 177, 216
Talal Asad "*Anthropology and the Colonial Encounter*" (1973), 98, 112
Targeting to 'find, fix and finish the enemy', 170, 174, 177, 216
Targeting, 8, 10, 21, 165, 167, 169, 172, 177, 216
Te Tiriti o Waitangi 1840, 137
Temporality of emergency, 3, 20, 158
Temporary 'safe house' accommodation, 183
Termination policy, 123
Thailand counterinsurgency controversy University of Sydney anthropology department, 106
The Fourth World: Nations Versus States (1994), 151
The Reds Take a City, 89, 91–92
The Third World War (1987), 151
Theory of Culture Change (1959), 117–118
Third World War Project, 142, 153, 157, 215
Tino rangatiratanga (sovereignty), 117, 137, 140
TMG domination of the Maori, 206
Traditionally high economic and social status of women expressed through kinship relations, 209
Transnational enemies, 5

Treaty of Waitangi Act 1975, 136
Tribal Research Centre (*see also* TRC), 108–109

UN Permanent Forum on Indigenous Issues (*see also* UNPFII) 2000, 17, 135, 144–145
Unarmed Truce Monitoring Group (TMG), 206, 220
Uncritical of Aboriginal policy and practice, 52
United Nations (UN) 'Working Group on Indigenous Populations' (*see also* WGIP), 15, 22
Uppsala Conflict Data Program (*see also* UCDP), 142, 155, 157, 215
Urgency from war and disaster justifies exception of civil–military intervention, 218
US Agency for International Development (*see also* USAID), 94

Victim danger from war and disaster justification for urgent exception of intervention, 3, 20
Viet-cong, 89, 94, 111, 212
Vietnam War, 7, 14, 46, 89–90, 92, 95, 97, 104–105, 108, 111–112, 121, 125, 212–213
Vine Deloria "*Custer Died for Your Sins*" (1969), 99, 123, 138

W. F. H. Stanner (1905–1981), 77–78, 81
Waitangi Treaty 1840, 24–25, 40, 42, 117, 137, 140, 214

Waitangi Tribunal, 136–137
War amongst the people, 163–164, 176, 216, 219
Wardship American Indians, 23, 25, 41, 211
Washington/Cambridge axis, 27
WGIP biocultural diversity, 16
WGIP ecology and ethnicity, 15
WGIP escaped anthropological attention, 15, 22, 214
WGIP global institution for indigenous identity, 15
'Who do the bad guys look like, they look like the people', 167, 205, 216
Whole of government coordination (*see also* WoG), 2, 19
William Robert Geddes (1916–1989), 84
WoG, NGO and volunteers on-ground 'taskforce', 180, 184
Women matrilineal landowners led protests, 197
World War II anthropology for control, management and advancement of colonised peoples, 86
World War II crisis of colonialism, 86
World War II professionalised anthropology in Australia and New Zealand, 86
WRA community analyst program, 62

Zone of exception, 185, 194

About the Authors

Dr David Hyndman was an academic anthropologist and Associate Professor with the University of Queensland for 30 years from 1972–2002, where he was a scholar actively engaged in teaching, research, and publishing in the area of political ecology, and conflict between nations and states over self-determination and natural resource management in the Asia-Pacific region. He moved to the Canberra district and established a vineyard wine business from 2002–2009 and continued consultant work as an anthropologist. He was an anthropologist with the Bureau of Rural Studies from 2003–2007, where he managed the National Landcare Program Monitoring and Evaluation Project. He was Contractor to the Commonwealth in the Australian Civil Military Centre from 2010–2011, where he was the Tertiary Education and Publications Manager. Together with Dr Scott Flower, he received a research grant in 2012–2013 for their project titled "Anthropology, Counterinsurgency and civil–military Relations for Stabilisation, Peace-building and Conflict Prevention" from the Australian civil–military Centre, and during the grant support period from 2012–2013, Dr David Hyndman was Visiting Associate Professor with the University of New South Wales Canberra, Australia. In 2015, he was Visiting Associate Professor with the University of Canberra, where he taught a course on Indigenous Perceptions of Landscape.

Dr Scott Flower is Fellow at the Melbourne Graduate School of Education at the University of Melbourne. He holds a PhD in Public Policy and a Master of Arts in Strategic Studies from the Australian National University,

(ANU). He has published in leading peer-reviewed academic journals including the *Journal of Islamic Studies*, *Novo Religio*, the *Journal of Muslim Minority Affairs*, *Islam and Christian-Muslim Relations*, the *Journal of Pacific Affairs*, *Journal of Pacific History*, and the *Australian Journal of International Affairs*.

Scott has been awarded a number of prestigious national and international research grants for his research. He was funded by the Australian civil–military centre to lead the project (with Dr David Hyndman) to deliver this book, *The Crisis of Cultural Intelligence: The Anthropology of Civil–Military Operations*, which investigates the use of the social sciences by Western militaries to develop sociocultural analytical capabilities for support civil–military stabilisation, peace-Building, and conflict prevention operations. Some of his other grant-funded research projects in the US and Canada were sponsored by the US Department of Defence and the Public Safety Canada respectively, and investigate conversion to Islam in each country and the radicalisation of converts there. Scott also has ongoing consulting and research interests in the Pacific region, particularly Papua New Guinea, where he has worked as a consultant in security and resettlement advisory roles for Exxon Mobil, BHP Billiton, and Xstrata.